Eros and Inwardness in Vienna

Eros and Inwardness in Vienna

in Vienna

❧

Weininger, Musil, Doderer

David S. Luft

The University of Chicago Press
Chicago and London

DAVID S. LUFT is professor of history at the University of California, San Diego. He is author of *Robert Musil and the Crisis of European Culture* and the coeditor and cotranslator of Robert Musil's *Precision and Soul: Essays and Addresses*, the latter published by the University of Chicago Press.

The University of Chicago Press, Chicago 60637
The University of Chicago Press, Ltd., London
© 2003 by The University of Chicago
All rights reserved. Published 2003
Printed in the United States of America

12 11 10 09 08 07 06 05 04 03   1 2 3 4 5
ISBN: 0-226-49647-3 (cloth)

Library of Congress Cataloging-in-Publication Data

Luft, David S.
    Eros and inwardness in Vienna : Weininger, Musil, Doderer / David S. Luft.
        p.   cm.
    ISBN 0-226-49647-3 (cloth : alk. paper)
    1. Vienna (Austria)—Intellectual life. 2. Vienna (Austria)—Social life and customs. 3. Austrian literature—Austria—Vienna—History and criticism. 4. Politics and literature—Austria—Vienna. 5. National socialism—Austria—Vienna. 6. Freud, Sigmund, 1856–1939—Influence.   I. Title.
    DB851.L84 2003
    306′.09436′13—dc21
                                                              2002009182

⊗ The paper used in this publication meets the minimum requirements of the American National Standard for Information Sciences—Permanence of Paper for Printed Library Materials, ANSI Z39.48-1992.

CONTENTS

∞

ILLUSTRATIONS

$\mathscr{P}$REFACE

❧

$\mathscr{T}$his is a book about an important and unfamiliar passage of European modernism that was located primarily in Vienna in the late nineteenth and early twentieth centuries. My book began as an attempt to understand more about the history of thinking about sexuality and gender in Vienna during the first half of the twentieth century. In the course of my research, I came to see the importance of two closely related tasks: characterizing the distinctiveness of Austrian intellectual life in the late nineteenth century as the context for this thinking, and looking more carefully at writers who have not received as much attention as Sigmund Freud or Arthur Schnitzler. Otto Weininger, Robert Musil, and Heimito von Doderer were attempting to come to terms with modern science in the context of a philosophical irrationalism that had little impact in the English-speaking world at that time, and they expressed themselves in terms of an idiom of gender and a preoccupation with sexuality. They challenged conventional assumptions and explored the relationship of sexuality and gender to ethics, imagination, and perception. Although the significance of what they have to say goes beyond sexuality and gender, all three chose to put this theme at the center of their work.

My book sets out from the mainly American literature on Austrian intellectual history, which has appeared in the past three decades, beginning with William Johnston (1972), Allan Janik and Stephen Toulmin (1973), and Carl Schorske (1980). Schorske's path-breaking articles, which he published together in 1980 as *Fin-de-siècle Vienna*, emphasized the cultural and intellectual life of Vienna around 1900 and the coherence of the liberal elite from

1848 to 1900. Schorske concentrated on figures such as Freud, Schnitzler, and Gustav Klimt who reached creative maturity in the 1890s, but he also touched on younger writers and artists who matured just before the First World War. Schorske also underscored the break in modern thought after Friedrich Nietzsche, while William McGrath (1974) explored the impact of Nietzsche (and his mentor, Arthur Schopenhauer) on Austrian thought in the 1870s. Janik and Toulmin shifted the focus of discussions of Vienna to the younger generation of Ludwig Wittgenstein, Karl Kraus, and Weininger and emphasized themes of language and gender. More recently, Jacques Le Rider (1993) has argued that this period constituted a crisis of masculinity, and Steven Beller (1989) has underscored the centrality of Jews to the liberal culture of Vienna. Anson Rabinbach (1983), Edward Timms (1986), Michael Steinberg (1993), John Boyer (1995), and Malachai Hacohen (2000) have continued to expand the discussion of Viennese intellectual life into the twentieth century. My argument characterizes the distinctive intellectual life of liberal Vienna, but I am less directly concerned than Schorske and McGrath with the political origins of Viennese modernism. My book sheds light on the significance of Schopenhauer and Nietzsche in combination with the powerful influence of the natural sciences in Vienna. I describe the distinctive qualities of this intellectual world and then interpret the creative work of three younger writers in relation to this context between 1900 and 1955.

The central figure in this book is Robert Musil, who has come to be regarded since 1980 as one of the most important writers of the twentieth century. Although Musil is a major figure in Austria and Germany, he has only recently become widely familiar to Americans. In *Robert Musil and the Crisis of European Culture, 1880–1942* (1980), I emphasized Musil's place in a Central European context and his rejection of an Austrian as opposed to a German identity. In *Eros and Inwardness in Vienna*, I am concerned with what is Austrian in Musil's background, especially in relation to his approach to thinking about sexuality and gender. Musil believed that the task of his generation was to rethink gender identity and conventions, that the move beyond bourgeois conventions about sexuality and gender was linked to the move beyond the bourgeois ego and to the exploration of the genuine sources of ethical motivation. Musil was searching for a deeper embedding of thought and the ethical imagination in the emotional sphere and in a more personal relation to the experiencing subject. His attempt at an ungrounded view of ethics and a "morality without interruption" emphasized the role of love in human knowledge and the significance of breaking out of the rigidities of the ego and the normal total experience of the world.

The figure who has often linked work in Austrian intellectual history to

German and European intellectual history is Freud. My book departs from that pattern, primarily because what is needed is an understanding of writers who are still not familiar in the United States and because the relationship between Austrian thought and the wider realm of German culture has still not been adequately clarified. I do not intend here to add directly to the literature on Freud but to reshape the way we see the intellectual history of Vienna in the early twentieth century. Writing this book, I have often found myself recalling my conversations with Louis Mink when I was an undergraduate at Wesleyan University in Connecticut. Mink was fond of pointing out that the principal problem with our understanding of Freud is that we remember virtually nothing else from the culture that produced him, that we have allowed ourselves to forget other intellectuals from Freud's culture who were thinking creatively about similar questions. As Musil once noted, it is easier to generalize about a culture if 95 percent of it is forgotten or simply left out, as is normally the case in characterizing past ages.

I begin with Weininger's extravagant attempt to give value to life after science and Nietzsche by way of Kantian morality and a critique of modern attitudes toward sexuality and science. I show that underlying his discourse about women and Jews are his concerns about philosophical irrationalism and modern science. Musil's intellectual significance becomes clearer in this context, both for thinking about sexuality and gender and for the larger concerns that informed Weininger's thought. Doderer was influenced by both Weininger and Musil, but his experience in the First World War transformed his reception of these themes in ways that initially made him open to National Socialism and then helped him to find his way beyond the ideological problems of his generation. My portrayal of Doderer takes the themes of Vienna 1900 into the First Republic and the fascist era. His magnum opus on Vienna in the interwar years appeared just as the Second Austrian Republic achieved independence in the midst of the cold war. The achievements of these three writers do not lie primarily in their thinking about politics or sexual science but in their reflections on the significance of eros and inwardness for ethical experience and for a meaningful relationship to the world.

$\mathscr{A}$CKNOWLEDGMENTS

෴

$\mathscr{T}$hree cities helped me write this book: San Diego, Vienna, and Philadelphia. And three universities: the University of California, San Diego; the University of Vienna; and Temple University. I am indebted to the University of California, San Diego, especially to the Committee on Research of the Academic Senate, for its support on this project and to the dean of Arts and Humanities for a research fellowship. I am grateful to the people in Vienna who helped me to acclimate to this unfamiliar cultural terrain, especially Hilde Spiel, Kurt Rudolf Fischer, Gertraud Diem-Wille, and Wendelin Schmidt-Dengler. In the last years of writing, I enjoyed the hospitality of Temple University, including the Medical School and the Departments of History and Religion in the School of Humanities.

In the course of writing this book, I have incurred many debts to students, friends, and colleagues. I am particularly indebted to my students, especially to those in my seminars since the mid-1980s, for helping to shape the intellectual community in which my work developed. Several of my friends read an earlier, somewhat differently conceived, version of this book: Robert Dowdy, Chris Norris, Earl Pomeroy, and Robin Ray. In more recent stages of writing I have been grateful to friends and colleagues who were kind enough to read my manuscript along the way: Frank Biess, Eugenie Carlstead, Steve Cox, Barnet Hartston, Russell Hvolbek, Elaine O'Brien, Fritz Ringer, Diana Reynolds, and Andrew Zimmerman. Allan Mitchell and Burton Pike encouraged this project from the beginning, as did my editor, Douglas Mitchell, and I am grateful to the readers of the University of Chicago Press, Gerald

Izenberg and Anson Rabinbach, who offered perceptive suggestions for revision. Over the final year of writing I appreciated the thoughtful readings of Don Wallace and Cecily Heisser. I am indebted to many other friends, but I especially want to thank Rick Harmon, John Lee, and John Marino for their support throughout this project. This book is for all my students, but especially for Jennifer Germain Luft, my most precise reader.

$\mathscr{I}$NTRODUCTION

&

$\mathscr{T}$his book is a study of three Austrian writers thinking about sexuality and gender during the first half of the twentieth century in Vienna: Otto Weininger (1880–1903), Robert Musil (1880–1942), and Heimito von Doderer (1896–1966). Weininger was a critic of modernity and Austrian liberalism who set the tone for his generation's moral intensity and nihilism. His view is a critique of sexuality in general, and of what he understood to be femininity in particular, although it was also a critique of the behavior and values of actual men in his society. Weininger committed suicide at twenty-three, just a few months after the publication of his *Gender and Character* in 1903.[1] Robert Musil belonged to Weininger's generation, but Musil lived to explore a richer, more complex view of sexuality and gender, most notably in his massive portrayal of prewar Vienna, *The Man without Qualities* (1930–1933).[2] Here, as well as in his earlier essays and fiction, Musil worked for a more balanced understanding of masculinity and femininity and for a less nihilistic view of modern experience. For Heimito von Doderer, thinking about sexuality was central to his own intellectual development and to his understanding of the social world of Vienna. His experience as a soldier in two world wars and his membership in the Austrian National Socialist Party during the 1930s reflect the dramatically different historical experience of the generation of intellectuals born around the turn of the century, and his postwar novels gave form to the experience of living in Vienna in the early twentieth century in the name of private life and the ordinary person. In *The Demons* (1956) Doderer described the German-speaking elites of the high

Bürgertum (haute bourgeoisie), who had dominated Austrian politics and culture in the late nineteenth century but were marginalized by modern mass politics and the collapse of the Habsburg monarchy after the First World War.[3]

Weininger, Musil, and Doderer lived and worked in Vienna during the period between the emergence of an identifiably modern society and culture in Imperial Austria and the founding of the Second Austrian Republic after the Second World War, roughly between 1900 and 1955. Their ideas about sexuality and gender appear in my book as metaphors for thinking about inwardness in the context of modern science and the crisis of Western traditions of spirituality after Nietzsche. My presentation of these writers sets out from the intellectual world of liberal Vienna in the late nineteenth century, a world that was dominated by the natural sciences, especially medicine and biology, and largely impervious to the historical and human sciences as they had developed in Germany in the context of German idealism and romanticism. But post-Kantian philosophy did have a powerful influence in liberal Vienna: in the guise of philosophical irrationalism, an intellectual tradition that grew out of Schopenhauer's conviction that the true basis "for all knowledge of human nature is the persuasion that a man's actions are, essentially and as a whole, not directed by his reason and its designs."[4] I emphasize the significance of this blend of scientific materialism and philosophical irrationalism for the intellectual context of liberal Vienna in the late nineteenth century; and, within this context, I consider the texts of three writers who were concerned with what Nietzsche called the "human soul and its limits, the range of inner human experiences reached so far, the heights, depths, and distances of these experiences, the whole history of the soul *so far* and its as yet unexhausted possibilities—that is the predestined hunting ground for a born psychologist and lover of the 'great hunt.'"[5]

The intellectual context of liberal Vienna provided a characteristic blend of attitudes that shaped discourse about sexuality: the recognition of a scientific, empirical view of the world, including an understanding of the body as a biological reality (and as the reality of the self), and a new understanding of the soul as feelings grounded in the body.[6] It is not surprising to discover that sexuality and gender were the themes through which these larger philosophical arguments were worked out or that novelists played a considerable role in this thinking. It is this combination of scientific materialism and philosophical irrationalism that shaped the thinking of Sigmund Freud (1856–1939) about sexuality. But my book is devoted to three less familiar and quite individual writers. They offer fresh perspectives on the significance of Vienna for the emergence of modern culture and serve as invitations to think about sexuality and gender in new ways. Weininger is certainly the most peculiar of the three writers, but he makes sense as an expression of the limitations of Austrian liberal culture and as a reaction against the scientific understanding of the world and the threats to the rational individual that emerged in the work of philosophical irrationalism. Of the three, Musil offers the most balanced perspective, advocating a sophisticated scientific view of the world against a variety of metaphysical perspectives, while also attempting to come to terms with the realities of the world of feelings. Finally, Doderer represents the political crisis of liberal culture and an attempt to reestablish literary realism on a new basis that includes a radical understanding of the unconscious and the feelings. All three of these thinkers explored these larger issues in relation to their understandings of sexuality and gender.

Although Otto Weininger is virtually unknown in the United States today, Jacques Le Rider argues that he was more famous than Freud during the first decade of the century, both in Vienna and among European intellectuals.[7] Weininger was a psychologist and philosopher who developed a theory of bisexuality and gender difference (partly under the influence of Freud and Wilhelm Fliess, Freud's friend and colleague). The moral intensity of Weininger's critique of his own culture is sometimes breathtaking, yet he was still closely tied to inherited assumptions about gender, as was his admirer Karl Kraus (1874–1936).[8] Weininger's uncompromising attitude made him a symbol of the nihilism of his generation of Austrian intellectuals, and he set the terms for his generation's exploration of philosophical themes in terms of metaphors of sexuality and gender. Weininger was so shaken by his failure to overcome his own sexuality that he committed suicide. Like Kraus, who attacked the masculine and defended the feminine, Weininger adopted a grammar of gender as a strategy for his attack on bourgeois culture, and his *Geschlecht und Charakter* (1903) was the most radical critique of sexuality to arise from a culture that was preoccupied with this theme. Scholars often see Weininger's critique of femininity and sexuality as conventional male prejudice in reaction to the early years of feminism in Vienna, but such readings fail to consider just how disturbing and unconventional Weininger was and obscure his value as a document of the emotional and intellectual life of liberal Vienna. Much of what Weininger has to say about women and Jews will seem unreadably misogynist and anti-Semitic to contemporary readers who might reasonably wonder what is the point of reaching back a hundred years to review prejudices that were all too familiar in the twentieth century. At the same time, we certainly cannot say that we understand (as well as we would like to) the power of anti-Semitism in Central Europe in the early twentieth century—or the nature of its links to misogyny and antifeminism.

Robert Musil was one of the great masters of twentieth-century German prose and probably the equal of anyone since Nietzsche in his intelligence and insight in the realm of the soul; more than any other writer of this period he found a way to reconcile the values implied in such polarities as masculine and feminine. Musil assimilated the importance of modern science and psychology while developing Nietzsche's understanding of ethics and aesthetics. His work represents an attempt to balance the polarized conceptions of masculinity and femininity in his culture, conceptions most radically defined and advocated by Weininger and Kraus. Musil explored what was fruitful in the attempt of his generation to see human experience in terms of the metaphor of gender, and he thought out the issues raised by historical changes in the roles of men and women. The metaphor of gender was central to his attempt to bring thinking and feeling into a more balanced relationship with one another and to develop his distinctive balance of science and imagination, irony and love.[9]

Heimito von Doderer was the most distinguished Austrian novelist of the generation after Musil.[10] Doderer's generation lived through the last stages in the collapse of liberal culture in Vienna, and his political experience (much like that of Martin Heidegger in Germany) offers some insight into the relationship of intellectuals to National Socialism. Doderer was a conventional child of late nineteenth-century liberalism who fought in the First World War as a young man and experienced the political polarization of the 1920s and 1930s. He was a member of the National Socialist Party between 1933 and 1938 (when it was illegal in Austria), and he served as an officer in the German Air Force in the Second World War. In the postwar era Doderer became one of the most articulate advocates of the conservative Austrian vision that helped to provide the Second Republic with an identity. But he was also a great writer, one for whom eros was central to his understanding of spirit.[11] Although he was younger than Weininger and Musil, Doderer was a product of the liberal culture of Vienna and shared for the most part in the same intellectual context.

Weininger, Musil, and Doderer all belonged to the culture of Austrian liberalism during its period of political defeat and intellectual crisis. Their lives and writings constitute a postliberal critique of liberalism from within the liberal tradition. They challenged liberal conceptions of human nature, of individualism and rationalism, and they drew attention to the limitations of this intellectual tradition in its understandings of religion and sexuality. These predominantly literary attempts to think about the feelings emerged out of a highly scientific, positivistic intellectual culture, one that was deeply committed to the objectivity of knowledge and to a rationality that was sharp and hard—and unsentimental—within the realm of scholarship. The writings of Weininger, Musil, and Doderer might be regarded as three decompositions: three decompositions of a culture. Weininger's critique is almost entirely destructive but in a way that makes a great deal visible about sexuality and liberal culture. Musil's view is the most complex and fruitful, but it also rises most above the culture it describes. Doderer's decomposition displays the limits and possibilities of this culture after the catastrophes of the fascist era. These writers represent three stages in a deepening crisis of liberal culture in Austria during the first half of the twentieth century.

The First World War is the midpoint of my narrative, after which politics plays a much larger role, but the intellectual context of liberal Vienna is largely continuous even after 1918. Weininger lived before the First World War (and died even before the dramatic political events around 1905). Musil was exactly Weininger's age, but his creative life was divided almost evenly between the prewar and postwar eras. Doderer was young enough that the war and his imprisonment in Siberia were the first experiences of his adult life. My discussion emphasizes three major works by these writers—*Gender and Character, The Man without Qualities,* and *The Demons,* respectively— but, for Musil and Doderer, these mature novels belong in the context of much longer, more complex evolutions. These three books appeared when their authors were twenty-three, fifty, and sixty, respectively. But even more significant perhaps is the simple distinction between a book written quickly by a very young man, and two books of maturity, written over periods of twenty to thirty years.

Much of my book will resonate with our understanding of Freud and with the ideas and language he helped to give prominence in modern Western culture. Yet very little of this story belongs to the history of psychoanalysis or to the history of these ideas as psychiatry might locate them. Over the course of the past century, no intellectual from the world of liberal Vienna has had more impact on Western culture than Freud. In this book, Freud appears mainly as an absent presence rather than a central figure. He has been so influential in Western culture, both explicitly and implicitly, that it is difficult to see him dispassionately in the context of other thinkers of his own period. Indeed, his influence has hardened into something more conducive to reactivity than to thinking. In a time when the literature on Freud continues to increase and when the polemical edge of these discussions is often surprisingly sharp, there is something to be said for looking at the perspectives of other writers nearby him. My book sets out from the discrepancy between the enormous amount of work that continues to appear on Freud in a wide variety of fields and the continuing invisibility of other important figures of the early twentieth century in Vienna.

We remember Freud best for his thinking about sexuality, a highly inward view of sexuality that emphasized the role of the unconscious in mental life. Freud's intellectual significance lies not so much in the details of his theory or of his scientific method as in his general approach to human nature: his emphasis on the enormous role that psychological matters play in human affairs, in particular, the importance of unconscious factors in determining behavior and suffering, and his development of the notion of a talking method within a human relationship as a means of cure by love. This view constituted a deviation both from conventional nineteenth-century views of human nature and from conventional views of science, medicine, and psychiatry as they were practiced in Freud's culture. In *"Dieses wahre innere Afrika,"* Ludger Lütkehaus argues that over the past century a colonization of the unconscious by the conscious mind has taken place, and he warns that our understanding of the unconscious mind may have ended with Freud (to be sure at a high point), rather than beginning with him.[12] Weininger, Musil, and Doderer were all aware of Freud, but all of them made distinctive contributions to thinking about sexuality, gender, and love. Although Freud had some influence on each of these writers, it is not their place within the psychoanalytic framework that is of interest here but rather their own ideas and language as they developed during the first half of the twentieth century.

Freud's liberal civilization ideology protected him against the full force of nihilism as it was experienced by younger readers of Schopenhauer and Nietzsche at the turn of the century.[13] Weininger, Musil, and Doderer all reached maturity in the early twentieth century. Their backgrounds were not in medicine or psychiatry or psychoanalysis but in philosophy, psychology, and literature in the largest sense. As with Freud, sexuality was central to their understandings of human experience to a degree that would be difficult to imagine in the philosophers of German idealism. All of them belonged to the intellectual world of liberal Vienna, which was marked by the intersection of positivism and scientific materialism with the post-Kantian tradition of philosophical irrationalism. My discussion of these two intellectual traditions offers fresh insights into Freud, but the full impact of this intellectual blend came after the turn of the century, especially in the generation of 1905, the generation of intellectuals who began to reach creative maturity in the decade before the First World War.[14]

I begin with liberal Vienna in the late nineteenth century in order to clarify what was distinctive (and not distinctive) in the intellectual world that produced these writers. Austrian intellectuals in the early twentieth century experienced the crisis of modernity in a form that was significantly different from what we associate with the German experience. My book is concerned with the intellectual history of Austria in a period when liberal intellectuals began to doubt the conception of human nature that we associate with the Enlightenment and classical liberalism. Carl Schorske's *Fin-de-siècle Vienna* has been the most influential attempt to come to terms with the intellectual creativity of this period of liberal political and ideological crisis in Austria, and my own work shares a good deal in common with Schorske's account of the first major crisis of Western rationalism.[15] I am particularly interested in thinking about sexuality and gender and the implications of this thinking for intellectuals who were living in post-traditional, postliberal culture. I emphasize the tensions between philosophical irrationalism and the dominant rationalism of the liberal political and scientific elite and the extent to which this revolt against rationalism took place in one of the leading centers of Western rationalism.

Several important terms require some clarification at the outset, notably, the sense in which "liberalism" was used in the nineteenth century. With the word *liberalism* I refer to the intellectual and political tradition that took distinctive shape in Western Europe and North America from the late seventeenth to the eighteenth century. This tradition emphasized individualism and rationalism and spoke particularly in terms of freedom—whether from political, economic, or religious regulation and authority. Kant put this conception of individual freedom positively as the self-legislation of rational moral laws. This specifically Kantian form may be regarded as the culmination of the European Enlightenment, and it is the form of the liberal tradition that is central to our understanding of German-speaking Central Europe in the nineteenth century.[16] But this Kantian tradition was not the form of liberalism that dominated the liberal era in Austria during the second half of the nineteenth century. Indeed, the post-Kantian tradition was generally resisted by Austrian intellectuals before 1900; although Viennese liberals were proud of their German culture, they were strongly influenced by French and English traditions of liberalism and by the German classicism and humanism of Lessing, Goethe, Schiller, and Wilhelm von Humboldt rather than by the familiar figures of post-Kantian idealism. In this context, what was emphasized after 1848 was primarily the liberation of the unbound man from the interference of the state in the development of capitalism and from the authority of the Roman Catholic church in education—and the new opportunities for men of property and education to participate in a representative political process.[17] With the term *scientific materialism* I am thinking of the most radical forms of positivism (or scientism) that drew on the ideas of Ludwig Büchner (1824–1899), Ludwig Feuerbach (1804–1872), Karl Marx (1818–1883), and Charles Darwin (1809–1882). Scientific materialism was intellectually and politically the most radical version of liberal culture after 1848, but it challenged liberalism in terms that were more or less continuous with its own assumptions. Scientific materialism was the hard edge of liberalism and positivism, and it was closely associated with science and medicine in the university and with radicalism in politics. Although Austrian intellectuals had been surprisingly resistant to German idealism before 1848, they *did* feel the impact of scientific materialism as it arrived from northern Germany in the context of 1848 and of the reform of the University of Vienna in the 1850s.[18]

Less easily assimilated to the assumptions of liberal thought was the tradition of philosophical irrationalism, which began to be influential in Vienna in the 1860s and 1870s and then even more after the turn of the century. With the term *philosophical irrationalism* I have in mind a tradition that denies that reason and consciousness are the dominant and defining features of human nature. Like Freud, thinkers in this tradition were sometimes advocates of reason, but they emphasized the powerful role of instinctual factors in human nature and in motivation. I use the term philosophical irrationalism as a way of adopting existing conventions for referring to nineteenth-century thinkers who had a certain family resemblance and who diverged from the dominant philosophical traditions. Intellectual historians of nineteenth-century Europe ordinarily emphasize two main philosophical traditions: positivism and idealism. Positivism, as an antimetaphysical way of thinking that attempted to apply the methods of natural science to human studies, was particularly strong in France. Philosophical idealism from Kant to Fichte to Schelling to Hegel was primarily a German tradition. British thought had strong roots in empiricism and utilitarianism, but after Romanticism many English intellectuals were strongly influenced by German idealism. The situation in Austria—particularly in the liberal culture of Vienna—was significantly different from any of these models. This was a distinctive intellectual culture, grounded in the Enlightenment, modern science, and German humanism, but thinking about the feelings in new ways.

When I speak of philosophical irrationalism, I am thinking primarily of Arthur Schopenhauer (1788–1860) and Friedrich Nietzsche (1844–1900), although Eduard von Hartmann (1842–1906) did a great deal to popularize Schopenhauer's ideas, and Soren Kierkegaard (1813–1855) was often included in this context once his ideas became known in the early twentieth century.[19] This tradition is sometimes characterized as *Lebensphilosophie* [life philosophy] or vitalism; in the English-speaking world, philosophical irrationalism became familiar after the Second World War as a kind of prologue to existentialism. Philosophical irrationalists emphasized the degree to which human nature is not under the control of the individual's conscious thought, reason, or intention.[20] Thinkers in the irrationalist tradition are interested in questions of character and life, in how the individual human being is constructed as a person, and they reject the idea of thinking of the self as a rational soul. Maurice Mandelbaum extends his definition of these thinkers (whom he refers to both as "voluntarists" and as "philosophical irrationalists") to the notion that external reality is irrational as well, but this seems to me less essential to what these thinkers share.[21] In principle, an irrationalist (again, one thinks of Schopenhauer and Freud as obvious examples) might think of irrational impulses as ultimately susceptible to lawful regularities, which may be utterly obscure from a subjective point of view. In this sense, irrationalism as I use it here is not necessarily incompatible with scientific materialism, but it does threaten rationalism (including German idealism). Moreover, insofar as rationalism has been associated with an optimistic view of historical teleology (in Hegel, for example), Schopenhauer may be regarded as its opposite: the denial of any sense of purpose or direction in history, and here Nietzsche and Freud come to mind as similar. The philosophical irrationalists were often quite sympathetic to reason, intellect, or even science, but they ordinarily emphasized the inadequacy of liberal and positivist views of these matters. This blend of scientific materialism and philosophical irrationalism was the distinctive feature of the intellectual world of liberal Vienna, although Weininger, Musil, and Doderer, like Freud, all combined these perspectives in different ways.

One other matter of definition requires comment here. I have not adopted firm, programmatic definitions of sexuality and gender. Even Freud did not define "sexuality" in *Three Essays on the Theory of Sexuality*, and no one knowledgeable about Freud would argue that his meanings were consistent and unambiguous from 1900 to 1930. I rely here on commonsense usage, despite the special problems created by crossing lines between German and English, and specify definitions more precisely in the context of each writer. I use "gender" in a sense very like Joan Scott, as something constructed and culturally, socially, and historically relative, although it would be anachronistic to attribute precisely this sense to my three authors.[22] Nonetheless, one claim of this book is that Weininger was beginning to make the distinction between sex and gender, at least in the sense of separating his understandings of male and female from conventional anatomical definitions—and that a similar notion of gender informs Musil's work, and perhaps even Doderer's.[23] At the same time, these writers were not social scientists, and I am concerned primarily with their thought rather than with behavior in their social worlds.

Because this is an intellectual history, I am interested in letting these authors speak for themselves as much as possible. At times this will make them seem quite conventional; at times, quite individual and creative.

My method aims at understanding—both within a particular historical context and within the texts these writers produced. Thus, with Weininger for example, it is a matter of trying to understand this person, of thinking along with him, while realizing that his language, like the culture that he lived, has a logic of its own. These writers are concerned with a kind of knowledge that is not entirely impersonal but connected in complicated ways to feelings and to the lives of these authors and the people to whom they speak. Musil and Doderer are most clear about this, while Weininger is ambivalent, vacillating between his scientific/scholarly apparatus and his frank confession of the autobiographical basis of his work. In the natural sciences the claim has often been made that independence from the personal reality of the knower is the positive goal; however doubtful these claims have been, they are certainly not appropriate here, which is not to say that these authors are entirely subjective. This book, then, is concerned with literature, not in the sense of fiction but in the sense of what the Germans call life wisdom, which inevitably includes mistakes and confusions, tangled relationships with the authors' lives and a problematic, disintegrating culture. I begin in chapter 1 with an extended discussion of the intellectual world of liberal Vienna in the late nineteenth century in order to qualify misleading contextualizations of German thought that are not appropriate for understanding Austrian intellectuals of the early twentieth century. I emphasize differences between Austrian and German intellectual life: the much weaker influence of idealism and historicism in Austria in the early nineteenth century and the distinctive blend of scientific materialism and philosophical irrationalism in liberal Vienna after 1848 that was different not only from Germany but also from France or England.

Figure 1. View of the *Ringstrasse,* c. 1900

௸

CHAPTER ONE

SCIENCE AND IRRATIONALISM IN LIBERAL VIENNA, 1848–1900

In 1848 Vienna was a city of 400,000, the capital of a mainly rural, multinational empire, ruled from the center by a German-speaking bureaucracy. By 1900 Vienna had become a modern city on the verge of universal manhood suffrage with a population of more than 1.6 million. In 1848 Vienna still retained its medieval shape; but the creation of the *Ringstrasse* in the 1850s and 1860s transformed the city, and by the turn of the century Vienna's districts extended far beyond the original inner city of the imperial palace, aristocratic residences, and gothic and baroque churches. The years between 1848 and 1900 were given their distinctive quality by the German-speaking *bürgerlich* (or bourgeois) elites, who took the lead economically and intellectually, and for a time, politically as well. These years were a period of transition between absolute monarchy and modern democratic politics, when liberal culture and politics shaped the life of Vienna, and it was in this context that the distinctive intellectual life of liberal Vienna emerged.[1]

The second half of the nineteenth century was marked not only by the modernization of Vienna as a city but also by the reception of intellectual influences that set the terms for thinking about sexuality and gender after 1900. The intellectual life of Vienna belonged to the Western cosmopolitan world of Paris, London, and Berlin, and in the late nineteenth century most intellectuals in Vienna regarded themselves as part of the broad stream of liberal progress, of reason and freedom, since the Enlightenment. Within the realm of German culture, liberal Vienna shared in the legacy of neohumanism and inward cultivation or *Bildung*. In relation to the wider European culture of high liberalism, the intellectual life of liberal Vienna had qualities that made it especially conducive to thinking about sexuality and feelings, in particular, its receptivity to currents of scientific and irrationalist thought after 1848.

Liberal Vienna

Austrian liberalism was not sharply defined or institutionally established before 1848. In this context, "liberal" referred to the broadly European emancipatory tradition, shaped by the German neohumanist emphasis on education and self-cultivation. In the absence of a parliamentary system before 1848, the liberal values of the Enlightenment and the unbound man found support in the state bureaucracy, in the theater, and in the banking and commercial elites. After the revolution of 1848, absolutism reasserted itself briefly, but it was clear that liberalism had become the transformative force in Austrian society and politics. The brief interlude of neoabsolutism in the 1850s yielded to liberal political institutions in the 1860s, and Liberals assumed parliamentary leadership and ministerial power. But even at the height of its power in the 1860s and 1870s, political Liberalism was a loose coalition of factions rather than a strongly organized party in the modern sense. By 1900 Liberalism in this narrowly political sense had ceased to be an important force in Austria, although the broad tradition of liberal culture and emancipatory values continued to shape Austrian intellectual life until the 1930s.

The culture of liberal Vienna grew out of the German Enlightenment and the bureaucratic reform tradition of the late eighteenth century, which had been established by Maria Theresa (1740–1780) and Joseph II (1780–1790). Between 1848 and 1900, as modern forms of liberal and democratic politics emerged, it was often difficult to make sharp distinctions between bureaucratic reformers and specifically bourgeois liberals. In Vienna these groups shared in the predicament of a German-speaking political and cultural elite within a multinational monarchy, and the mainly secular culture of this elite formed the basis for intellectual life. Liberal Vienna was powerfully shaped by the German humanism of the eighteenth century, which was given its distinctive Austrian form primarily by the bureaucratic and professional strata and by the secularized Jewish culture that made its home in modern German culture both before and after 1848.

Central to Austrian liberalism as it emerged out of German humanism was the idea of the free personality, "the element of the freedom and dignity of the human being." This broad, universal, undoctrinaire aspect of Austrian liberalism went beyond any particular party or interest and amounted to a belief in the "freedom and worth of the human being as human being against the state."[2] The "fundamental liberal principle of the personality, individualism," was strongly shaped by German humanism's ideal of *Bildung*. The original force of the eighteenth-century word *Bildung* is often lost in English translation, where it appears routinely as "education" or even as "culture"; but "self-cultivation" gives the sense of why it was like a religious ideology. This view of individuality was at the heart of the religion of humanity that emerged out of the German Enlightenment in the work of Goethe, Schiller, Lessing, and Humboldt.[3] In Austria, this secular, emancipatory vision was a challenge to the Roman Catholic Church as well as to the absolutist state, and it had complex implications for education and language in a multinational empire.

The basic ambiguity of liberal Vienna in the late nineteenth century was the tension between the broad emancipatory tradition of German humanism and the actual practice of a political and economic elite that briefly dominated in the 1860s and 1870s. This tension in liberal ideology was present from the outset in the sense that the individuality of the *Bildung* tradition was different from the competitive individualism of liberal economics and politics.[4] Austrian liberalism began by emphasizing the ideal of the free personality, but in the late nineteenth century political Liberalism came to stand for economic competition, social ambition, and the bourgeois culture of achievement; and Liberalism was identified with the class interests of the high *Bürgertum*. As in Germany, *Bildung* began as an ideal of education and self-cultivation, but it could easily become a Philistine indicator of achieved status.

The distinctive shape of Austrian liberalism emerged from the reception of the Enlightenment by the German-speaking bureaucratic stratum of this multinational, Roman Catholic state.[5] Although the process of reform, centralization, and state formation began under Maria Theresa, in retrospect the accomplishments of reform absolutism were associated primarily with her son, Joseph II. The intellectual, political, and ecclesiastical traditions that grew out of these eighteenth-century reforms were known as Josephinism, which stood for rationalism, progress within the parameters of the centralist state, reform within the church, and an affinity for modern science. Austria's bureaucratic stratum was influenced by the individualistic, humanistic tradition as it emerged in German culture in the eighteenth century.[6] Joseph II did a great deal to encourage the reception of German culture and Enlightenment values in Austria, and his decision in 1781 to grant freedom of worship to established Protestant, Jewish, and Greek Orthodox congregations was an important step toward modernization that facilitated the development of liberal intellectual life. By the 1830s and 1840s, Josephinism began to merge with the early signs of liberalism, and after 1848 liberalism and neo-Josephinism worked together to create the distinctive blend of absolutist and liberal elements in the constitution of Austria after 1867.[7]

Between 1792 and 1848 the bureaucratic centralism established by Maria Theresa and Joseph II lost its reformist impulse and declined into the conservative, mainly passive rule that prepared the way for the liberal and national revolutions of 1848. But, despite the censorship of this period, much that was distinctive and distinguished in Austrian culture flourished. This was particularly true in literature, where the achievements of Franz Grillparzer (1791–1872), Adalbert Stifter (1805–1868), and Johann Nepomuk Nestroy (1801–1862) set a standard that arguably was not surpassed by the writers of Young Vienna in the 1890s.[8] Vienna was also the center of European music in this period; and the salons of second society, frequented by the financial and bureaucratic elites and by the lower nobility, established the high cultural tone that continued into the late nineteenth century.[9] The intellectual culture of second society took on its characteristic form in the relatively apolitical and preparliamentary world before 1848. The central figures of this salon culture of the high *Bürgertum* were Fanny von Arnstein (1758–1818), Caroline Pichler (1769–1843), and Josephine von Wertheimstein (1820–1898).[10]

In Vienna the revolution of 1848 brought to expression the conflict between the conservative forces of the Habsburg monarchy and those who advocated freedom from traditional bonds and the participation of citizens in shaping public life. The April Constitution established universal manhood suffrage, and in June the Constituent Assembly completed the emancipation of the peasantry begun by Joseph II. Prospects seemed good for liberal and democratic rule both in the Habsburg Monarchy and in a new Germany, and local self-government was established in Vienna. By the end of the year, the revolution had been defeated in the Habsburg monarchy, and Austria had been separated from the process of German unification in Frankfurt. The events of 1848 unleashed such chaotic forces that Austrian intellectuals such as Franz Grillparzer became skeptical about nationalism and resigned toward a conservative monarchy that might at least allow the nationalities of Central Europe to coexist in peace.[11] For Germany, the liberal revolutions of 1848 represented the first step toward national unification, but for Austria these upheavals meant near disintegration and a reminder of cultural and national difference.[12] What seemed to have been established in the spring of 1848 was realized only gradually and partially during the second half of the nineteenth century in the age of liberal Vienna.[13]

After 1848 Vienna began to change from a culture dominated by bureaucratic and financial elites in a mainly stagnant political and economic order to a more rapidly modernizing society. Although 1848 nearly destroyed the Habsburg monarchy, it also reinvigorated political and economic life: it led to liberal institutions in Vienna, to university reform along liberal and German lines, and to a new social mobility that transformed Vienna and other Austrian cities in the late nineteenth century. Most of what we associate with bourgeois society—in terms of capitalism, educational reform, local self-government, internal migration, and the emergence of a modern press—followed after 1848, and yet the monarchy, the army, and the central bureaucracy remained largely in charge until the end of the empire.[14] In the 1850s the bureaucracy tried to create the basis for a modern society, including the reconstruction of Vienna and the encouragement of modern economic life. In this sense, neoabsolutism was dependent on the German-speaking high *Bürgertum*, which played an increasingly significant role in political affairs down to the liberal reconstitution of Austria between 1861 and 1867. The construction of the *Ringstrasse*—and of the symbolic buildings of the bourgeois liberal era, the Burgtheater, the Rathaus, the Reichsrat (or parliament), and the University—and the creation of Vienna in its modern form stamped the period of political and economic dynamism in the 1860s and 1870s.[15] This physical transformation of the medieval city came to symbolize the new role of the liberal *Bürgertum* in Austrian public life.[16]

This period also witnessed a dramatic movement of population from the countryside to the cities. What had particular significance for liberal politics and culture was the migration of Jews to Vienna from Bohemia, Moravia, Galicia, Bukovina, and Hungary; the Jewish population of Vienna grew from just a few families in 1848 to nearly 150,000 people by 1900.[17] Under these circumstances, the German language appeared to most Jews as a symbol of freedom, progress, and culture. Secularized Jews ordinarily identified strongly with Austrian liberal politics and culture, and in the late nineteenth century Jews seem to have felt more at home in Austrian society than in Bismarck's Germany.[18] Jews received full civil rights in Austria in 1867 and played important roles in the political and intellectual life of liberal Vienna.[19]

The years of high liberalism between 1867 and 1879 were shaped by the exclusion of Austria from Germany and by the division of the Habsburg lands into a dual monarchy: the Ausgleich (or Compromise) of 1867 gave the Magyars a free hand in the eastern half of the empire while the German Liberals were left to take the lead in Austria and Bohemia. The most conspicuous aspect of the high liberal era was the brief period of political success of the Constitutional Party (Verfassungspartei) in the Austrian Reichsrat between 1867 and 1879, but Liberal political leadership in Austria was fragile and problematic from the start. Although Liberalism benefited initially from the economic dynamism of the *Ringstrasse* era, as the Austrian *Gründerzeit* was called, the limitations of its economic, cultural, and electoral base were apparent even then; and its active hostility to Roman Catholicism awakened divisions within the *Bürgertum* even before the major political challenges of the 1880s.[20] The political successes corresponded to the early successes of capitalism in Austria with railroads and stock markets, but in this respect as well disappointment came swiftly—in the Crash of 1873 and the ensuing period of slowed economic growth, which lasted until 1896. In the midst of its successes, political Liberalism in Austria was, for the most part, class bound and conservative, oriented to property and education and indifferent to the experience of people in other social strata.[21] In political terms, the liberal era in Austria was a mixed phenomenon. On the one hand, it represented the gradual victory over absolutism, the development of representative government and civil rights, the emergence of a modern capitalist economy, freedom of religion, the limitation of Catholic ideological dominance, and the assimilation of Jews into the mainstream of public life. Jews, Czechs, and other minorities were permitted to participate in public life on the basis of the German language, which was perceived not only as the language of state but also as the language of education and culture. On the other hand, these achievements were limited by the continued roles of the monarchy, the aristocracy, and the bureaucracy. Franz Joseph (1848–1916) remained on the throne throughout this period, retained the power to dissolve parliament, and continued to control the army and foreign policy. German liberal elites kept the franchise limited and enjoyed the privileged status of a wealthy, educated stratum; and Czechs, who comprised a substantial minority in Austria and Bohemia, struggled for full recognition in the political system.[22] Liberalism as a political movement came to be identified with the narrow interests of the high *Bürgertum* and its limitations in extending its own values to other groups, whether other nationalities, the lower *Bürgertum*, the working class, or women.[23]

After 1879 Liberalism lost its leading position in Vienna, first in the Austrian parliament and by 1897 in city hall as well. Between 1880 and 1900 three political parties emerged in Vienna to challenge Liberal political leadership: the German Nationalists, the Christian Socials, and the Social Democrats.[24] All three parties intended to be more democratic than the Liberals, and they constituted the main political alignments of modern Austria after the collapse of the monarchy in 1918. The Social Democrats attempted to continue the emancipatory tradition and the rationalism of Liberalism; the

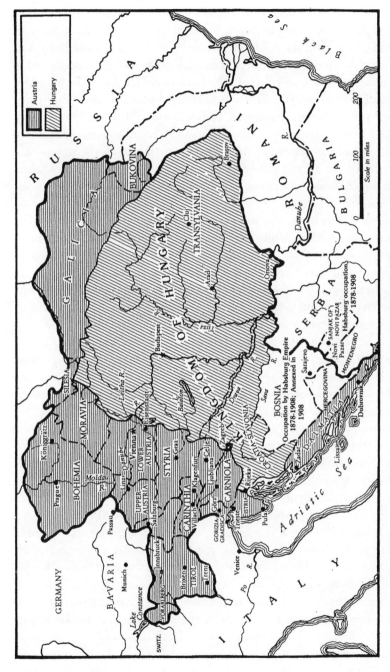

Figure 2. Austria-Hungary, 1867–1918. The dual monarchy was both Austrian and Hungarian, imperial and royal, *Kaiserlich und königlich*.

Christian Socials, although representing Catholics from the lower *Bürgertum*, were in many respects continuous with the values and conventions of the high *Bürgertum*; the German Nationalists under Georg von Schönerer were the clear precursors of Adolf Hitler, but even they began as a democratic movement that was linked both to the anticlericalism of the Liberals and to the revolutionary moment of 1848. The German Nationalists (who hoped for a greater Germany) and the Christian Socials (who became the leading party in Vienna after 1897) were anti-Semitic as well as antiliberal and antirational. But these qualities in the new mass parties ought not to obscure the extent to which political Liberalism had itself become ineffective by the 1880s—and often merely illiberal and self-aggrandizing. Indeed, Austro-German Liberals did little to stand up for Jews as political anti-Semitism increased during the 1890s.[25]

Liberal culture after 1880 was marked by a lack of intensity and purpose that was a function not simply of new mass parties but also of the realization of the aims and interests of the professionals and businessmen of the high *Bürgertum*. This stratum enjoyed the world of Viennese high culture—of opera, theater, and music—a center of elite culture comparable to Paris in the late nineteenth century. Carl Schorske has emphasized the aestheticism of this liberal elite and the attempt of bourgeois and Jewish intellectuals to assimilate to an aristocratic culture of grace and elegance. He argues that the function of art had changed by the end of the nineteenth century from assimilation to escape: "Elsewhere in Europe, art for art's sake implied the withdrawal of its devotees from a social class; in Vienna alone it claimed the allegiance of virtually a whole class, of which the artists were a part."[26] In Vienna, even more than in Paris, the culture of bourgeois leisure merged with a more rebellious aestheticism.

In *Hofmannsthal and His Time*, Hermann Broch (1886–1951) characterized Vienna around 1880 as "a city of decoration," a culture of theater like Paris, a culture of cynicism, hedonism, and "operetta wisdom." Vienna seemed to Broch "cheerful, often idiotically cheerful"—the epitome of a word coined in Munich at that time to describe decorative art that offered a pleasant escape from reality: *kitsch*, the best word the twentieth century found to describe dishonesty and artificial prettiness in art. "And as the metropolis of kitsch, Vienna also became the metropolis of the value vacuum of the epoch."[27] Broch emphasized the cynicism of late nineteenth-century aestheticism and how the refinement and aestheticism of this cultured elite, particularly in France and Austria, became a reductio ad absurdum of the bourgeois goddess of kitsch. If the art movements of Paris in the late nineteenth century were largely designed to shock the rational, practical values of the bourgeoisie, in Vienna writers and artists were alienated along with the high *Bürgertum* as a whole in an ideology of pleasure and aestheticism.

The aesthetic and highly eroticized elite culture of the 1890s was in many respects the realization of German humanism's ideal of the free personality. But it also expressed a revolt against the rationalism of liberal culture and, even in its dandyish individualism, uncertainty about the reality and coherence of the self.[28] Schorske underscored the generational aspects of the 1890s: Freud and the writers of Young Vienna as the children of the founders of the liberal constitution in the 1860s. But Schorske also pointed out that these intellectuals of the 1890s were alienated together with their whole class precisely because of the situation in which political Liberalism was no longer effective. In this sense, Viennese modernism belonged to the established liberal culture of the fathers: "The writers of the nineties were the children of this threatened liberal elite."[29] Writers such as Arthur Schnitzler (1862–1931) and Hugo von Hofmannsthal (1874–1929) and painters such as Gustav Klimt (1862–1918) expressed the alienated, passive situation of their social class as a whole.[30] Schorske described the "ill-reconciled moralistic and aesthetic components" of this liberal elite; in the midst of a culture of ornament, subjectivism, and erotic play, liberal intellectuals continued to suffer "the persistent presence of conscience in the temple of Narcissus."[31]

Liberal Vienna was a culture that respected individuality, education, and creativity—as well as courtesy and grace. It is not surprising that such a culture produced exemplars of these values such as Hofmannsthal and Schnitzler, but these sons of liberal culture also experienced the tensions between these liberal values and the divisions among classes, status groups, and genders within the society. Works on Viennese modernism generally emphasize the generation that reached creative maturity in the 1890s. I am interested in the intellectual context of the late nineteenth century as the basis for those who reached maturity after 1900.[32] As Schorske puts it: "Only in the last decade before World War I does there appear alienation of the intellectual from the *whole* society."[33] The generation that reached maturity after 1900 did not grow up, like Freud and Schnitzler, with the illusion of liberal Vienna but instead with the failure of Liberal politics and the realities of anti-Semitism and Christian Social dominance in Vienna. The first decade of their adulthood was marked by the Revolution of 1905 in Russia, by the introduction of universal suffrage in Austria, by the new diplomatic alignments of the Entente, and by signs that a revolutionary era was under way. The generation of 1905 experienced the bankruptcy of liberal politics and institutions—and went to war.

Younger intellectuals like Doderer went into battle before their mature political and intellectual views had been formed, and yet the continuity of intellectual life remained in the midst of the upheavals of war, political collapse, revolution, and counterrevolution. The nature of liberal Vienna became a feature of the political and ideological debate, but the patterns of intellectual life it established were continuous down to the Anschluss and the Second World War. In the midst of the decline of political Liberalism, the social basis of Liberalism was more apparent, and the high *Bürgertum* became more isolated from other parts of society. By the 1930s Austrian Socialism and National Socialism seemed to many intellectuals to offer more democratic alternatives than either Liberalism or political Catholicism.

Nonetheless, the culture of liberal Vienna provided a fruitful context for intellectual life and for thinking out the conditions of life in modern civilization, not only for the generation of intellectuals who rebelled against the liberal fathers and created Viennese modernism but also for younger writers such as Weininger, Musil, and Doderer. What is sometimes overlooked in emphasizing Viennese aestheticism and decadence is the distinctive intellectual qualities of liberal Vienna that shaped creative thought after 1900, particularly the receptivity of liberal Vienna to currents of German thought after 1848.[34] Especially striking is the powerful influence of scientific materialism in this Roman Catholic culture of elegance and grace, theater, and opera.

SCIENTIFIC MATERIALISM

What set the intellectual world of liberal Vienna apart from other European traditions was the dominance after 1848 of the natural sciences (especially medicine) in the absence of either a strong social science tradition (as in France) or a strong tradition of idealism or historicism (as in Germany). In Vienna, scientific materialism, emphasizing the natural sciences and medicine, had enormous institutional and ideological power among the liberal intellectual elites, especially with the reform of the University of Vienna and the medical faculty after 1848. If idealism set out from the assumption that the subjective experience of the human being was the key to understanding the nature of reality, scientific materialism assumed that knowledge of the objective, natural world revealed the truth about reality. In the nineteenth century, *positivism* was often associated with the origins of the social sciences, especially in France, whereas the term *scientific materialism* was ordinarily related to developments in the natural sciences, particularly in Germany and Austria.[35] The central figures who shaped these ideas from the 1840s to the 1860s were Ludwig Feuerbach, Ludwig Büchner, and Charles Darwin. Karl

Marx belonged to this period, but he primarily influenced the working-class movement later in the century.[36]

Modern German intellectual historians ordinarily emphasize the Protestant context for German thought, the emergence of the modern university between 1740 and 1830, the history of philosophical idealism, and the broad impact of idealism and romanticism in the early nineteenth century. The context of Austrian intellectual history in the nineteenth century was substantially different, although German language and culture dominated Austrian intellectual life. Unlike Prussia and most of northern Germany, Austria had been Roman Catholic since the Counter Reformation, and it had modernized not through Protestantism but through the Enlightenment.[37] Austria was influenced only slightly by German idealism in the early nineteenth century, and after 1848 German thought arrived in Vienna in the context of the belated creation of a modern university and the powerful impact of scientific materialism. The intellectual worlds of northern Germany and Austria were increasingly similar after 1848; but in Austria enthusiasm for science dominated the intellectual world of the late nineteenth century in the virtual absence of the German idealist tradition.

German-speaking Austria was separated from the distinctive evolution of German culture and intellectual life in the early nineteenth century not only by the division between Protestantism and Catholicism but also by the diplomatic isolation of Germany north of the Main during the decisive years of German idealism and romanticism.[38] Austria's political and intellectual isolation from northern Germany during the Romantic era and the Prussian reform movement meant that Austrian intellectual life was almost untouched by the ideas of Fichte and Schelling, Hegel and Schleiermacher, between 1795 and 1815.[39] Instead, a distinct philosophical and literary tradition emerged in Austria, influenced by Goethe and neohumanism, by G. W. Leibniz and Christian Wolff, as well as English and French thought; in Austria, Enlightenment values of reason, nature, and humanity blended with a reformed Catholicism that emphasized the objectivity and reality of God's world.[40] Austria developed a mainly realistic tradition in philosophy that was resistant to Kant and even more so to his successors in the idealist tradition. Johann Friedrich Herbart (1776–1841) and Bernard Bolzano (1781–1848) were the figures who shaped Austrian philosophy in the early nineteenth century, and Bolzano became influential after 1848 through his student, Robert Zimmermann (1824–1898), who taught at the University of Vienna.[41] Austrian intellectuals seem to have felt at home with the merely empirical reality sometimes disdained in the post-Hegelian atmosphere of German culture.[42] In this sense, liberal intellectual culture in Austria after 1848 was not concerned with overcoming philosophical idealism or recovering from Protestant subjectivity. The intellectual world of Vienna after 1848 was largely continuous with the Enlightenment and German humanism, and it easily absorbed the German scientists and scholars who arrived in Vienna in the 1850s and 1860s, including Franz Brentano. Even Catholic realism could be reconciled with modern science, as Brentano showed.

Although Vienna's faculties of law and medicine were established in the 1750s, the University of Vienna did not emerge as a modern institution comparable to other German universities until a century later, thanks to the reforms after 1848 and the founding of the Second Vienna School of Medicine. Unlike the University of Berlin two generations earlier, Vienna did not take shape as a modern university in the context of *Bildung* and Wilhelm von Humboldt, as well as Ranke and Hegel, but unambiguously in the context of the natural sciences and the ideological confidence of materialism. The Prussian universities were reformed and modernized when idealism was at its height; the Austrian universities underwent a comparable transition after 1848. It is not surprising that German universities continued to emphasize philosophical idealism, history, and human studies even after they took the lead in modern scientific research, while Austrian universities concentrated on scientific research and scientific materialism. Fritz Ringer has emphasized the antiscientific ideology of the German mandarins, the university-certified bureaucrats and professionals.[43] In Austria, the educational ideology of the late nineteenth century was more strongly shaped by scientific materialism than by idealism, historicism, and the human sciences. To be sure, the training in the law faculty was not in the natural sciences, but the worldview of the liberal elite as a whole in Vienna was sympathetic to the natural sciences and strongly influenced by its medical school.[44]

Under the leadership of Count Leo Thun-Hohenstein, the neo-Josephinist bureaucracy reformed and modernized the University of Vienna in the 1850s, principally by inviting German scientists and scholars to join the faculty. The Catholic University of Vienna looked to Protestant, liberal Germany for a model of the university: *Lehrfreiheit* [freedom of teaching] and *Lernfreiheit* [freedom of learning] and faculty as something more than state bureaucrats who would prefer other, higher positions.[45] In 1848, university professors had assumed a leading role in the political life of Germany, and universities became bastions of liberalism, where *Wissenschaft* [science or scholarship] was a kind of liberal religion. This way of thinking gained prominence in Austria after 1848, especially at the University of Vienna and the reformed Second Vienna Medical School. The reform of the gymnasia in Austria also required calling faculty from Germany, and together the gymnasia and the universities became the foundations of liberal culture in the late nineteenth century.

Scientific materialism in the nineteenth century was much more strongly influenced by biology than in the seventeenth and eighteenth centuries. Progress in anatomy, physiology, and cell biology had enormous influence in universities, and in the 1860s Darwin's ideas were added to make biology a powerful basis for the materialist worldview. Scientific materialism in the late nineteenth century emphasized empiricism and reason, and refused to contrast philosophical thinking in any fundamental way to the methods of natural science.[46] The classic statement of nineteenth-century positivism was the French ("social science") version formulated by Auguste Comte (1798–1857) in the 1830s. His law of "the total development of the human intelligence" distinguished three stages: "the theological or fictitious, the metaphysical or abstract, and the scientific or positive."[47] In this view "positive" was equated with "scientific" and set in opposition to less developed religious and metaphysical ways of thinking. In less dogmatic or articulated form, this positivist ideology was widely influential among bourgeois intellectuals in Europe after 1848. John Stuart Mill was enthusiastic about it, and positivism had a powerful impact on thinking about society, often in conjunction with the new importance of biology. However, it was aimed primarily at the social sciences and had relatively little influence in Austria at this time. What did have impact at this stage was an emphasis on empiricism, facts, and science, usually in the context of the natural sciences, especially biology.[48]

A physician, Ludwig Büchner (1824–1899), became the principal advocate of scientific materialism in the 1850s in Germany and Austria. Büchner's *Force and Matter* (1858), despite its metaphysical emphases and its challenge to philosophical rationalism, for the most part simply argued a modern research view that emphasized the facts. Büchner advocated the empirical sciences against academic philosophy, but he also acknowledged his affinities with materialism, sensationalism, and determinism and his opposition to "every form of supernaturalism and idealism."[49] The humanist materialism of Ludwig Feuerbach (1804–1872) was both a materialist rendering of German idealism (knowledge of God is knowledge of man) and a logical continuation of the secularization common to the German *Aufklärung* and Josephinism. Feuerbach's critique of Christianity and his vision of man as species-being inspired Marx in the early 1840s, but Feuerbach also had enormous impact on Austrian intellectuals in the following decade and after.[50] Feuerbach's materialist transformation of Christianity, which saw Jesus as the recovery of the human essence of religion, was a reformulation of the

Protestant tradition and subjectivist theology quite different from Austrian realism and Catholicism. But it converged after 1848 with liberal humanism in Austria, and it underscored the perspective of modern science in opposition to Catholicism. Büchner and Feuerbach gave élan and passion to atheist humanism after 1848, and these views were warmly received in Vienna, especially at the university and in the medical school. Victor Adler (the founder of Austrian socialism), Arthur Schnitzler (the leading literary figure of Young Vienna), and Sigmund Freud were all students of medicine at the University of Vienna in the 1870s and 1880s when these ideas were dominant.[51]

The influence of Charles Darwin (1809–1882) was only part of a much wider scientific materialism in liberal Vienna. The center of this intellectual excitement was the newly reformed university, where Darwin was enthusiastically received, whether by Carl von Rokitansky (1804–1878), the founder of the Second Vienna Medical School, or by Freud, the young student of physiology. Within the medical school itself, philosophical materialism was more rigorously scientific, experimentalist, and methodological, along the lines of Hermann von Helmholtz (1821–1894) and Ernst von Brücke (1819–1892), but also practically shaped by biology, physiology, and neurology. Darwin changed the whole discussion about human nature when he made human beings decisively part of the animal world; he also brought philosophy and psychology closer to physiology and made reproduction and survival central philosophical themes. Darwin's ideas about the evolution of species, natural selection, and the survival of the fittest had wide influence throughout the Western world in the late nineteenth century, and Frank Sulloway has reminded us of the importance of biology and Darwin in the genesis of Freud's ideas.[52]

At the end of the century, the German biologist Ernst Haeckel (1834–1919) published a summation of nineteenth-century materialism, *Die Welträtsel*, which was immediately translated into English as *The Riddle of the Universe: At the Close of the Nineteenth Century* (1900). Haeckel's popularization of Darwin and evolutionary biology, ordinarily referred to as monism, was widely influential among Vienna's liberal elites. Haeckel's book was a confident assertion of the values of the late nineteenth-century man of science. In his evolutionary ethics and religion, Haeckel managed to capture something of the afterglow of German idealism and humanism in the context of biology. But his enthusiastic advocacy of science and progress also contributed to the dark sense of fatalism and determinism that accompanied scientific materialism by the end of the century, helping to shape Weininger's view of the place of the individual in the universe as well as the somber positivism and determinism that broods in Freud's work. Moreover, Haeckel's ideological influence was symptomatic of the drift of scientific materialism from 1848 to 1900: from being the hard edge of revolutionary liberalism and democracy to a more conservative view that was sympathetic to the biological reductions of sex and race.[53]

Two creative minds who were important for what came to be known as Austrian philosophy in the twentieth century emerged out of this scientific context: Franz Brentano (1838–1917) and Ernst Mach (1838–1916). Brentano was one of the German scholars who arrived in Vienna during the high liberal era, but he was also a Catholic priest whose proofs for the existence of God gave pause to the young Freud. How resistant Austrian philosophy remained to German idealism even after 1848 is apparent in Freud's account of Brentano's views. Brentano emphasized his admiration for Locke, Leibniz, and Hume as well as his qualified approval of Kant, who Brentano thought was overrated. As Freud reported, "[W]hat makes Kant important is his successors, Schelling, Fichte, and Hegel, whom Brentano dismisses as swindlers (you can see how close he comes to the materialists in this regard)."[54] We may think of Brentano as the continuation and modernization of the Austrian tradition in philosophy, although Brentano himself was educated and trained in Germany rather than Austria. Brentano had his own quite distinctive approach, but he represented an attempt to reconcile Catholicism and modern science that was more at home in Vienna than in Berlin.

Ernst Mach may be regarded as the continuation and modernization of the secular tradition of scientific materialism in Austria. His critical positivism was more sophisticated epistemologically than the sociological positivism associated with Comte. Moreover, Mach's positivism was grounded in the physical sciences and psychology (and to some extent in biology in his practical, economical concept of knowledge).[55] He was the equivalent in Austrian philosophy of Wilhelm Dilthey (1833–1911) in Germany. Just as Dilthey's achievement was to move German idealism to the methodologically more sophisticated ground of the modern cultural and social sciences, so Mach moved thinking about the natural sciences away from the metaphysical style of scientific materialism. If Dilthey liberated the human sciences from the methodological tyranny of the natural sciences, Mach developed a critical positivism that was designed to further modern science by assuming a purely methodological standpoint. Although Mach was a physicist, he did not assume the metaphysical primacy of physics. He simply assumed the unity of human knowledge based on understanding the relations among sensations. For Mach, physics, biology, and psychology all deal with the same sensations, but each organizes them from different points of view. Mach hoped to free modern science from pointless metaphysical quarrels between materialism and idealism and to open the way to a scientific method that simply described relations among sensations.[56]

Brentano and Mach remain the principal points of reference in the late nineteenth century for philosophers and intellectual historians attempting to locate an Austrian tradition. But both of these philosophers were important primarily for their influence after 1900 on academic philosophy—in Vienna and elsewhere. Brentano influenced Edmund Husserl (1859–1938) and Martin Heidegger (1889–1976), the principal figures in phenomenology and existentialism, both of whom became major figures in German philosophy in the early twentieth century.[57] In addition to his impact on modern physics, Mach is generally regarded as the father of logical positivism and the Vienna Circle, and he came to stand for the modern sciences in Vienna and for views that were associated with literary impressionism and naturalism.[58] Brentano and Mach are important as the most familiar symptoms of the receptivity of liberal Vienna and the University of Vienna to scientific philosophies in the late nineteenth century.[59] Brentano and Mach began to have some influence in Vienna before 1900 (for example, on Freud and on the writers of Young Vienna), but it was the wider enthusiasm for scientific materialism that was the palpable reality within this intellectual culture by 1900.[60] Weininger, Musil, and Doderer all confronted the powerful influence of the scientific worldview, but they reacted very differently. Mach's insistence that the ego must be given up appealed to Musil but represented a terrible threat to Otto Weininger.[61] Weininger recoiled from the dominance of the natural sciences in the intellectual world of liberal Vienna, Musil embraced it, and Doderer tried to find a way beyond it.

PHILOSOPHICAL IRRATIONALISM

Along with scientific materialism, the major influence of German thought in Austrian liberal culture after 1848 was not the German idealism of Fichte, Schelling, and Hegel but, rather, the "other" post-Kantian tradition: from Kant to Schopenhauer to Nietzsche.[62] This less familiar strand of post-Kantian thought was alert to the power of nonrational and nonconscious elements in human thought and behavior, and its positive contribution to Austrian thought in the early twentieth century was a heightened awareness of the role of feelings and an attempt to develop a more balanced understanding of human personality.[63] Philosophical irrationalism seems to have arrived in liberal Vienna in three main waves: first, the influence of Arthur Schopenhauer (1788–1860) on the most distinguished minds of the liberal elite in the 1860s; second, the influence of Schopenhauer in combination with the young

Friedrich Nietzsche (1844–1900) and Richard Wagner (1813–1883), all of whom were enthusiastically received by students at the University of Vienna in the 1870s in the context of German nationalism and a critique of liberal rationalism and individualism; and third, the influence of Schopenhauer and the late Nietzsche at the turn of the century, primarily in the generation of 1905.

Arthur Schopenhauer's *Die Welt als Wille und Vorstellung* (1819) became one of the most influential books of the late nineteenth century, and it was associated by 1880 with fashionable talk of the unconscious, although the idea of the unconscious [*das Unbewusste* and its variants] goes back at least to Leibniz's *petites perceptions* (unconscious apperception and reflection).[64] Schopenhauer represents perhaps the most significant break with the classic rationalism of academic philosophy and with the subject-object conventions of modern thought. He was as important for European intellectual history in the second half of the nineteenth century as Hegel was for the first half, but Schopenhauer's views were the opposite of Hegel's: pessimism, lack of faith in historical progress, and a critique of liberal assumptions about rationalism and individualism. Schopenhauer set out from Kant's Copernican revolution of the mind as the point of departure for modern thought as well as the justification of modern science: the view that our understanding of the lawfulness and coherence of phenomenal reality is a function of the categories of human understanding. Kant emphasized the limits of human understanding and the impossibility of knowing the ultimate nature of reality, the thing-in-itself. Schopenhauer believed that he had discovered this unknown X, which he called the Will, by which he meant the senseless impulse and need of the body rather than the conscious purpose and intentionality often associated with the will. According to Schopenhauer, this mindless force at the heart of phenomenal reality expressed itself in human beings as the illusion of individuation and the will to live.[65] Schopenhauer believed that ultimate reality was what he called the Will—the opposite of the conscious will of the individual. The Will expresses itself in organic matter as the will to live—it is neediness, demand, suffering, force, sex, hunger, and survival.

Schopenhauer's philosophy was close to a biological view of human nature and to materialist and positivist approaches to knowledge, although in Kantian form. Schopenhauer had begun his own university studies in medicine, and his ideas were often attractive during the nineteenth century to physicians and biologists because of his emphasis on unity and conflict in nature and on the role of suffering in human life. Schopenhauer was received enthusiastically by many people who admired Darwin. While Darwin emphasized our status as animals, Schopenhauer underscored our dependence on a senseless metaphysical Will at the heart of the universe. Although Schopenhauer wrote a half century before Darwin and emphasized a metaphysical vision of the world as Will, many nineteenth-century observers noticed the complementarity between his views and Darwin's.[66] Both thinkers imagined human beings at the disposal of nature and saw human behavior in terms of survival and need.[67] For both, reason and civilization introduced new capacities for consciousness and knowledge, but the deeper destiny in nature was more fundamental. In the 1860s Schopenhauer was an important point of reference for the leading minds of liberal Vienna, whether Carl von Rokitansky (1804–1878), the dominant figure in the medical school, or Ferdinand von Saar (1833–1906), the master of prose style. Although Schopenhauer's critique of progress and individualism influenced leading figures of the liberal elite in the 1860s, philosophical irrationalism had an even wider impact in the 1870s in the context of Wagner's music and Nietzsche's early works.[68] In the 1870s these ideas were often associated with German nationalism and democratic politics, and they were attractive to young intellectuals such as Freud, Gustav Mahler (1860–1911), and Victor Adler (1852–1918).

Richard Wagner became the most influential interpreter of Schopenhauer's ideas to the late nineteenth century. Wagner represented a revolution in music and a spiritual critique of liberal rationalism and individualism, both of which were influential in Austria. In combination with Nietzsche's *The Birth of Tragedy*, Wagner had an enormous impact on the communitarian critique of Austrian liberalism; the enthusiasm of the young Nietzsche as well as the even younger Freud, Adler, and Mahler is evidence of the fit between Schopenhauer's ideas and Wagner's music.[69] But Wagner also advocated an anti-Semitism that influenced German nationalism in Austria in ways that obliged Freud and others to withdraw from it. Wagner's "higher" anti-Semitism gave respectability to the Jew-baiting of the German nationalists around Schönerer. This spiritual form of anti-Semitism continued to be influential in Vienna down to Houston Stewart Chamberlain's *The Foundations of the Nineteenth-Century* (1899).[70] Chamberlain was both Wagner's son-in-law as well as an important influence on Hitler's ideas, a significant link between the Wagnerian ideology of music and Hitler's own gift for speaking directly to the feelings.[71] Nietzsche moved away from Wagner, but the creative force of the music and the ideas of the 1870s continued to be important for intellectuals after the turn of the century. Wagner had only limited intellectual significance, but he was important on popular and political levels, and he offered a model of genius to the educated elite, including Weininger and many of the people Musil knew as a young man. Wagner's philosophical significance lies at the point where his enthusiasm for Schopenhauer and his achievement as a musician intersect: in his artistic rendering of the world as feelings.

Although Nietzsche was personally and intellectually close to Wagner as a young man, his thought was more deeply connected to Schopenhauer. Nietzsche shared Schopenhauer's tragic pessimism, but he attempted to transform the Will toward life—to give value to human existence and to create a new culture that went beyond the asceticism of priests and scientists. Schopenhauer had a powerful sense of the horror of existence, whether in his own immediate experience of pain and need or in his observation of the brutality of nature and the self-aggrandizement and futility of human life. He counseled the renunciation of the Will, whether through the aesthetic contemplation of the phenomenal world or in the ascetic renunciation of the Will at the heart of ethical and religious life. For Nietzsche, Schopenhauer was the culmination of Western nihilism and a deeply appealing worldview for creative, ethical people; thus, Schopenhauer was both Nietzsche's principal precursor and the central intellectual problem of his work. Despite his debt to Schopenhauer, Nietzsche spent most of his intellectual energy trying to overcome him.

Nietzsche announced the death of Western morality and culture as well as the death of Western religion and philosophy, and he pointed to what is problematic in morality and motivation. Although his account of Western nihilism was both an assertion of the truth of human existence and a recognition of untruth as the basis of life, his critique of Christianity and its successor ideologies was also an attempt to overcome Western nihilism as he saw it embodied in Schopenhauer (and, in a different sense, in modern science). From his earliest works, Nietzsche developed a critique of the liberal culture of knowledge, which he believed was cut off from the reality of human existence and from the genuine sources of creativity. Indeed, one might characterize his *Schopenhauer as Educator* (1874) as a critique of the decline of the *Bildung* tradition in the name of an even more demanding statement of this ideal of self-creation.[72] His work as a whole is the most important continuation of the irrationalist tradition after Schopenhauer—a series of histories of the forms of human feeling from *The Birth of Tragedy* (1872) to *The Genealogy of Morals* (1887); in his attempt to understand the history of morality and the feelings beneath the surface, Nietzsche interpreted moralities as "a sign language of the affects."[73] Perhaps the clearest formulation of his reworking of the irrationalist tradition appears in *The Gay Science*, in one of the sections he added in 1887:

My idea is, as you see, that consciousness does not really belong to man's individual existence but rather to his social or herd nature. . . . Fundamentally, all our actions are altogether incomparably personal, unique, and infinitely individual; there is no doubt of that. But as soon as we translate them into consciousness *they no longer seem to be*.[74]

Schopenhauer and Nietzsche took on significance in the context of liberalism's obtuseness about religion and ethics. This was the point of vulnerability of the liberal tradition as it hardened in the late nineteenth century into a culture of reason, pragmatism, and achievement in which the aesthetic appeared as kitsch and the ethical appeared as a set of unmotivated rules. Schopenhauer's challenge to the dominant culture of achievement, competition, and control appealed strongly to creative people in the late nineteenth century, and after the turn of the century, Nietzsche was important for the intellectuals of the generation of 1905 for awakening new ways of drawing on the ethical and aesthetic imagination.

Whereas scientific materialism tended toward an idealization of nature (and an optimistic, evolutionary view), philosophical irrationalism was more ambivalent about unconscious instincts and feelings. What is too often overlooked, however, is the extent of common ground between scientific materialism and Nietzsche.[75] Nietzsche's view was not merely a critique of scientific materialism but an attempt to experience the full implications of this way of thinking, the simultaneously nihilistic and ethical implications of modern scientific knowledge. Scientific materialism and philosophical irrationalism shared common ground except that irrationalism made explicit important aspects of human experience that scientific materialism generally ignored. Both of these ways of thinking threatened liberal individualism and rationalism. In an early essay about Schopenhauer, Nietzsche argued that Germans in the late nineteenth century were living "on the inherited capital of morality which our forefathers have accumulated, and which we only squander instead of increasing." Against the inertia of conventional existence, Nietzsche advocated the human being who "voluntarily takes the pain of truthfulness upon himself, and this suffering serves to kill his individual will to prepare that complete revolution and reversal of his being, the attainment of which is the actual meaning of life."[76]

Nietzsche's announcement of the death of God and Western culture and his invitation to a creative morality found an intellectual world in Vienna that was prepared to receive these ideas. But his influence on Young Vienna in the 1890s was still very slight by comparison with his importance for writers and philosophers after 1900, including the philosophers of the Vienna

Circle. Throughout Central Europe, in Austria as well as in Germany, it was the intellectuals of the generation of 1905 who responded most strongly to the late Nietzsche.[77] In part, this was simply because Nietzsche's later works did not appear in print until the 1880s or, in some cases, until after his death in 1900. But the literary impressionists and modernists of Young Vienna seem not to have had ears for the whisperings of Schopenhauer and Nietzsche. The leading figures of Young Vienna in the 1890s avoided their influence to an extent that would have been unimaginable after the turn of the century.[78] Gustav Klimt provides the conspicuous exception in the generation of the 1890s. His erotic vision of reality in the University paintings drew on the inspiration of Schopenhauer and Nietzsche in challenging the liberal view of reason, science, and medicine advocated by Friedrich Jodl. Klimt's *Philosophy* of 1900 and his *Medicine* of 1901 offer a far more intense vision of sexuality and the irrational forces at work in human life than anything in Schnitzler or Hofmannsthal. Schopenhauer and Nietzsche never strongly influenced Schnitzler. Hofmannsthal recalled his belated understanding of philosophical irrationalism in reading Rudolf Kassner: "[N]ever before were continuous thoughts of Schopenhauer, of Nietzsche or the like, capable of giving me such inner happiness . . . such an understanding of why one writes poetry . . . and what it has to do with existence."[79] Kassner set the tone for his generation's reception of philosophical irrationalism in Austria, arguing that at first the Germans had not read Nietzsche "at all, and then they became hysterical, and Schopenhauer was for them the prophet of suicide."[80] By contrast with the reception of the early Nietzsche in the 1870s, however, it was a more cerebral, less romantic, more individualistic Nietzsche who was influential at the turn of the century, although Nietzsche's critique of scientific knowledge remained.[81]

The dramatic influence of philosophical irrationalism in Austria, of Schopenhauer and Nietzsche as well as Kierkegaard, came with the essayists, novelists, and philosophers who reached creative maturity in the first decade of the twentieth century: Rudolf Kassner (1873–1959), Karl Kraus (1874–1936), Martin Buber (1878–1965), Grete Meisel-Hess (1879–1922), Otto Weininger (1880–1903), Robert Musil (1880–1942), Ferdinand Ebner (1882–1931), Hermann Broch (1886–1951), and Ludwig Wittgenstein (1889–1951).[82] Philosophical irrationalism was important in the generation of 1905 for thinking about art, ethics, feelings, religion, and gender; and it shaped the ideas of these writers about masculinity and femininity, and about the relationships between ethics and aesthetics and between thinking and feeling. In the context of scientific materialism and philosophical irrationalism, intellectuals were ready to think about sexuality and gender in new ways that were

Figure 3. Gustav Klimt, *Medicine.* University paintings, 1901.

less encumbered by traditional assumptions about human nature. This worldview combined a biological vision of material reality and a view of human subjectivity as fundamentally irrational, acting out of unknown motives and senseless need. And this combination of perspectives was also often close to the anxiety of masculine rationalism about these threats, perhaps most eloquently expressed in Nietzsche's opening to *Beyond Good and Evil:* "Supposing truth is a woman—what then?" The blend of scientific materialism and philosophical irrationalism in liberal Vienna combined an awareness of the dying value structures of traditional religion with a frankly biological view of human nature.

Philosophical irrationalism established sexuality and whatever the mind cannot control as philosophical issues; in this tradition, sexuality, women, religion, and the unconscious appeared as threats to reason, usually negatively but sometimes positively. Irrationalism was the most explicit and important modern misogynist tradition, but it was also the only nineteenth-century philosophical tradition centrally concerned with gender and sexuality as well as with the relationships between thinking and feeling, consciousness and unconsciousness. In retrospect, what is interesting about Schopenhauer is not so much that he was a misogynist but rather that he had as much clarity as he did about the significance of sexuality and gender in European culture. European intellectual life in the nineteenth century, including the variation of it that developed in Vienna, was dominated by men and by assumptions about reason, consciousness, and knowledge that were rarely questioned within the university or, for the most part, in other areas of public discourse. Within these assumptions, sexuality, women, the feminine, and irrationality were closely associated with one another, and the meanings of these words often elided and blurred. It was this general area of concern that made philosophical irrationalism both so important, because of its conscious interest in these issues, and so misogynist, because of its conviction that the realm suggested by these words threatened human individuality, freedom, and consciousness.

The distinctive blend of scientific materialism and philosophical irrationalism that characterized liberal Vienna did not change in fundamental ways after the First World War, but politics came to play a larger role in virtually everyone's thinking. Concerns with race and national community became more central, and the spiritual anti-Semitism of Wagner took on new importance. There is a strong rational component in philosophical irrationalism, not only in Schopenhauer and in the late Nietzsche but in Freud, Weininger, and Musil. Moreover, the importance and power of the scientific tradition at work in Vienna (especially at the medical school) is sometimes

overlooked in the emphasis on fin-de-siècle decadence, aestheticism, and irrationalism. It is only in this scientistic context that it becomes interesting to
find in these thinkers such alertness to the irrational and such a willingness
to move away from the liberal, rationalist view of human nature in which
they were reared. In 1900, however, thinking about sexuality for the most
part still lagged behind the possibilities opened up by these ways of thinking.
Discourse was strongly influenced by scientific materialism but less so by irrationalism, and Freud represented the only clear sign of combining these
ways of thinking before 1900.

THINKING ABOUT SEXUALITY AND GENDER

> Sexual feeling is really the root of all ethics, and no doubt of aes-
> theticism and religion.
> > Richard von Krafft-Ebing, *Psychopathia Sexualis* (1886)

> We are unknown to ourselves, we men of knowledge. . .
> > Nietzsche, *Genealogy of Morals*

There is general agreement about the importance of Vienna in the 1890s as a
historical location for thinking about sexuality. Austrian writers, physicians,
and painters of the 1890s have attracted considerable attention for their interest in sexuality, in sexual behavior and sexual convention, but also for their
emphasis on the power and threat of femininity for men. In the early twentieth century Viennese writers were acknowledged within the wider sphere
of German culture for their distinctive preoccupation with sexuality:

> In all areas Austrians—poets, novelists, psychologists, cultural critics—
> transmitted to their German audience their obsession with decadence
> and their attempt to come to terms with eros: Sigmund Freud, Hugo von
> Hofmannsthal, Karl Kraus, and Arthur Schnitzler had as many readers in
> Berlin, Munich, and Frankfurt as they had in Vienna—perhaps more.[83]

At the same time the emphasis on sexuality and gender in Vienna after
1900 was often a way of addressing other issues. As Edward Timms puts it,
in "turn-of-the-century Vienna sexuality became the 'symbolic territory'
where the fundamental issues of the age were debated: the crisis of individual identity, the conflicts between reason and irrationalism, between domination and subservience."[84]

In relation to Europe and the wider realm of German culture, there was little to set Vienna apart in 1900, whether in bourgeois social convention or in thinking about sexuality and gender. The sexual conventions of the upper *Bürgertum* conformed for the most part to European standards—from prostitution to proper marriage—and the social realities of sexuality and gender in Vienna offered little to challenge nineteenth-century assumptions. Thinking about sexuality and gender in Vienna before 1900 was not fundamentally different from such thinking elsewhere in Europe and the United States. The men who wrote about sexuality in Austria, whether for medical journals or for the theater, generally shared the values and perceptions of educated European men in the late nineteenth century. Freud had not yet published his views on sexuality and gender, nor had Karl Kraus published his attack on the Austrian legal system and his defense of sexual freedom. Except for hints of psychoanalysis in the work of Josef Breuer and Freud in the 1890s, medicalized discourse about sexuality and gender in Vienna was still firmly embedded in the European norms of the nineteenth century.

Both social convention and scientific research in liberal Vienna set out from the assumption of deep and fundamental differences between men and women.[85] The polarity of gender was a European-wide phenomenon in the nineteenth century, although in Vienna the conventions of cavalier grace and style, learned by bourgeois sons in their year of military service, may actually have exaggerated perceptions of this polarity common to European culture as a whole. In terms of our contemporary discourse about gender, a great deal still remained concealed under the word *Geschlecht*, which meant both "sex" and "gender" and which was the conventional German prefix for "sexual," to say nothing of its associations with everything from grammar to species. Ordinary language routinely blurred these issues in much the same way that the word "sex" does in English: that is, a discussion of sex was a discussion of gender.[86] In much the same way, Austrian literature drew on conventional European stereotypes about women, sexuality, and love.[87] But these issues were not yet formulated in ways that are familiar to the late twentieth century. For example, there was no clear distinction in the 1890s between "sex" and "gender," but most physicians and most other writers matter-of-factly assumed fundamental and more or less bipolar differences between men and women. The realities of sexual pleasure (let alone some norm of average experience) are one area in which the limits of historical knowledge become conspicuous. Scholars are not even in rough agreement about the realities of sexual life in bourgeois marriage, to say nothing of its national variations.[88] For the Victorian world of England and the United

States, Steven Marcus's view of repression and the woman is often cited, but Peter Gay has argued that reality was less repressive and that the woman was more involved in sexual experience than has often been supposed.[89]

The men who wrote about sexuality and gender in Vienna were all strongly influenced by the tensions within the liberal tradition on these issues. The great nineteenth-century liberal, John Stuart Mill (1806–1873), wrote one of the classic statements on women's emancipation, but liberalism also belonged to the conventions of *bürgerlich* life in the nineteenth century. The emancipatory tradition of liberal humanism and individualism influenced early feminism and brought a large number of men into the early women's movement, and yet the University of Vienna did not make a place for women as matriculated students until 1897 in the sciences and the humanities (philosophy faculty) and until 1900 in medicine.[90] As in Germany, Austrian bourgeois liberal goals of emancipation called up the woman question, and bourgeois emancipation through education was allied with liberalism and the natural sciences at the university. At the same time, women's emancipation conflicted with bourgeois notions of the family, and very little had changed by the 1890s.[91] Although Liberalism was the leading advocate of women's rights in nineteenth-century Austria, most liberal men assumed the limitations of reproduction, family, and the management of the house. And these ways of thinking were informed by the powerful realities of disease, unwanted children, and death in childbirth.[92]

Mill had great influence on liberal Vienna in almost every respect, but *The Subjection of Women* (1869) seems to have found little resonance among liberals. Despite widespread admiration for Mill, the Viennese high *Bürgertum* did no better with the theme of women than other European liberal elites in the late nineteenth century. The ambivalence of Austrian liberalism on the woman question is perhaps most evident in Theodor Gomperz (1832–1912), whose credentials as a liberal and as Mill's translator are not in doubt.[93] Although Gomperz was one of the most prominent men in the women's movement, he seems to have had difficulty appreciating Mill's essay on women. Mill's wish to extend liberal conceptions of humanity and education to women met with incomprehension even from Gomperz, who regarded higher education and professional life as suitable for women only in exceptional cases, but as not relevant to the majority of women.

Ernest Jones recounts Freud's perceptions of his own views on women in reference to Freud's 1880 translation of Mill. Freud regarded Mill as "perhaps the man of the century who best managed to free himself from the domination of customary prejudices":

On the other hand—and that always goes together with it—he lacked in
many matters the sense of the absurd; for example, in that of female emancipation and in the woman's question altogether. I recollect that in the essay
I translated a prominent argument was that a married woman could earn as
much as her husband. We surely agree that the management of a house, the
care and bringing up of children, demands the whole of a human being and
almost excludes any earning, even if a simplified household relieve her of
dusting, cleaning, cooking, etc. He had simply forgotten all that, like everything else concerning the relationship between the sexes. That is altogether
a point with Mill where one simply cannot find him human.[94]

Although many readers will be inclined to think of this passage as a commentary on Freud, it represented the enlightened view of an educated young
man from the Viennese liberal *Bürgertum* in 1883. In the context of bourgeois conventions about the family and the management of a house, Mill's
views seemed simply "inhuman"—and utterly out of touch with the realities
of social and biological life. For Austrian liberals, the principal obstacles to
Mill's kind of feminism were reproduction and the family, and Freud reacted
much like other liberals such as Gomperz or Eduard von Bauernfeld (1802–
1890). This view allowed for exceptions but not for fundamental changes in
social life.

A more extreme opposition to feminism came from a German scholar
whose views were familiar in Vienna around the turn of the century. P. J.
Möbius (1853–1907) emphasized the biological obstacles to equality and contended that the average woman would never be capable of intellectual or professional life, or at least not for a very long time to come.[95] Möbius argued
that intellectual differences between men and women were grounded in biological differences. He believed that average differences between men and
women in his own time were evident and considerable, and that, in spite of
individual exceptions, talk of equality injured society, because it injured
women and the best conditions for reproduction. He rejected the "American
wisdom" that women should enter the workplace, and he argued that women
were needed in the home. Möbius represented one way in which the biological reduction could be used to justify gendered roles in society, whereas Mill
offered the most eloquent nineteenth-century application of the emancipatory tradition within the liberal movement.

The principal advances of women's rights in Austria before 1900 coincided
with the achievements of Josephinism and liberalism. The Code of Civil Law
of 1812 gave women rights of property and inheritance. In these and other

respects Austrian women were actually better endowed with legal rights than women in other European countries. The February Constitution of 1861 granted women who were large property owners the right to vote in Lower Austria, and progressive reform of public schools in 1869 allowed women a larger role in education. In the last third of the nineteenth century, the main goals of the women's movement in Austria were equal employment and equal opportunity in secondary education, but the movements for suffrage and women's rights were weak.[96] The women's movement was at an early stage in Vienna in 1900, involving a small number of key figures and supported mainly by socialists and liberals, as well as a variety of writers and philosophers.[97] Women in Austria began to contribute to this public discussion at the end of the nineteenth century. Most significant in intellectual terms were Irma von Troll-Borostyáni (1847–1912), Grete Meisel-Hess (1879–1922), and Rosa Mayreder (1858–1938), though only Troll-Borostyáni had much impact before the turn of the century. Mayreder, intellectually the most interesting representative of the women's movement at the turn of the century, did not publish her most important work until after 1900.

The intellectual world of liberal Vienna was almost exclusively male. The most conspicuous exceptions to this generalization—Marie von Ebner Eschenbach (1830–1916) and Josephine von Wertheimstein—recall the elevated social status of the exceptions and confirm the impression that the public world of culture was largely shaped by men. This tendency to acknowledge exceptions appears in the granting of an honorary doctorate to Eschenbach, one of liberal Vienna's finest writers, in 1900, the year that women were first permitted to matriculate in medicine at the University of Vienna.[98] Thus, public discourse about sexuality and gender in liberal Vienna was dominated by men, both in medicalized discourse about sexuality and in literary portrayals of sexual life. Austrian feminism in the early twentieth century did not constitute a very significant threat to the power of men. As with much of feminism in Germany, the emphasis was on valuing motherhood and feminine qualities within the larger context of the family and patriarchy. Certainly Austrian intellectuals such as the young Weininger were not confronted with a movement comparable to the Anglo-American suffrage movement.

The issue of concern for male writers in Vienna around 1900 seems not to have been the strength of the feminist movement, which was still in its early stages, but the power of femininity and female sexuality over men, or put differently, the uncertainty and confusion of men as they encountered their own feelings and sexuality. The power, intensity, and threat of sexuality were apparent in the paintings of Klimt; and the hypocrisy and destructiveness of the social conventions surrounding sexuality in bourgeois Vienna were most evident in the stories and plays of Schnitzler. The social conventions of sexuality seemed obviously unsatisfactory (whether seen through the eyes of Schnitzler, Weininger, Kraus, or Mayreder), and Freud's early attempts to give some order to the realm of the feelings were still virtually unknown among educated people. In the stylized decade of the 1890s, women were both idealized as decorations and demonized as threats to reason.[99] Women and the feminine served as symbols of kitsch and escape from reality, but they were also threats to masculine rationalism.

In Austria, as in other European countries at the turn of the century, medicine and literature did the most to shape discourse about sexuality. Medicine was strongly influenced by a scientific materialism that ordinarily took for granted great differences between men and women and sought to impose conventional conceptions of sexuality and gender. Within this context, a few writers were beginning to work toward a more modern notion of sexuality.[100] Medical research on sexuality was important in Vienna, especially work on the psychopathology of sexual life and childhood sexuality, but this was not distinct from other work in Europe and the United States in its attitudes toward women, children, and masturbation. Freud had very little influence within the medical profession, and even he did not publish his first important work on sexuality (in relation to the general nature of neurosis) until 1905 in *Three Essays on the Theory of Sexuality*. Freud had still not met Schnitzler, whose plays offered realistic portrayals of the sexual customs of fin-de-siècle Vienna.

Literature was at once the medium for the culture's clichés about gender identity and the location for tentative attempts to understand human irrationality and the links between passion and social convention. Viennese modernism was preoccupied with sexuality—and in Arthur Schnitzler Viennese literature produced an important social critic of European stature. Schorske characterizes Schnitzler as describing "the social matrix in which so much of twentieth-century subjectivism took form: the disintegrating moral-aesthetic culture of *fin-de-siècle* Vienna"; and Schorske describes Young Vienna as a movement that "challenged the moralistic stance of nineteenth century literature in favor of sociological truth and psychological—especially sexual—openness."[101] Although there were only very minor personal and intellectual connections between Freud and literary Vienna, Michael Worbs argues that the concerns of nineteenth-century psychiatry and Austrian literature converged in an introspective *Nervenkunst:* both psychoanalysis and Young Vienna developed psychological, inward visions out of the naturalism and positivism of the late nineteenth century. The most striking similarities are between Freud and Schnitzler, whom Freud regarded as his *Doppelgänger* [double], but the other writers of Young Vienna had little interest in psychoanalysis, and Hofmannsthal regarded the founder of psychoanalysis as "'absolute mediocrity.'"[102]

The most dramatic development in thinking about sexuality in the 1890s came in *Studies on Hysteria* (1895) by Freud and Josef Breuer, particularly in their emphases on the significance of internal processes, the rationality of apparently irrational feelings and behaviors, and the role of transference in the relationship between the patient and the physician.[103] These new ways of thinking emerged out of the mainstream of psychiatric research on hysteria in France and Austria, and all of this work was available to students of physiology and psychology at the turn of the century such as Weininger. But these developments in the medical profession were influenced very little, if at all, by the literary and artistic movements of the 1890s. Freud's *Interpretation of Dreams* appeared in 1900, but it had only slight impact at the outset, especially by comparison with the work of his younger contemporary Otto Weininger.[104] Indeed, Sander Gilman emphasizes both Weininger's influence on Freud's thinking between 1903 and 1910 and Weininger's significance as a summation of late nineteenth-century thought.[105]

Weininger attempted both to clarify what his culture meant by "masculine" and "feminine" and to distinguish these notions from actual individual men and women, and his work offers insight into the gendered values of male, liberal culture in Vienna around 1900. Weininger's book draws attention to the significance of gender and sexuality as a way of thinking about central problems in philosophy for Viennese intellectuals after 1900. The theme of sexuality and gender provided these writers with ways to think about science, modern society, and resistance to modernity in the German-speaking culture of Central Europe but without the customary emphasis on German nationalism. In the creative minds of Vienna after 1900, sexuality and gender became metaphors for thinking out human experience in the wake of scientific materialism and philosophical irrationalism. It was in this context that Weininger's radical critique of sexuality and gender appeared, which adopted the grammar of gender to interpret the central philosophical issues of modern culture in the aftermath of positivism and the work of Nietzsche.

Figure 4. Otto Weininger (1880–1903)

CHAPTER TWO

⟡

OTTO WEININGER'S VISION OF GENDER
AND MODERN CULTURE

In the end we are always rewarded for our good will, our patience, fairmindedness, and gentleness with what is strange; gradually, it sheds its veil and turns out to be a new and indescribable beauty. That is its *thanks* for our hospitality. Even those who love themselves will have learned it in this way; for there is no other way. Love, too, has to be learned.

Nietzsche, *The Gay Science*

*O*tto Weininger's book on sexuality and gender appeared in Vienna in May 1903. His suicide a few months later, in the house where Beethoven died, drew attention to the author and his book, and twenty-five reprintings appeared in German over the next twenty-two years. In the preface to *Geschlecht und Charakter*, Weininger announced his intention to understand the nature of gender not by means of "'inductive metaphysics'" but rather by means of the "step-by-step psychological deepening" of themes that were familiar to everyone. Weininger acknowledged that his work would be read as antifeminist, even though it was directed against men "in a deeper sense than the women's rights people imagine," and he made clear that he was more concerned with the deeper, fundamental issues of human existence than with the applause he could expect for his negative view of women. He was also conscious that some philosophers might find it offensive to have the highest and ultimate questions treated in the context of a problem of "no very great dignity." He conceded that he shared this feeling but argued that "the special problem of the polarity of genders constitutes more the point of departure than the goal of the deeper exploration."[1]

Weininger's study of gender is largely devoted to a critique of femininity, which culminates in a critique of Judaism that identifies female qualities with the male Jew.[2] *Geschlecht und Charakter* offers important evidence for the power of antifeminist and anti-Semitic discourse in the liberal culture of Vienna, and Jacques Le Rider argues that the "partial identity of the anti-Semitic and antifeminist elements constitutes the originality of Weininger's writings."[3] Weininger is ordinarily regarded as an instance of misogyny and Jewish self-hatred, and Peter Gay has emphasized his appeal to "an oddly assorted collection of misogynists and anti-Semites. . . ."[4] But most people who met him at the turn of the century regarded him as an obviously brilliant and creative person. Robert Calasso emphasizes the indebtedness of other intellectuals to Weininger, particularly "writers who abhorred the 'milieu of the educated': Karl Kraus, August Strindberg, Ludwig Wittgenstein."[5] In retrospect, it is easy to discount Weininger but more difficult to understand why he seemed to serious minds of his generation to have ethical and intellectual significance. His appeal extended beyond misogynists and anti-Semites to some of the best minds of the generation of 1905, including Austrians such as Kraus, Wittgenstein, Musil, Hermann Broch, Franz Kafka, Arnold Schönberg, Georg Trakl, Italo Svevo, and Ferdinand Ebner, as well as non-Austrians such as James Joyce, D. H. Lawrence, and Gertrude Stein.[6] Ebner, who was two years younger than Weininger, argued that his generation of Austrian intellectuals had to "overcome four 'spiritual-intellectual illnesses': Richard Wagner, Otto Weininger, psychoanalysis, Karl Kraus."[7] Weininger was also important for the next generation of Austrian writers, including Heimito von Doderer and Elias Canetti.

What is sometimes lost in evaluations of Weininger is the nature of the philosophical and moral issues at stake for him and his significance as a representative of a crisis of Western values on the threshold of modern culture. Apparent on the surface of Weininger's text are his misogyny and his anti-Semitism, but within these limitations he attempted to deconstruct conventional understandings of gender identity.[8] Moreover, Weininger represented for serious minds an exemplary moral intensity and a critique of liberal Vienna that spoke to the central philosophical problems of his time. He was also a dramatic example of the connection between philosophy and the preoccupation with sexuality and gender in Vienna at the turn of the century. His work constituted an attempt to save the free, rational, conscious self from the realities identified by philosophical irrationalism—the threats summarized by sexuality and woman—and from the reductions of modern science and empiricism. Weininger introduced the theme of a grammar of gender—and the radical nihilism of his generation. Central to his thought was the task of overcoming nihilism, of confronting the meaninglessness and lack of value in modern life. He was a misogynist of a rather peculiar and unabashed type, although he was not a sexist in anything like the conventional sense of this word.[9] He becomes more readable when we bear in mind his ideal-type method: he wanted to try to characterize M and F, male and female, as abstractions that do not exist in reality, and he made creative contributions to discussions of sexuality and gender by moving away from nineteenth-century assumptions about sex. This is crucial to understanding why Weininger was so important to Viennese intellectuals. The breadth of his appeal can probably be explained by his misogyny and anti-Semitism, but this does not explain his significance to Wittgenstein, Mayreder, Broch, and Musil. I have no desire to make Weininger's prejudices more appealing, but I wish to understand what was actually at stake for him and for creative writers who read him. What is central to Weininger's thought is not misogyny or anti-Semitism but rather a crisis of liberal rationalism and individualism in the face of modern society and two powerful intellectual challenges: philosophical irrationalism and scientific materialism. Weininger attempted to give value to life after modern science and Nietzsche by way of Kant and a critique of modern attitudes toward sexuality and science.

GENDER AND CHARACTER

As a man who wrote a critique of femininity and as a Jew who wrote an attack on Judaism, Weininger's intellectual work was closely connected to his person.[10] It would be difficult to think of a creative person whose work has been more consistently judged by his character—or whose character is more consistently inferred from his work. A significant portion of the early scholarship on Weininger was not only biographical but specifically psychological. This was conspicuously true of one of the first studies to appear after Weininger's suicide, a psychiatric biography by Ferdinand Probst entitled *Der Fall Otto Weininger: Eine psychiatrische Studie* [The Case of Otto Weininger: A Psychiatric Study] (Wiesbaden, 1904), which established the tendency to regard Weininger as a psychological case study. Forty years later, a Norwegian psychoanalyst wrote about Weininger with considerably greater sympathy and understanding in what is still the most comprehensive biography of Weininger in English: David Abrahamsen's *The Mind and Death of a Genius* (New York, 1946).[11] Abrahamsen's account echoed another early theme of Weininger scholarship: Weininger as the genius who inspired his generation, a notion that became the dominant motif for Kraus, Hermann Swoboda, Emil Lucka, Moriz Rappaport, and Carl Dallago.[12] In 1907, Robert Saudek argued that Weininger was either the "hysterical" author of an anti-feminist book or a genius of "enormous depth."[13] Most of the early work on Weininger emphasized his genius, his moral intensity, and his critique of women.[14] Surprisingly, feminists were sometimes sympathetic to Weininger: Charlotte Perkins Gilman, for example, criticized his "'andro-centric view of humanity'" but admired "the 'intense moral earnestness' and 'lofty scope' of Weininger's work."[15] Beginning in the 1930s anti-Semitism emerged as the central theme with Theodor Lessing's chapter on Weininger in his book on Jewish self-hatred, *Der jüdische Selbsthass* (Berlin, 1930), which inspired a large literature, from Weininger's National Socialist admirers to Allan Janik's recent critique of arguments about Jewish self-hatred.[16] Weininger did not receive a great deal of attention in the twenty-five years after the Second World War, but this began to change in the 1970s with the appearance of Janik and Toulmin's *Wittgenstein's Vienna* (New York, 1973), in which Weininger figured prominently.[17] The reprinting in 1980 of the original edition of *Geschlecht und Charakter* was followed by Le Rider's biography of Weininger in 1982 and by a collection of articles by Le Rider and Norbert Leser.[18] By 1990, Hannelore Rodlauer could characterize the new interest as a "Weininger Renaissance."[19] This assessment was confirmed in the English-speaking world in 1995 with the collection of essays edited by Nancy A. Harrowitz and Barbara Hyams, *Jews and Gender: Responses to Otto Weininger* and, more recently, by Chandak Sengoopta's *Otto Weininger: Sex, Science, and Self in Imperial Vienna* (2000).

Despite the recent interest in Weininger's work, it continues to be true that Weininger's person is often the issue and that the scholarly discussion is largely ad hominem. This tendency is most evident in accounts of his mental illness, religious conversion, self-hatred, and sexual orientation. Characterizations of Weininger's sexual orientation have been especially casual, although Le Rider provides some clarification of assumptions in the scholarship that Weininger regarded himself as a homosexual.[20] I am less interested in psychologizing Weininger than in understanding the ways of thinking that were available to a brilliant, creative young man in Vienna around 1900 and why Weininger chose sexuality and gender as the way to summarize his critique of philosophy and science. Weininger was a problematic person and his arguments are often offensive, but what is lost in ad hominem accounts of his work is his distinctive critique of philosophy and science, his reasons for choosing sexuality and gender as his subject, and what this means about Vienna 1900.

Weininger was born in Vienna on April 3, 1880, to parents from the lower *Bürgertum*. His grandparents on both sides of his family had been part of the migration of Jews to Vienna after 1848 from other regions of the empire, from Hungary, Moravia, and Bohemia. His father, Leopold Weininger, was a craftsman whose work in gold, china, and enamel became known throughout Europe.[21] Although Leopold Weininger was not part of the *Bildungsbürgertum*, he participated in the broader currents of liberal Vienna and cosmopolitan culture, and his enthusiasm for languages and music played a large role in his son's education. He married Adelheid Frey in 1878, and in the next twenty years she gave birth to seven children, the last when she was forty-one and Otto was eighteen. Otto was the first son and the first child to survive childhood.

Most of what we know about Otto's childhood and youth concerns his intellectual intensity and his appetite for knowledge.[22] He was a precocious student, very much under the influence of his father, whom he seemed to mirror in his intellectual gifts and in his withdrawn emotional life. Otto's mother appears in the sources as attractive, hardworking, and gifted at languages, but her husband clearly dominated the family; she was ill much of the time and died of tuberculosis. Judging from the accounts of Otto's sister, Rosa (who admired both her father and Otto), and from the complete defection of his brother Richard to the United States, the emotional world of Otto's youth was probably not very happy. The fact that Otto was intellectually more mature than other children derived in part from his father's attentions and from Otto's tendency to retreat from his family into a world of books. He was sometimes difficult to deal with in the *Volksschule,* and Abrahamsen is probably right to imagine him as aloof and superior and not particularly well adjusted as a boy. Otto received the classical gymnasium education of a Viennese intellectual. He studied very little mathematics or science until the university, but he excelled in history, literature, logic, philosophy, and languages. He read Latin and Greek in the gymnasium and learned English, French, and Spanish from his father, who was astonished at the ease with which his son mastered new languages.[23] Observers of Otto as a child emphasized the strong will that allowed him to challenge not only his teachers but eventually even his father, who had wanted him to attend the Consular Academy.

Weininger arrived at the University of Vienna in the fall of 1898, where he left the philological world of the gymnasium for the natural sciences, beginning with physics and mathematics and turning by 1900 to biology, medicine, and philosophy.[24] His interests in science and empiricism drew him into the mainstream of academic life at the university. He was a member of the Philosophical Society of the University of Vienna, which was regularly attended by both students and faculty.[25] His mentor, Friedrich Jodl, played an active role in the society, to which almost all of Brentano's students belonged. Among the speakers during the time Weininger was involved were Houston Stewart Chamberlain (who spoke on Richard Wagner), Richard Kralik, Josef Breuer, Franz Wickhoff, Alöis Riegl, Sigmund Exner, Robert Reininger, Wilhelm Jerusalem, Christian von Ehrenfels, and Jodl. Weininger's friend Hermann Swoboda (1873–1963) gave a lecture for the philosophical society on arguments against solipsism. These talks covered a wide range of themes from Darwinism to art and music, and the speakers were generally the leading figures in their fields. Participants in this intellectual world recalled Weininger as a serious, inhibited, physically awkward young man of extraordinary intellectual gifts, who devoted long hours to intellectual labors. The best minds among his contemporaries in psychology sought his friendship and intellectual leadership, and Swoboda emphasized Weininger's free intelligence and consuming intellectual life. By the age of twenty, Weininger had a strong sense of being prepared for important intellectual contributions, and in 1900 he participated in a debate at the fourth international congress of psychologists in Paris, where he emphasized the significance of introspection for psychological research.[26]

During these first years of study at the university, Weininger's work proceeded in the spirit of scientific research; although he was apparently not very good at experimental work, his intellectual sympathies went in the direction of empiricism and the two most sophisticated advocates of the purely empirical standpoint: Richard Avenarius (1843–1896) and Ernst Mach.[27] In the context of his research on talent and sexual education in children, Weininger began to develop ideas for his dissertation. In the fall of 1900, his work received a fresh impulse through his friend Swoboda, who was a patient of Freud and two decades later a mentor to Doderer. What Swoboda seems to have passed along to Weininger from Freud was the idea of bisexuality, or at least the word, which had entered Freud's practice by way of Wilhelm Fliess, Freud's friend in Berlin.[28] The idea of a blend of masculine and feminine qualities in human beings was not new with Fliess; this notion emerged repeatedly in the Western tradition from Plato to Margaret Fuller.[29] But academic subspecialities sometimes have very local notions of originality, and these ideas seem to have been more threatening in the late nineteenth century than they had been to the Romantics. Weininger decided to develop the notion of bisexuality on the basis of existing empirical research. In a few weeks during the summer of 1901 he wrote "Eros und Psyche," the sober, scientific first part of what eventually became *Geschlecht und Charakter;* it was this manuscript that Freud read and criticized in October 1901.[30] By the end of 1901 Weininger's ideas came into focus, and Jodl and Laurenz Müllner agreed to sponsor his dissertation.

The last two years of Weininger's life were marked by dramatic changes on three distinguishable but interconnected levels. First, Weininger experienced an intellectual rupture of the most fundamental sort, a conversion from philosophical monism and scientific empiricism to German idealism and a more intuitive method of developing his ideas. The main feature of this revolution in Weininger's thought was the move from the critical attitude of Mach and Avenarius toward the "unsalvageable ego" [das unrettbare Ich] to an intense commitment to the intelligible ego of Kant and Fichte. Second, this change in philosophical worldview was accompanied by an extraordinary burst of creativity, which seems to have been inspired by his conviction that there was a connection between gender and philosophical dualism and which produced not only *Geschlecht und Charakter* but also the shorter work that appeared posthumously in 1904: *Über die letzten Dinge* [On Ultimate Things].[31] Finally, Weininger's personality began to undergo the changes that culminated in suicidal crises in November 1902 and October 1903.

The consensus among those who knew Weininger was that he experienced a transformation of his worldview about two years before his death. Swoboda emphasized that the change was more apparent in 1902 (at least by March), but the letters Weininger wrote to him in Leipzig in 1901 already display the new way of thinking very strongly. The two most conspicuous features of this change were his enthusiasm for Kant and his insistence that ethics (conceived in a powerfully dualistic manner) was all that mattered. As his revolt against monism developed, Weininger tended to emphasize his debts to Plato, Augustine, Plotinus, and the Christian tradition, but all of this took place in an intellectual context that was powerfully influenced by Schopenhauer and Nietzsche. Weininger belongs to a large extent to the intellectual world of late nineteenth-century neo-Kantianism, but his extreme emphasis on the will to value had a heroic quality that was not at all academic.[32] He also shared in the wider reception of north German and Scandinavian thought in Vienna around 1900 through writers such as Rudolf Kassner: Schopenhauer and Nietzsche, Ibsen, and Strindberg, although apparently not Kierkegaard.[33] By 1902, Weininger was a Kantian, but he tended to develop Kant's transcendental idealism in ways that owed a good deal to Schelling.[34] By the summer of 1902, Weininger had found his way via

German idealism to his distinctive version of Christianity and his conversion to Protestantism on July 21, 1902, the day he received his doctorate.[35]

Weininger's main preoccupation during these years of intellectual revolution and creativity was the writing of *Geschlecht und Charakter*, which he completed in three stages: (1) the short draft of 1901, which Freud saw and which includes the scientific material of the first part; (2) the six-hundred-page manuscript, now missing, which Weininger submitted to Jodl and Müllner for the doctorate in the spring of 1902; and (3) the final published version, which Weininger completed during the winter and spring of 1903, in which the antifeminist and anti-Semitic themes were apparently more pronounced than in the dissertation.[36] After 1901, intellectual and emotional issues became steadily more difficult for Weininger to distinguish. Although the ideas for his dissertation were very much a part of the revolution in his own thought, this intellectual transformation was accompanied by an intense emotional process that culminated in his suicide. The account by his friend Lucka makes clear how much Weininger mirrored the deepest concerns of a wider intellectual circle that was discouraged by the intellectual and moral emptiness of positivism and determined to create something of greater value. Thus, for intellectuals in Weininger's generation such as Lucka and Artur Gerber (and later Karl Kraus), Weininger was an intellectual hero, even when some of his views seemed to them misguided. Along with the inner transformation of Weininger's intellectual interests came his growing contempt for his earlier scientific work and an inclination to interpret every detail of his own life in categories of good and evil, guilt and salvation. In the last two years of his life Weininger's striving for truth took on an ethical dimension, because science always searches only for "truths" but "not the 'Truth.'"[37]

Weininger's emotional crisis was already underway before he wrote the final version of *Geschlecht und Charakter*. By September 1902, when he returned from travels in Germany and Norway, his personality had altered substantially. Weininger's father and Artur Gerber were as worried as Weininger himself, who said: "'I have the chill of the grave in me.'"[38] One night in November, Weininger's depression reached a severe crisis; Gerber, who helped Weininger past this extreme point, reported that Weininger's only explanation for his depression was that he was a "born criminal," a "born murderer."[39] That winter, Weininger was apparently able to work with his accustomed concentration once more, but in the summer of 1903 he spoke again of his criminal nature. The essays in *Über die letzten Dinge* underscore the mounting intensity of his dualistic view, and in the aphorisms and letters of the last months this process built to complete intellectual and personal crisis. He was "almost always close to despair," and in September 1903, when he returned from a trip to Italy, he was exhausted from this struggle with himself.[40] He shot himself, despite neurotic attempts to ask his father and his friend for help. But, just as he had made his own life as difficult as possible, so did he give others very little opportunity to help him.[41]

Weininger's suicide was clearly related to the intellectual changes that occurred as early as 1901, although it is a mistake to interpret his suicide as a reaction to the unsatisfying reception of his book, much less as a reaction to Freud's disapproval, as some commentators have argued.[42] Weininger's near suicide of November 1902, recounted by Gerber, makes clear that Weininger was suffering from more than an abstract philosophical decision about departing from the empirical world. On the other hand, his ways of thinking about human experience offered him little help during this period of extreme crisis. He steadily intensified his own isolation and his standards of judgment. His friend Lucka saw him as someone who preached endlessly to himself and was always ready freely to commit suicide if he was too weak. And it is hard to avoid the impression of a cold life that excluded any hint of sexuality or comfort.

The skeptical psychologist Swoboda was probably right to assert that the conflict in which Weininger found himself was "unavoidable" and to suggest that it was "a matter of complete indifference what occasion made it break out."[43] Insofar as Weininger's suicide had anything at all to do with the book, the significant point is the agreement among Swoboda, Carl Dallago, and Weininger himself that either Weininger or the book had to die, in other words, that Weininger was in no position to live according to his own ideas. Unfortunately, he was equally unable to renounce his book.[44] But this is not so much a matter of the book itself as it is a question of the burden he had to bear because of his worldview and the pressure it put on everything that was broken or undeveloped in his own personality. Swoboda, like Probst, emphasized the hysterical symptoms of his repressed sexual drives, but what is certain is that Weininger suffered under his own severe moral judgments: "Only when someone strives for extreme purity do they become really dirty; whoever wants to avoid every disturbance will never be free of disturbances; whoever wants to escape the world entirely only then becomes really entangled in it."[45] Weininger was the victim of the solitude and the moral purity he valued so highly. His suicide is not to be imagined apart from terrible emotional conflicts, but it is also clear that it was precisely Weininger's philosophical views that made these psychic conflicts unbearably severe.

Until his suicide Weininger seemed destined to become one of the major creative minds of the early twentieth century in philosophy and psychology. However atypical and psychologically problematic he may have been as an individual, Weininger's ideas had tremendous impact on the best minds of his generation in prewar Vienna. *Geschlecht und Charakter* is an important document of the intellectual and spiritual life of Vienna in the early twentieth century and an attempt to map every significant human problem on the polarities of gender. But it is a mistake to see Weininger simply as a symptom, sign, or voice of his times. Although Weininger reflected customary prejudices within his culture, he was certainly not the typical male of his society. Nor did Kraus, Wittgenstein, and Musil respond to him because they were typical of their "times."[46]

Gender and Method

> Only male and female together constitute the human being.
>   Kant, as cited by Weininger[47]

Geschlecht und Charakter is divided into two parts: an empirical section that summarizes the state of scientific research on gender and sexual characteristics and a section that aims to clarify ideal types or models of masculinity and femininity. The first part argues that all human beings are mixtures, while the second part attempts to define the types. Weininger explained in his preface that his struggle to "free himself from biology in order to be able to be entirely a psychologist" was reflected in the tension between the part of the book that appealed to natural science and the part that was more concerned with "inner experience." The second (and much longer) section, he continued, did not set out from a positivist worldview but attempted to defend the rights of a "nonbiological, nonphysiological psychology."[48]

Weininger's achievement was to separate discourse about gender from literal assumptions about individual men and women—or at least to argue for this in a serious way. What makes his argument interesting is his attempt to deconstruct his culture's understanding of gender and to develop a methodology that distinguishes male and female types from individual men and women. The fundamental idea of *Geschlecht und Charakter* is that the human being is bisexual, that every human individual consists of masculine and feminine qualities. Weininger's argument set out from scientific sources that confirmed the gradations of sexual types—that all biological forms are borderline cases, physiological and psychological mixtures rather than pure types. But his goal was not so much an inductive theory as an attempt to understand the sexual types; "male and female are to be understood only as types," as concepts M and F, which never appear in the world in their pure forms.[49] At the same time, his discussion was informed by his own strong prejudices and by the prejudices that shaped scientific discourse about women (and Jews) in the nineteenth century.[50]

One of the most overlooked aspects of Weininger's argument is how much trouble he takes to underscore the diversity and variety of sexual types. He argued that purely male and female types do not exist in nature: "[T]horoughgoing sexual distinctions between all men, on the one hand, and all women, on the other, are not demonstrable."[51] In short, his point was the opposite of the one that is often attributed to him: he was arguing the biological reality of androgyny. He contended not only that empirical work in the biological sciences demonstrated this but also that anyone who had lived in a large city had confirmed the wide variety of sexual types with his own eyes. "Sexual differentiation is never complete."[52] He noted that embryos in the fifth week have still not taken on sexual characteristics, although these must already be present in some form, and he tried to establish something like a genetic account of intermediate sexual forms.[53] He emphasized the slow pace at which the human fetus begins to display sexual differentiation, although the state of biology in 1903 did not allow him to say how sex is inscribed in organisms even before they begin to develop:

> Thus, male and female are like two substances, which are distributed among
> living individuals in various proportions, in such a way that the coefficient
> of one of the substances does not become zero. We may say that male
> and female do not appear in experience, but only masculine and feminine.
> Therefore, we may no longer label an individual A or an individual B simply
> as "male" or "female." (10)

Instead, the task was to locate the individual "at a specific point" between "the two extremes" (99). The virtue of Weininger's method was that it allowed him to distinguish gender from sex, although he did not quite have the words for this. The problem with his method was that he was constantly driven to clarify ideal types as if they were essences, when they expressed prejudices that were personal or cultural.

Weininger explored some interesting methodological possibilities that are easily lost in the standard English translation, but his inconsistencies allow his prejudices about gender to come through.[54] On the most empirical level, Weininger distinguished between individual men and women, between *Männer* and *Frauen*. More central to his argument is a second distinction between *Mann* and *Weib*, which I translate as a distinction between male and female, although this has sometimes been rendered as Man and Woman; this distinction refers to what Max Weber would have called ideal types, that is, models that do not correspond to empirical men and women. It is important to note that Weininger uses the same word on the masculine side in both distinctions. In the first pair, *der Mann* refers to individual men; in the second, to the ideal of humanity—an ambiguity that haunts the text throughout. Weininger failed to justify the identification of human being with man, *Mensch* with *Mann*, although both German and English have always tended in this direction. Moreover, there are ambiguities in Weininger's text, which translation sometimes flattens unavoidably: *Mensch* means human being or man; *Mann* means man or male. Thus, Weininger uses the same word—*Mann*—to refer both to the highest human type and to the gender "male," but he was also underscoring nuances that were present in nineteenth-century German.

Weininger's references to women and femininity suffer from the opposite problem: here he employs two different words, *das Weib* and *die Frau*. In his ideal-type distinction, he uses the word *Weib*, a word for woman or female that had much more negative and usually sexual connotations within his culture than the word *Frau*. Thus, even the methodological categories are loaded from the outset to idealize the masculine and disparage the feminine. Or, to put it differently, Weininger epitomized everything he valued with the word *Mann* and everything he condemned with the word *Weib*. Finally, when Weininger wanted to make absolutely clear that he was dealing with a pure ideal type, he distinguished between *M* and *W*, which I render in English as *M* and *F*. In German *das Weib* is neuter, and Weininger consistently refers to it with the pronoun "es" [it], which Freud used as a noun that has been translated into English as "id."[55] Weininger uses the terms *die Frau, das Weib,* and *W* to express different degrees of abstraction, which I translate as "the woman," "the female," and "F," but it is never quite clear just how these terms are related to empirical individuals. Thus, Weininger can generalize about the memory of F without referring to empirical women.[56] At times, Weininger's practice was even more irregular and less precise, as, for example, when he referred to empirical women as *Weiber*, implying that actual women embody the values of the female. A strange footnote on page 108 of *Geschlecht und Charakter* helps to account for some of the contradictions that appear later in Weininger's argument. He notes that "in what follows 'the man' will always mean M, and 'the woman,' F, not men [Männer] or women [Frauen]." Here Weininger very unobtrusively extends his method in a way that the reader is likely to miss, that is, the singular is always supposed to mean the ideal type and not real people, whether for "Mann" or for "Weib" and "Frau." The effect is to idealize M and to make F as negative as possible—although neither term refers to real people. In this sense, Weininger anticipates his own sloppiness later in the text.[57] Weininger seems, gradually and unevenly, to give up on the method he outlined at the outset. Thereafter, he is less attentive to his earlier distinction between woman [Frau] and female [Weib], and the argument slides more conspicuously in an antifeminist direction.

Weininger's arguments are often circular, even when he is claiming to be empirical. Thus, he has a tendency to argue that, if a woman is creative, she is masculine; or, if a woman writes music that Weininger likes, he is inclined to describe the music as masculine.[58] When women display what Weininger regards as masculine qualities, he assumes that these have been unnaturally imposed from the outside and dishonestly received by the women who display them. On the other hand, when women display "feminine qualities" of sexuality and mating, Weininger assumes that these are natural expressions of woman's essence and purpose in the universe.

Weininger never took the trouble to sort out the various levels of contradiction in his book, usually between his stated methodology and his spontaneous expressions of prejudice. In practice, Weininger relied a great deal on his own personal observations about real women, which often undermines his claim that he is simply trying to understand absolute M and absolute F. At times, he argued that, at any given moment, individual human beings are always either male or female and that there is an oscillation in individual human beings between masculine and feminine elements. "In short, bisexuality will not display itself in a single moment but can reveal itself psychologically only successively" (65). In this context he cautioned against any final labeling of human beings. Yet elsewhere he argued that the man can become female, but the woman cannot become male (241). At times he seems to assume that a man can become 100 percent male, although a woman cannot; and, at times, he did not allow the possibility that a particular woman can be more than fifty percent male or rise morally above the most inadequate man (404). He does seem to be saying that an empirical woman is less likely than a man to be able to become an ideal human being, although this argument is frequently inconsistent.

Weininger's biological argument for androgyny drew on the deeper sources of the Western tradition. In developing the idea of bisexuality, Weininger emphasized his debt to the account of human sexuality in Plato's *Symposium*.

The presentiment of this bisexuality of all living things (through sexual differentiation that is never quite complete) is age-old. Perhaps it was not foreign to Chinese myths; in any case in ancient Greece it was extremely lively. The personification of the hermaphrodites as a mythical form testifies to this; the story of Aristophanes in the Platonic symposium; yes, even in later times, for the Gnostic sects of the Ophites, the original human being was masculine-feminine. (13)

In the *Symposium* Aristophanes distinguishes three genders (male, female, and hermaphrodite), which correspond to three sexual orientations: homosexual, lesbian, and heterosexual.

Our original nature is not what it is now, but quite different. For one thing there were three sexes, rather than the two (male and female) we have now. The third sex was a combination of these two. . . . Secondly, each human being formed a complete whole, spherical, with back and ribs forming a circle. They had four hands, four legs, and two faces, identical in every way, on a circular neck.[59]

Aristophanes describes human beings as male, female, and male-female, then divided. "When man's natural form was split in two, each half went round looking for its other half" (191).

That is why we have this innate love of one another. It brings us back to our original state. . . . We're all looking for our "other half." Men who are a fragment of the common sex (the one called hermaphrodite), are womanisers, and most adulterers are to be found in this category. Similarly, women of this type are nymphomaniacs and adulteresses. On the other hand, women who are part of an original woman pay little attention to men. Their interest is in women; lesbians are found in this class. And those who are part of a male pursue what is male. (191d–e)

Robert Calasso argues that the

dark point from which the whole book [i.e., *Geschlecht und Charakter*] arises is the phantom of the androgyne. That bisexuality, which Plato and the Cabbalists and Jakob Böhme and the alchemical texts down to Balzac's *Séraphîta* had so wonderfully described, which had become lost again like an elusive chimera, blossomed once more over subterranean and dreary ways in the young Weininger—as well as, and over no less dreary ways, in the somewhat older Fliess and Freud.[60]

This understanding of bisexuality shaped Weininger's account of androgyny and gender identity.

Weininger wanted to recast traditional understandings of sexual attraction with an eye to the significance of types. He later discovered that Schopenhauer had already formulated "the law of sexual attraction," which Weininger cites: "'Sexual union always requires that a whole male [M] and a whole female [F] join together, even if distributed in each case in different proportions between the two different individuals.'"[61] In order to explain this, Weininger offers a number of quasi-scientific formulas, but his simple example is perhaps most helpful: That an individual whose constitution is $3/4$ M and $1/4$ F will find "his best sexual complement in an individual whose constitution is $1/4$ M and $3/4$ F," this is to say "[t]hat male and female attract each other as sexual types" (35).[62] This always implies the imaginary instance in which X (100 % M and 0 % F) meets Y (0 % M and 100 % F), that is, in which a pure male meets a pure female, but only as a sum of the two people. In Weininger's view, homosexuality (what Weininger and his contemporaries called contrary, or inverted, sexual feeling) was only a special case of the general laws of sexual attraction. "The contrary sexual feeling thus becomes for this theory not an exception to natural law, but only a special case of it. An individual who is approximately half male and half female requires for his completion (precisely according to the law) another, who also has about equal portions of both sexes." Weininger explained that this is why those who are not homosexuals only very rarely find themselves in this social world; "sexual attraction is mutual—and it is the most powerful factor influencing the fact that homosexuals always immediately recognize each other." On the other hand, those who did not share these feelings seemed to react violently: "A professor of psychiatry at a German university seriously proposed as recently as 1900 that one ought to simply castrate homosexuals" (59).

Perhaps the most significant implication of Weininger's analysis of gender was his rejection of stereotypes and gender roles:

> For until now we have educated the intermediate sexual forms (particularly among women) in the sense of approximating as nearly as possible the conventional ideal of a man or a woman. We have practiced a spiritual orthopedics in the fullest sense of a torture. In this way we not only drive a great deal of variation out of the world but also repress a great deal that is present

as a seed and could strike roots, force others into unnatural situations, and breed artificiality and dissimulation. (69)

Weininger's opposition to the "spiritual orthopedics" of his culture would hardly be suspected on the basis of most of the literature about him.

Weininger also drew into question the conventional notion (held by Freud) of "the greater intensity of the sex drive in the male" and the tendency to regard this as the fundamental distinction "from which all others may be derived." Weininger wondered whether the word "sex drive" referred to "anything unambiguous and really measurable," and he mocked "the phrase that is so popular today, that 'everything' is only 'sublimated sex drive'" (108–109). In any case, he rejected the view that the intensity of the sexual drive is greater for M than for F and noted that it seems to be variable among both men and women. Thus, he argued that there is no real distinction between the sexes with respect to the drive for sexual intercourse. Weininger did, however, see a difference in the tendency of men to seek release from sexual tension and a tendency for women to seek to sustain "a state of sexual arousal" (111):

> For the woman the condition of sexual arousal simply means the highest intensification of her whole existence, which is always and entirely sexual. F is completely absorbed in the sphere of mating and reproduction, that is, in the relationship to the male and the child. She is completely filled out by these things in her existence, while M is not only sexual. Here then in reality lies the distinction, which we sought to find in the variable intensity of the sexual drive. (112)

But Weininger often forgets that "male" is a sexual type at all. He treats the male as a sexual type in the first part and as something else, nonsexual and nonnatural, in the second. He perceives this disparity only partially, although on certain levels he makes a point of it.

Indeed, Weininger seems to lose track of the fact that the distinction between male and female is a sexual distinction. Thus, one might expect him to discuss the male in terms of aggression or power or sexual desire or the ability to provide for women and offspring, and indeed, people in his society thought in such terms. But Weininger was struck by the way in which his society defined women in exclusively sexual and reproductive terms. "The psychology of the sexes will always coincide with the psychology of F." This could simply mean that the existence of women makes a psychology of the genders necessary, or it could mean that female (or F) means sexuality (106), which he also argued. Here the asymmetry of Weininger's view was much like Freud's: he began with the man as normatively human and attempted to explain the significance of women as secondary or even epiphenomenal.[63] Being a male for Weininger meant not being entirely enslaved by the tasks of reproduction. But Weininger refined this relative definition into a type, which is, of course, not present in its pure form in men either.

Weininger's deductive psychology of types begins with the distinction between male and female, but he goes on to argue that the female is to be understood either as mother or as prostitute. For Weininger, the types of the mother and the prostitute are opposites, although he does allow for a type of the lover who falls between these two main types (282). Weininger regards motherhood as "something inward that does not simply refer to the fact that a woman has given birth" (283). Likewise, he points out that the type of the prostitute includes "not only the girl who is for sale [das käufliche Mädchen], but also many among the so-called respectable girls and married women, yes even those who never violate their marriages" (283). For Weininger, the mother-type (the most feminine type) is committed to humanity, to the preservation of the species. But precisely this makes her a negative type, because she is not much concerned with the individuality (or genius) of the people she loves, especially her own children (295–296). The mother serves the purposes of the species, while the prostitute stands outside these purposes in the name of individuality (294).[64] The prostitute turns out to be Weininger's positive type (one of the significant connections to Kraus): "The spiritually most developed women (everything that in some way becomes muse for the man) belong in the category of the prostitutes: the women of the Romantic era belong to this, the Aspasian (or hetaera) type" (297). "Significant people have always loved only prostitutes," to which he adds in a note that he is obviously not speaking here of women who sell themselves on the street (297). "Just as the mother is a principle that is friendly to life, so is the prostitute a principle that is inimical to life" (311). Weininger defined ethical individuality in opposition to what he regarded as the feminine drive to pair, whether through marriage or sexual intercourse.[65]

Weininger was alert enough to his own method to see that it was not merely an ideal-typical methodology but also an induction from the society in which he lived, from his own experience of women. He was conscious that his typology was not only an ideal image but also a critique of his own society, a description of the education of the sexes in Vienna 1900: "[H]ow women are today, that is the issue" (112). Weininger makes this point on the same page with his harshest remarks about women, and it is difficult to bear in mind while reading Weininger's text that the issue is not how women are universally but how women were in his culture and historical period. Weininger himself was inclined to confess that in discussions of gender, even more than elsewhere in human studies, projection is a constant danger, aside from the routine probability of generalizing from one's own narrow basis of personal experience.

Weininger comments on the widespread notion among women in his society that all men are pretty much alike, which he explains by pointing out that any particular woman is likely to meet similar men during her life. "Thus, in this way we may also explain some, gently put, daring assertions of many women's rights people about the male and the alleged untrue superiority of the same: from the sort of men precisely they as a rule get to know well" (71). Of course, this might bear on Weininger's understanding of women as well. At times he seems to see this and to conclude that the feminine man is in the best position to give an account of the psychology of the female:

> Never—is even this only a consequence of male oppression?—for example, has a pregnant woman brought her sensations and feelings to expression in some way, whether in a poem, in memoirs, or in a gynecological treatise; and this cannot be the result of excessive shame, for—here Schopenhauer was right to point out—there is nothing so remote from a pregnant woman as shame about her condition. (107)

This means that men who write about the female must depend on "what is feminine in men themselves. The principle of intermediate sexual forms reveals itself here in a certain sense as the presupposition of any genuine judgment of a man about a woman" (108).[66]

According to Weininger, "the genuine female, F, wants nothing to do with the emancipation of the female." He distinguished his conception of women's liberation from "the wish for external equality with the man," emphasizing instead "the will of a female to become inwardly equal to the male, to achieve his intellectual and moral freedom, his interests and his creative energy." He argued "that F has no need, and consequently no capacity, for this emancipation. All women who really strive for emancipation, all women who have a certain right to be famous and somehow intellectually distinguished, always display numerous masculine qualities; and anatomically masculine qualities (a physical appearance that approximates the man) are always recognizable to the keen observer" (80). The kind of women's emancipation that Weininger favored was "[f]ree access to all, no obstacle in the way of those whose true psychic needs drive them to masculine activities, always in accordance with their physical constitution, for women with masculine

qualities. But away with building *parties,* away with *inauthentic* revolution-
izing, away with the whole women's *movement,* which creates in so many
people anti-natural and artificial, basically dishonest striving" (87). Weininger's quarrel with the women's emancipation movement was that the "true
liberation of the human mind" cannot be achieved by political "armies" but
only by "the solitary individual alone. Against whom? Against whatever in
one's own temperament works against it. The greatest, the only enemy of the
emancipation of the woman is the woman" (93).

 Weininger's idiosyncratic argument is constantly generating problems
and contradictions. Why was it that men who are homosexuals can be creative in fields where, according to Weininger, women have made few contributions? Or, why was it that women who are lesbians can achieve important
literary or philosophical or scientific work, although "[e]ven the most masculine femininum probably has hardly more than 50 per cent M" (87–88)?
Weininger might more reasonably have come to the conclusion that the mixtures are the highest types spiritually; he does argue that intermediate sexual forms are entirely normal.[67] Or he might have argued that the absolute M
does not desire emancipation any more than the absolute F, but Weininger
eventually reaches a conclusion that is not justified by his own theory: that
the man "can become a female," whereas *the woman can never become a
male*" (241). Here Weininger seems to mean something like this: the man can
be wholly trapped in his body but a woman can never entirely overcome her
connection to nature. Here Weininger reaches a turning point in his argument, which appears to be based primarily on his own experience, which is
that he has met many men "who were psychologically almost completely,
and not only half, female" but "never yet even a single woman who would
not still have remained fundamentally a female" if this femininity had not
been concealed in a variety of ways even from the person herself (241–242).
Later in his argument he refers back to chapter 1 of part 2 to remind the
reader that a person is "either male or female, regardless of how many characteristics of both genders may be present" (242). This of course still leaves
the essential question undecided, but Weininger settles it for the reader on
the basis of nothing: "[B]ut while there are anatomical males who are psychologically females, there are no persons who are physically females and still
psychically males." This is the crucial move that makes him a misogynist in
his argument and undermines the possibilities of what he is doing.

 Weininger explores at least three different overlapping and contradictory
arguments, which are woven together erratically throughout his book. The
argument about variety and androgyny dominates in his part 1 and in the
manuscript of "Eros und Psyche" that he wrote in 1901. The theoretical

assumption behind this view is that the whole human being is male and female, but this argument is not coherently developed in the book, although it
was arguably the crucial inspiration. This view emphasizes that each human
being is a mixture of male and female and indicates that a full human being
is male and female together. This argument seems at times to point toward an
ideal of androgyny, of the union of male and female in the human being, perhaps even toward a third type.[68] A second argument, the deductive theory of
types, dominates part 2 and is the one that is most clearly developed: this interpretation of Kant's moral theory regards male as good and female as bad
with the assumption that human liberation means becoming male and end-
ing sexuality. In this argument Weininger rejects sexuality, relationships, and
androgyny as well, acknowledging the validity of the male type only—the
male as free, rational subject. (The contradiction between these two views is
mirrored in other passages when Weininger comments on whether individuals can be all male or all female, or whether it is possible for a female or a
woman to become male.) Finally, the whole book tends toward what seems to
be a critique of women or a view that is sometimes described as "antifeminist." This is the argument that implicitly shapes the later parts of the book
and the one that most readers draw from it.

But Weininger was not a conventional misogynist, and his book is a critique of conventional male attitudes toward sexuality and women. He un-
equivocally rejected the stereotypical vision of the woman as child bearer or
sexual object. It is not entirely misguided to think of him as a martyr of human liberation: for human autonomy, for the person, and against the woman
as child, slave, or toy. For Weininger, the roles of mother and prostitute are
obstacles to the real tasks of human freedom and maturity. A woman who ac-
quiesces in these roles becomes a victim of *das Weib*, and a man who con-
tributes to them opposes the human freedom of that person. In Weininger's
view, human beings can become free only as individuals, and there is no reason to postpone this until stereotypical roles are completed. The duty of human freedom is immediate and for everyone. For Weininger, questions about
the future of the species were, in this context, simply irrelevant and immoral.

Weininger frankly considered the view that his theory, if taken seriously,
would lead to the extinction of the human species. This was not a serious argument for Weininger, since the realization of humanity lies always and only
in the individual and not in the species. In this sense, Weininger offers the absolutely principled alternative to Marx and his notion of species-being. But
Weininger points out that it is unlikely that anyone ever engaged in sexual
intercourse out of moral concern that the species not die out. According to
Weininger, Augustine ought to have opposed sexual intercourse entirely but

lost his nerve because the logical consequence would be the end of the human race. Even Augustine, when he required chastity of all people, had

> to consider the objection that in such a case humanity would very quickly disappear from the earth. In this remarkable fear, for which the most terrible thought seems to be that the species could die out, lies not only the most extreme lack of faith in individual immortality and an eternal life of the moral individual; it is not only despairingly irreligious. With it one also demonstrates cowardice and an incapacity to live beyond the herd. Whoever thinks in this way cannot imagine the earth without the swarms and throngs of human beings on it; he becomes anxious and fearful not so much before death as before solitude. (457)[69]

Weininger's book on gender turns out to be not an attack on women but an attack on sexuality and reproduction, the two things he believed enslave women and make human liberation impossible. What is central to Weininger's critique of sexuality is not conventional asceticism but rather a radical and somewhat peculiar application of Kant's categorical imperative to the realm of sexuality. Weininger refused any sexual form that was predicated on the objectification of any person, allowing another person to become a means to an end, whether the man is used as a means to the child or the woman is used as a means to the man's pleasure.

Gender and Ethics

> The most sublime book in the world, *The Critique of Practical Reason*, led morality back as to its lawgiver, to an intelligible ego, which is utterly different from all empirical consciousness.
>
> Weininger, *Geschlecht und Charakter*

Weininger was convinced that there was a significant relationship between the *Mann/Weib* (male/female) distinction and two basic philosophical approaches to the world: the idealist, largely Kantian view and the Machian, scientific, empirical, psychological view. Swoboda describes what this must have meant to Weininger: "Weininger discovered one day to his unspeakable joy that M alone has an intelligible ego; and he found further—with what pleasure one can estimate from the boldface type—that the Platonic distinction between Being and Non-Being is completely equivalent to M and F: The female is not only *nothing*, but rather altogether *not*."[70] Weininger believed that "the most heroic act of world history" was the moment when Kant came to the understanding that he was morally responsible only to himself. This was "the birth of Kantian ethics," the discovery of the categorical imperative (209). Kant's view distinguished the self-legislating, intelligible ego from the empirical world of sensation and causality. For Kant, the moral subject is the intelligible ego or rational subject, not the empirical, psychological self; this distinction parallels the distinction between morality and scientific knowledge. And Weininger set out from Kant's view to emphasize the opposition between a scientific view and one that emphasizes the moral-religious self, which Weininger thought of as rational and masculine.

Weininger defined the male type [M] in terms of Kant's categorical imperative of moral law and rational freedom: "Act only according to that maxim by which you can at the same time will that it should become a universal law."[71] The idea of a self-legislating moral being was identical for Kant with the injunction never to treat another human being as a means but always as an end.[72] This second formulation is crucial to Weininger's understanding of morality and sexuality. M is the microcosm in relation to the universe, while F is the will to pair, to join with another, whether through marriage or intercourse. Put differently, Weininger was powerfully affected by the Kantian emphasis on "the starry heaven above me and the moral law within me." On the one hand, the human being is a speck in a sea of matter and, on the other hand, a moral intelligence, independent of the world of sensation (209–210). For Weininger, the distinction between M (male) and F (female) summarized the received dualities of Western experience: between consciousness and unconsciousness, subject and object, freedom and slavery, chastity and sexuality, individuality and pairing, spiritual faith and the material world. The male type for Weininger meant freedom, consciousness, everything rational, logical, and moral in the sense of Kant's categorical imperative, while the female was unfree, unconscious, irrational, alogical, amoral, and without memory, without awareness of the sublime demands of the categorical imperative. M meant the highest ethical individuality, while F was defined by sexuality and therefore, according to Weininger, stood in opposition to human essence.

Weininger understood the connection "between the self and the universe" (248) in terms of the eternal demand on the human being to achieve the identity of being and thinking, that is, truth, which would be the unity of the self and the universe. He believed that the moral responsibility of being the male type led to unhappy solitude beyond society. The will to union and reproduction was, for Weininger, the resistance to true humanity, which he believed is always achieved in the full realization of individuality.

The human being is alone in the universe, in eternal, monstrous solitude. He has no purpose outside himself, nothing else for which he lives—he is far removed from being a slave or wanting to be a slave or having to be a slave: all human society disappears far beneath him, and social ethics sinks beneath him; he is alone, alone. (210)[73]

The defining image of *Geschlecht und Charakter* is the solitary, unhappy individual in relation to the cosmos—at once genius and saint—in contrast to the image of pairing as an escape from true humanity and adulthood.[74]

For Weininger, the moral issue about sexuality is simply that the woman becomes a means rather than an end in herself as a person, an object rather than a subject, an instrumentality rather than a self. Weininger claimed that this, and not asceticism, was his only argument against sexual intercourse, but it is difficult not to suspect that Weininger mistrusted pleasure in a more general way. According to Weininger's views, it is hard to imagine the possibility of a genuinely human and moral sexual life, but for him at least one thing was certain: "It can be right for the man to honor and respect the woman, however, only when she herself stops *wanting* to be object and material for the man" (459). Weininger saw only what was problematic about *das Weib* as a cultural formation, and he identified the masculine (also a cultural form, of course) with humanity, reason, and freedom in the most universal sense. Weininger's argument draws attention to the extent to which the idea of humanity in the West took form in the Enlightenment (especially in Kant) in a way that inclined toward rationality and a particular notion of masculinity, but Weininger's critique of femininity was actually a critique of the sexual polarity as such:

Thus, coitus contradicts the idea of humanity in every case; not because asceticism is a duty but, above all, because in it the female becomes an object, a thing, and the male really does her the favor of regarding her only as a thing, not as a living human being with inner psychic processes. Therefore, the man also despises the woman momentarily, as soon as he has possessed her, and the woman feels that she is now despised, even though two minutes earlier she knew she had been made into a goddess. (459)

This account only slightly overdraws a common Viennese view of the sexual dynamic, but Weininger believed that it would be better for the human race to die out than to have this continue. For Weininger, the central moral failure of his society appeared in the realm of sexuality and in the division of labor between men and women, their sexual as well as their social and spiritual relations. His conclusion was simple: the woman must no longer be feminine (F) but rather become fully human, which for Weininger meant the assumption of masculine values by women. "A woman who has really renounced, who really wants to seek peace within herself, such a woman would no longer be a female" (460). And, in the concluding words of his book, Weininger asked:

> Will the female finally subordinate herself to the moral idea, to the idea of humanity? That alone would be women's emancipation. (461)

Weininger's book is not so much about women as about the emancipation of women, about the possibility of being a human being and freeing the self from F, which for him meant being a genius, a Christian, and an ethical individual.[75] Although the gender polarity appears as his fundamental metaphysical assumption, his ethical goal was to abolish this polarity entirely; thus, his idealism assumed the complete rejection of nature and reality, while at the same time it was tainted with the biological and social one-sidedness of his masculine definition of true humanity. Although Weininger could be characterized as an antifeminist or as a misogynist, Gisela Dischner is probably right when she emphasizes that "in order to circumvent sexual slavery" Weininger saw in his own time only the possibility of chastity.[76]

Weininger believed that women have to begin to want to be free and that men have to risk everything on this possibility as the only hope for humanity. According to Weininger, most men do not regard women as moral equals, and women are happy to enjoy this. Weininger cites Kant's view of women's emancipation: "That the step to competence is held to be dangerous by the far greater portion of mankind (and by the entire fair sex)—quite apart from its being arduous—is seen to by those guardians who have so kindly assumed superintendence over them."[77] Weininger continues:

> But [women], supported by men who believe them, have nearly been able to persuade the other sex that sexuality is the man's most important and genuine need, that he ought to hope for satisfaction of his truest and deepest wishes only from the female, that chastity constitutes something unnatural and impossible for him. (442–443)

Strangely, there has been very little interest in what troubled Weininger about the female, a type that was not even capable of evil because it was unable to come to conscious awareness of other human beings as ends in themselves, unable to respect the individuality of other beings.[78] Weininger's female was simply absorbed in herself.[79] Weininger thought that the intellectual basis for this way of being lay in modern science, in empiricism, and in the psychological understanding of the self. Jacques Le Rider concluded that Weininger confused nature and culture, but this is itself simply a point of departure.[80] If it is true that a culture constructs its notions of gender, then these are as objective as the biological realities it takes literally. If we may say that Weininger had a problematic construction of gender, it is crucial to know what construction of gender this was. Weininger clarified his understanding of the concept of the female by defining its opposite: the genius, which he regarded as the highest form of consciousness.

As Weininger turns to the connection between genius and M, he falls away from his ideal-type method and toward his prejudices against women. He begins his argument about genius with a discussion of henids, which is his neologism for unclear ideas, for the stage of unclarity before an idea comes fully to consciousness. He points out that Leibniz (and later J. F. Herbart) tried to describe this aspect of mental processes, a feeling of association or connectedness that is not yet clear or conscious (118). Weininger uses this distinction to clarify his account of M and F: "The male has the same psychic contents as the female in more articulated form; whereas she thinks more or less in henids, he already thinks in clear, distinct representations. . . . For F 'thinking' and 'feeling' are one and undivided; for M they must be kept separate. F thus has many experiences still in the form of henids, when for M clarity has long since emerged" (127–128). Weininger, however, emphasizes in a note that there is neither an "absolute henid" for the female nor "absolute clarity" for the male. This distinction has implications for a matter that concerns Weininger more than gender: genius: "[T]here are doubtless females with qualities of genius, but there is no feminine genius, there has never been such a thing and never can be" (242). Masculine for Weininger means ethical and logical, and for him these are the crucial qualities of a genius. Whether people who are anatomically female can have these qualities is an entirely different matter. Weininger is obviously prejudiced in favor of honesty and logic, but he provides no real, empirical basis for arguing that anatomical females can never have these qualities to a high degree.

Weininger begins his chapter on masculine and feminine psychology by explaining that the first eight chapters of the second part have primarily been concerned with demonstrating "the soullessness of the female" (that is, the female's lack of a transcendental ego), including that "the woman lives in henids, the man in ordered contents, that the feminine gender leads a less conscious life than the masculine" (243). Rational consciousness is what is at stake for Weininger: it is the key to his idea of the soul, while unconsciousness is the great threat. Indeed, for Weininger, "transcendental subject and soul are interchangeable concepts" and "all being is consciousness" (243); even when a man is working with henids, he is making his way toward concepts, whereas the female "is not at all suited to concepts, whether in perception or in thinking." If Weininger is going to define the female as soulless, it is clear that he will argue that the female cannot be a genius. But what he is attacking is actually a view of the human being that regards the individual simply as a fragment of empirical reality, that is, the scientific view.[81] The scientific way of thinking is not itself feminine but rather grounds and justifies the feminine worldview. Weininger was not always quite clear about this himself, but it explains why he believed that only men could contribute to science even though the scientific view is distinctively connected to the feminine.

Weininger distinguished two different ways of thinking: "a conceptual-masculine and an unconceptual-feminine" (245). But this "unconceptual nature of the female" amounts to the same thing as a lesser degree of consciousness (not really a form of thinking at all) and a proof "that she [es] has no self" (245). He argued that the gliding style of the thinking of the female was similar to the intellectual style of Young Vienna, and he criticized the state of intellectual life in Germany and Austria more generally as a period of the unconscious in philosophy. He believed that the philosophy of the age had "become in more than one sense the unconscious"; for Weininger "greatness is consciousness, before which the fog of unconsciousness disappears as before the rays of the sun" (150).[82] It was not enough for Weininger to distinguish different styles of thinking: he felt obliged to choose between them, to say that one of them was good and the other, bad. It is one thing for Weininger to have valued a certain constellation of moral qualities, another to regard them as masculine, and yet another to identify them with actual men. It would be possible in principle either to reject these values altogether or to deny that they are distinctively linked to masculine qualities or to actual men.

Weininger's central concern was to hold on to the coherence and reality of the self in the face of the reductions of science.[83] His understanding of individuality was primarily Kantian, rational, and moral, but it blurred at times with Schelling's intuition and a scientific vitalism that emphasized the individuality of organisms—and with variants of mysticism, both Eastern and Protestant. The self at issue for Weininger in this argument was not the self-promoting ego of the marketplace or the political arena, but the subject of perception and experience—also for Weininger the moral subject. He emphasized the early Schelling's belief in the capacity of each person to transform the chaos of external experience into the eternal within. "This intuition

[Anschauung] is the most inward, genuine experience, on which everything, everything that we know and believe about a suprasensuous world depends" (215).

> This intellectual intuition appears when we cease to be an object for ourselves, when, drawn back into itself, the intuiting self is identical with the intuited. In this moment of intuition, time and space disappear: it is not *we* who are in time, but rather time—or, much more, not time, but rather pure, absolute eternity—is *in us*. It is not we who are in the intuition of the objective world, but rather it is lost in our intuition. (215)

Weininger was not as confident as Schelling that the dualism of subject and object is ever entirely overcome in the sense of Plotinus or the Indian Mahatmas, but Weininger was willing to settle for the experience of the self or ego. He emphasizes that the significant person always lives more intensely and has a stronger and more differentiated consciousness of guilt. Thus, the significant person is more conscious of the division between spirit and nature in the cosmos and of "the need for salvation, the need for an inner miracle" (216). Here Weininger makes the transition from the theme of contrasting M and F to the contrast between his own way of seeing the world and the scientific way of seeing: "[T]he significant person has the whole world in himself; the genius is the living microcosm" (220). And, "The scientist takes appearances as they are for the senses, while the significant person or genius takes them for what they mean" (221).

> Beside the realm of causes is a realm of purposes, and this realm is the realm of the human being. A complete science of being is a totality of causes, which wants to rise to the highest cause; a complete science of morality is a totality of purposes, which culminates in a final highest purpose. (229)

For Weininger, the realm of purposes is masculine, the realm of causes feminine; the first is the realm of morality, the second the realm of science. The realm of scientific objects, rather than the way of thinking of scientists, is feminine in Weininger's sense.

Weininger wants to see morality in terms of a "'center of apperception,'" that is, "the personality," and for this he turns to Kant and to the problem of the subject (195).[84] He rejects Mach's view that "the ego is not a real, but only a practical unity; that it is unsalvageable; therefore one can (happily) renounce individual immortality; still it does no real harm to behave here and there, especially for the purposes of the Darwinian struggle for existence, as if one did possess an ego [or self]" (198). For Weininger, it is a mystery how someone as knowledgeable as Mach could have failed to take any notice of the fact that all organic life, unlike inorganic matter, is composed of more or less indivisible beings or organisms—although this is presumably what Mach meant by a practical unity. Here Weininger connects to the scientific vitalism of his time and conflates the vitalist argument for the coherence of the organism with a quite different idealist argument about the rational ego. Weininger rejects the idea that organisms are simply "waiting rooms for sensations," and he argues that even animals color their experience in individualized and distinctive ways. Weininger slides from Kant's intelligible ego to Schelling's intuition to a scientific vitalism that emphasizes the individuality of organisms. In opposition to Mach's denial of the subject, Weininger argued that there is something continuous in human identity that goes beyond the immediate occasions and sensations (205). Weininger did not want to see psychology reduced to being an annex of biology and physiology, which is where Avenarius and Mach pointed. All this led Weininger to oppose psychology as an empirical science, because it is doubtful that empirical psychology "can ever be compatible with soul" or "with the freedom of thinking and willing" (273). For Weininger, science and scientific psychology were the greatest threats to the self, the masculine, the genius, and the religious view of the world, which relies on the concept of character, "the concept of a constant, unified being" (102).

> For someone for whom there are only sensations [Empfindungen], all sensations are necessarily of equal value, the prospects of one no greater than another of becoming the building block of a real world. Thus it is precisely empiricism that annihilates the reality of experience, and positivism reveals itself, despite its "solid" and "real" sounding title, as the true nihilism. (247)

For Weininger, scientific positivism is the true nihilism because it cancels meaningful individual experience that goes out from a center of apperception and a soul—and does so in the name of a reductive abstraction of a total world of imagined sensations.

Weininger wanted to drive the theory of sensations (Mach and Avenarius) out of psychology entirely. "It has been the misfortune of scientific psychology that it allowed itself to be influenced most vigorously by two physicists, by Fechner and Helmholtz" (101). On the other hand, the "two most subtle among the empirical psychologists of the last decade, William James and Richard Avenarius, are also the only two who have at least instinctively felt that psychology ought not to begin with skin-sense and muscle-sense, while all other modern psychology is more or less sensation-paste" (102). Stumpf, Meinong, Höfler, Ehrenfels, Mach and Avenarius—the scientific and Austrian philosophical traditions—appear in Weininger's text in opposition to a tradition that was idealist and German: Windelband, Cohen, Natorp, Husserl, and Dilthey.

Weininger argued that logical and ethical phenomena (or more correctly, "the logical and the ethical phenomenon") compel "the assumption of an intelligible ego or a soul, as a being of highest, hyperempircal reality."

> In a being like F in whom the logical and ethical phenomenon is lacking, the reason to make that assumption is also not applicable. The completely feminine entity knows neither the logical nor the moral imperative, and the word law, the word duty, duty to oneself, is the word that is most foreign to it. Thus, the conclusion is completely justified that it also lacks the suprasensuous personality. (239)

"*The absolute female has no self*" (239–240). Weininger points out that he is hardly the first person to hold this view. He notes that ancient Chinese tradition denied that the female had a soul, and he points to the tendencies in this direction in Islam. He cites Aristotle's association of the masculine principle with soul and form, although he admits that Aristotle, like most Greeks, had little to say about women altogether; and he contrasts Tertullian and Origen to Augustine's resistance to misogyny in the Christian tradition. Weininger argues that the absolute F cannot even mention the notion of the identity of A = A, since one notion does not endure in her memory until the next (189). "For the absolute female there is no principle of identity" (191), and a being who cannot understand A = A can have no inhibition about lying or any memory in the proper sense. For Weininger, "[t]he man is obligated to logic, the woman is not" (192). This link between logic and memory is at the heart of his whole discussion of the male, genius, and timelessness. Someone who cannot understand why lying is flatly wrong cannot understand Weininger's view. For Weininger, all this connects to his notion of universal apperception and the continuity of the personality.[85] He argues that the "universal recollection of all experience is therefore the most dependable, universal, and most easily established mark of genius" (146).[86]

> For the more significant a person is, the more human beings, the greater number of interests that come together in him, the more comprehensive his memory must become. Human beings have in general altogether similar

opportunities to "perceive," but most "apperceive" only an infinitely small part of the infinite amount. The ideal of a genius would have to be a being whose combined "perceptions" were just as many "apperceptions." There is no such being. But there is also no human being who never apperceives but rather always merely perceives. For this reason alone there must be all possible gradations of genius; at least no masculine being is entirely without genius. But complete genius also remains an ideal: there is no human being without any, and no human being with, universal apperception. (147)

Weininger contrasts the unity and continuity of the universal apperception in the genius to the female's hanging on to individual moments that are discontinuous with previous experience, and he argues that whoever experiences his inner life as something more than bodily life will not easily give himself up to death. "The question of the 'euthanasia of the atheists,' which was so frequently raised in the eighteenth century, is thus by no means senseless, and not merely a historical curiosity, as it was treated as being by Friedrich Albert Lange" (164).

Weininger argues that women (here he does not say "females" or "woman") lack any need for immortality, despite the fact that anxiety in the face of death is common to both men and women. He links this indifference to immortality to the lack of living in one's own past, the lack of piety toward one's own life in women. Weininger argues that "a woman is *never* solitary; she does not know the love of solitude or the fear of it. The woman lives continuously, even when she is alone, in a condition of *fusion* with all the people she knows: a proof that she is not a monad, since all monads have boundaries. Women are by nature without boundaries" (255).

> The woman [he returns here to the singular] does not honor the pain of her fellow human being with silence; she believes she can cancel it out by talking at it: so much does she feel herself bound up with the other person, as a natural not as a spiritual-intellectual being. (256)[87]

For Weininger, the woman's pity is "only a form of sexual fusion" even when it is related to "someone of the same sex," and her willingness to demand pity from other people is a form of "psychic shamelessness," which arises from making herself an object among other objects and thus relinquishing her identity as subject (256–257). According to Weininger, "no suffering can be as shameful as pity and love, because they both bring most strongly to consciousness the impassable limits of each individuality" (257). He sees evidence of the lack of shame in women in "the naïve enthusiasm with which all women, wherever social convention simply permits it, display their décolletage" (257). The key to his discussion of shame, whether with respect to tears or décolletage, is the woman's willingness, even desire, to be an object for others—and even for herself. For Weininger, this is the opposite of being a human being, a subject, a microcosm, a consciousness. He emphasizes that "the genuine woman" judges herself not in terms of the development of her personality and freedom but in terms of her husband and her marriage: "[S]he lacks the self-value of human personality. Women always derive their value from other things, from their money and property, the number and splendor of their clothes, the level of their loge in the theater, of their children, but above all, of their admirers, of their men" (261). Weininger not only falls away here from his distinction between the female and the woman, but he also slides into a much broader critique of bourgeois society. He argues that when a woman fights, she does so with themes such as "social station, wealth, reputation and title, but also the youthfulness and number of her husband's female admirers" (261). Weininger imagines men as people who are ashamed to draw their value from anything external. Such people would be human beings in Weininger's sense.

On the basis of his own argument, Weininger's examples about women and men can only be suggestive and culturally relative, although Weininger seems often to lose track of this himself. The center of his argument is the opposition between wanting to be a subject and wanting to be an object. The two major problems that arise from this are, first, the extent to which Weininger was justified in identifying this opposition with man/woman, masculine/feminine and, second, whether he was right to value being a subject so exclusively in the way he did. Weininger identified a constellation of values, which he thought of as feminine. What is overlooked by readers who react primarily to his antifeminism is the complex process of sorting that is involved either in rejecting these values or in revaluing them. Many people, whatever their ascribed gender, have no intention of experiencing life in a conscious way or of treating other human beings as ends in themselves. Weininger's morality is not set in opposition to women but in opposition to the whole process of attraction, manipulation, and seduction in sexual relationships.

Ironically, it has become quite common over the past century to distinguish how men and women express themselves or form relationships or perceive other people. Weininger was at least able to see that this way of speaking is a heuristic oversimplification, although he may not have seen how easily it can become crass and trivial. Separated from its misogynistic elements, Weininger's argument reads something like this: There are no ideal human beings in the world, no human beings as we ought to be (no males in

Weininger's sense), but, given the current state of education and culture, men have a far better chance of approximating the ideal of humanity than women do. Indeed, he believed (a bit like Freud), that men were almost certainly more highly motivated to do so. But perhaps it is a problematic ideal in any case, and Weininger pointed to this at times himself. Much of Weininger's argument aims at the deconstruction of the romantic idea of love as it was understood by the Viennese *Bürgertum*. Weininger argues that those who defend women are motivated by feelings that arise out of eroticism; and he distinguishes "eroticism" from "sexuality" (which among animals constitutes everything about the relations between the sexes and plays by far the greater role among human beings). Weininger rejects the notion, which he ascribes to Kant and Schopenhauer, that sexuality and erotic love amount to the same thing, that love is simply a sublimation of sexuality (315):

> In coitus lies the most profound devaluation of the female, in love the highest elevation. That the female demands coitus and not love means that she [es] wants to be devalued and not elevated. *The ultimate opponent of women's emancipation is the woman.* (447)

For Weininger, "[l]ove and desire are such different, completely mutually exclusive, indeed opposed conditions that in the moment when a human being really loves, the idea of physical union with the loved being is completely unthinkable" (317). For Weininger, the split between sexual desire and higher, romantic love was in the nature of things—a view that informed the notion of *Fernliebe* that descended to Weininger from Plato and the German Romantics. Although he insists that eros and sexuality vary inversely, he refuses to accept the view that eros is sublimated sexuality.

> There is then such a thing as "Platonic" love, even if the professors of psychiatry don't think so. I would even say: there is only Platonic love. For what is otherwise called love belongs in the realm of the sows. There is only one love: it is the love for Beatrice, the adoration of the Madonna. For coitus the Babylonian whore is there. (318)

Weininger rejected the sophisticated sexual ethos of Vienna's social elites, but he also rejected the tradition of romantic love (or eroticism) in the West. This is part of what he means by saying that his argument is directed against men far more than people imagine, against the sentimental idealization of the woman to meet the man's psychological need. He emphasized the projection and false consciousness that were involved in this version of the man's relationship with women. Weininger links eros to romantic love but also to religious and philosophical love, whereas he distinguishes sexuality as something utterly different. For Weininger, eros was specifically masculine, associated with figures such as Kant and Jesus in opposition to purely feminine sexuality, which was the basis for selfishness and possessiveness—simply the extreme instance of what is least valuable in human beings. Weininger attacks the tendency in modern culture to identify love with sexuality—or with family and the nurturing role of women.[88] He thought of eros as Christian, as masculine and rational (in something like Kant's sense). Le Rider argues that Weininger's "entire error, and his unhappiness, consisted in not wanting to distinguish between the sexuality he denied and eroticism, a superior form of acceptance of life, the affirmation of an individuality freed from illusions of individuation."[89] This is an interesting observation, which seems to idealize "eroticism" along Laurencian lines, but Le Rider apparently means that Weininger distinguished between sexuality and eroticism in the "wrong" way.

An easily misunderstood aspect of Weininger's argument is his critique of the way in which men idealize women in the context of romantic love. This is sometimes read primarily as another denigration of women that argues that women do not have the positive qualities that men attribute to them. Lost in such a critique is not only Weininger's view of sexuality and eroticism but also his insight into the mind of the male type in love and the kind of function women have provided for men in the history of Western creativity. Weininger could be right about male eroticism quite apart from whether he has a correct view of what qualities real women may be capable of achieving.

> In all love, the man loves only himself. Not his subjectivity, not that which he really represents as a being burdened by all weaknesses and vulgarity . . . ; but that which he completely wants to be and completely ought to be, his own deep, intelligible essence, free from all the rags of necessity, from all the lumps of earthliness. (322)

The man "projects his ideal of an absolutely valuable being on another human being, and it is this and nothing else that it means, when he loves this being. . . ." But this is simply to say that "love is the highest and strongest expression of the will to value," and it is in love that "the real essence of the human being comes into view, an essence that is banished between spirit and body, between sensuousness and morality, participating in the divine as well as the animal. The human being is in every regard only then entirely himself when he loves" (323).

Weininger argues that "the beauty of the female and the love of the male are not two different things, but rather one and the same fact. Just as ugliness comes from hating, so does beauty come from loving. And this is also the reason that beauty has as little to do with sexual drive as love does" (321).[90] Weininger believed that the "beauty of the female is only morality made visible, but this morality is itself that of the male, which he has transposed to the female in the highest intensification and perfection" (325). This is Weininger's account of what was going on in nineteenth-century European romantic love, but it is also his model for understanding the relationship of the creative person to the world: "Just as love creates a new female for the male instead of the real female, so does art, the eroticism of the cosmos, create the fullness of forms out of the chaos of the universe" (325).[91]

Projection is central to Weininger's argument because it is the key to understanding the relationship between male and female and the confusion between eros and sexuality. It also applies in all sorts of ethical contexts, including his critique of Western religion. One would never suspect this psychological subtlety (one might almost say self-irony) in Weininger from most of the accounts of his argument in the scholarship:

> Just as all hatred only projects negative qualities that one possesses onto fellowmen, in order to show them there in an even more terrible union; just as the devil was only invented in order to represent the evil drives in the human being outside him, . . . so does love also have only the purpose of easing for the human being the struggle for goodness, which he is still too weak to comprehend as a thought in itself alone. Both, loving and hating, are, therefore, cowardice. (327)

"From the person whom I love, I want something, at the very least I want the other person not to disturb my love through unbeautiful gestures or common qualities. . . . I want out of the hands of a fellow human being nothing less than myself—I want me!" (328).[92]

Weininger seems to want to argue that the human being in love reveals a capacity for love and a will to value that contradict the scientific understanding of the human being as a body with needs for pleasure and reproduction. He argues that what happens in the conventional form of romantic love is that the male projects value on the female, and Weininger happened to believe (or to argue by definition) that the female is not capable of this projection of value (340). Indeed, this is the real denigration of the female. For Weininger, this is the substance of the contrast between male and female. But this is not the crucial point, since falling in love with any particular person is, for Weininger, always a falling away from what is most important. It is really at this point that Weininger's respect for Jesus and Kant becomes most clear—and it becomes apparent what Weininger's attempt to be a religious genius might have looked like, had he lived. For Weininger, romantic love is the moment that simultaneously reveals what is most important and valuable in the human being and distorts it in the direction of something local and empirical. For Weininger, Jesus and Kant understood that there can be no narcotic escape from the individual's obligation to love and create value. This is what he means by M, by masculine love. It is eros that makes the human being aware of his own hybrid nature:

> For eros is a middle thing between having and not having; no god, but a demon; eros alone corresponds to the place of the human being between mortality and immortality: the greatest thinker knew this, the divine Plato as Plotinus called him (the only human being who really, inwardly *understood* him . . .). Love is thus in reality not a "transcendental idea"; for it corresponds only to the idea of a being who is not purely transcendental—a priori but also sensuous-empirical: the idea of humanity. (340)

According to Weininger, the female is at home in the merely empirical, while the man is "not only empirical, conditioned, but also intelligible, free subject" (375).[93] Thus, the man is a hybrid ("a middle thing" like eros). Weininger was reluctant to extend his argument to the woman, although he regarded the female hysteric as one of the decisive points of intersection of masculine and feminine. He saw the hysterical constitution as "a mimicry of the masculine soul," but he believed that hysterical women were precisely the highest feminine types, the women who were always adduced as "proofs of feminine morality" (372–374). Instead of taking the hysteric as the decisive instance of a hybrid nature, however, Weininger regards the hysterical woman as the site of a conflict between her unconscious nature and imposed masculine values that are not her own. Indeed: *"Hysteria is the organic crisis of the organic mendacity of the female"* (358).[94] Nonetheless, Weininger claimed that he would renounce his whole theory if he were mistaken about it in even one instance:

> It is clear that if even only a single very feminine being were inwardly asexual or stood in a true relationship to the idea of moral self-worth, *everything* that was said here about women would have to lose its general validity as a psychic characterization of her sex, and thereby the whole position of the book would be invalidated at a stroke. (353)

Weininger distinguished human qualities that are shared by animals (or organic life in general) from qualities that characterize human beings alone, especially the human male. He developed a set of characteristic oppositions: individuation and individuality, recognition and memory, desire and value, sexual drive and love, limitation of consciousness and attention (that is, apperception), drive and will (378). For Weininger, the second member of these pairs describes "the idea of the eternal, higher, *new* life of religion and especially of Christianity" (379); and the conflict "between the higher and the lower life . . . constitutes the main theme of all history of the human spirit: this is the theme of world history" (380). Weininger's goal was "the moral rebirth of the human being" (379), and he seems at times to imply that his account of gender concerns the biological limitations of human beings, while the idea of spiritual rebirth transcends these limitations. According to his definitions, the more nearly female a person is, the more difficult it will be to overcome the empirical self. Weininger simply assumes that the male participates in the new, higher life, while the female does not; he identifies the higher life with reason—and that, in turn, with eternal life and immortality. Weininger's intent was not to impose conventional understandings of gender but to challenge empiricism, positivism, materialism from the perspective of Kant's transcendental ego. "If the female should become masculine, by becoming logical and ethical, she would then no longer be so suitable as the passive substrate of a projection" (452). Weininger argues that women must no longer be educated simply to serve the needs of men and children. "Overcoming femininity is the issue. If, for example, a woman were really to want the chastity of the man, she would in this way have overcome the female" (453).

> A woman [eine Frau] who has really renounced, who really sought peace within herself, such a woman [Frau] would no longer be a female [Weib]. She would have received the inner baptism in addition to the external one.
>
> There is no absolute female, and yet the affirmation of this question is for us like the affirmation of a miracle.
>
> The female will not become happier through such an emancipation: it cannot promise her bliss [Seligkeit], and the way to God is still long. No being between freedom and unfreedom knows happiness. But will the female be able to resolve to give up slavery in order to be unhappy?
>
> Not to make the woman holy; it cannot so quickly be a matter of that. But only: can the female achieve a candid awareness of the problem of her existence, of the concept of guilt? Will she at least want freedom? It is simply a matter of carrying out the ideal, of seeing the guiding star; can the

categorical imperative come to life in the female? Will the female finally subordinate herself to the moral idea, to the idea of humanity?

For that alone would be women's emancipation. (460–461)

Weininger's book *is* a critique of the women's movement but in a rather peculiar way that argues for what Weininger regarded as true women's liberation. His argument drew heavily on his personal experience, which in turn reflected a particular culture and historical period—and its conventional expectations for the genders. By the end of his book, it is not clear whether Weininger even remembered what he had said earlier: not how women are essentially, but how they were in 1903.

GENDER AND MODERNITY

Weininger believed that sexuality and gender were central to understanding modern culture and that the theme of Judaism was closely connected to them. However problematic his discussion of the female may be, we may say that Judaism has nothing to do with his subject at all; and, however tangential Judaism may seem to his subject, he nonetheless placed his chapter on Judaism at the culmination of the book's argument. His critique of Judaism was in part his attempt at a psychology of the male, but it was also a summary of the metaphysical issues that motivated his argument throughout.[95] Weininger believed that Judaism was "the hardest and most to be feared opponent of the views developed here" (405). He identified the Jew with the scientific worldview and modernity, which he believed was the way of thinking that gave legitimacy to the female. What he meant by Judaism was the scientific, materialist, empirical way of seeing the world. "Jewish is the spirit of modernity, however one regards it. Sexuality is affirmed, and the contemporary sexual ethic sings hymns to coitus. . . . females and Jews pair, it is their goal: to let human beings become guilty" (441). For Weininger, "Jewish" meant external and cynical, and his critique of Judaism was aimed at overcoming cynicism, empiricism, and positivism.[96] Weininger's view is problematic in the extreme—one might see it as the culmination and incarnation of the issues that concerned Nietzsche—but the problem is not the one that is usually raised. His central concern is not anti-Semitism, but the problem of value and of the value of life.

Weininger is perhaps the most dramatic case of someone from a Jewish background embracing an intellectual tradition of anti-Semitism. Houston Stewart Chamberlain was probably the main influence in this regard, but there were others, including Richard Wagner and Weininger's father. Weininger explains to his readers that he is "himself of Jewish heritage" (406n), but he apparently had very little institutional experience of either Judaism or Christianity. Much as in his argument about gender, Weininger confronts an idealized Christianity with a diminished Judaism. As prejudicial as Weininger's view of real women and real Jews is, he makes clear that the objects of his criticism are not women and Jews but rather qualities that are threats to everyone. As in his discussion of gender, Weininger develops an ideal-type methodology, but he speaks of Jews, as he does of women, in ways that allow his readers to forget this. "I am speaking about Judaism as a Platonic idea—there is no absolute Jew, any more than there is an absolute Christian; I am not speaking of individual Jews, so many of whom I would in no way want to cause pain, who would be done a real injustice if what I am saying were applied to them" (418). Weininger tries to make clear "in what sense I speak of Judaism. For me it is not a matter of a race and not a matter of a people, still less, to be sure, is it a matter of a legally recognized denomination. One may only regard Judaism as a mental tendency or constitution, which constitutes a possibility for all human beings and has simply found in historical Judaism its most grandiose realization" (406). But, however one may read Weininger and his contradictions, it is difficult to avoid the labels he chose for what he thought most worthy of opposition: Judaism and femininity—the socially determined conventions in which Weininger located his own discourse.

Weininger argues "that one ought not to confuse Judaism with the Jews. There are Aryans who are more Jewish than some Jews, and there are real Jews who are more Aryan than certain Aryans" (407). This is the kind of point that is often overlooked in discussions of Weininger, but one must still ask why Weininger wanted to talk this way at all. Like many liberal intellectuals of his day, including many Jews, Weininger accepted as a matter of course ways of speaking that can only seem racist and sexist today.[97] But there is still the question of what Weininger was trying to say in this discourse, even of what problem he was trying to solve. What makes an attitude Jewish, according to Weininger, is regarding and valuing "individuals only as belonging to a species or type [Gattung]" (418). Oddly, of course, this is precisely what Weininger seems to be doing when he writes about the female and Judaism, and he is known primarily as a proponent of what he regarded as the principal moral and intellectual mistake. Weininger found a powerful antidote to sexism and racism, and yet he left the impression that he was a misogynist and an anti-Semite as well as conventionally prejudiced against non-Europeans. Nonetheless, he believed that the North was the just party in the American Civil War, that a man has no right to control a woman because he is married to her, and that men and women have equal rights. If we may say that at twenty-three Weininger's experience of people and of women, in particular, was slight, his experience of non-European peoples and cultures was even more meager. Here he was thrown back almost entirely on the prejudices and conventions of his intellectual environment. And Weininger's way of talking about bodies belongs to the bizarre, highly metaphorical discourse described by Sander Gilman in *The Jew's Body*. Many passages in Weininger read like familiar anti-Semitism, but his argument turns out to be somewhat different. One could say that Weininger pays his respects to the racist norms of his day, but Peter Gay is right, in the main, to emphasize that Weininger's argument is not racist. For Weininger, his negative remarks about women (or about Jews and Negroes) are only evidence of the necessity of emancipation. "The lower the female stands, so much more necessary is it that she be emancipated. Ordinarily one concludes the opposite" (594).

Weininger's view of Judaism is a critique of Western religion and monotheism that was strongly influenced by Schopenhauer and Nietzsche. In Jesus, Weininger saw the highest individuality as well as a new concept of God, which he interpreted as the overcoming of Jewish tradition, God, and family. In theological terms, Weininger expressed Nietzsche's critique of God as a critique of Judaism: "Schopenhauer once offered the following definition: 'The word "God" means a man [einen Menschen] who created the world.' At least for the God of the Jews this is accurate." Weininger contrasted this notion to the idea of "the divine in the human being, of 'the God who dwells in my breast'; that which Christ and Plato, Eckhard and Paul, Goethe and Kant . . . meant" (420).[98] In Weininger's critique of the notion of God as an external power and lawgiver, the influence of Nietzsche is unmistakable, but Weininger's move toward a more inward notion of spirituality was strongly influenced by Kant and Protestant mysticism as well.

Weininger uses the word "Jehovah-slave" to describe anyone who is determined morally by an external lawgiver, by a man who created the world.

> Certainly it is true that most people need Jehovah in some way. Very few—they are the geniuses—do not live heteronomously at all. The others always justify what they do and do not do, their thinking and being (at least in their minds) before someone else, whether it is a personal Jewish God, or a loved, respected, feared human being. Only in this way do they act in formal, external conformity with the moral law. (208)[99]

Weininger was criticizing a notion of God that he associated with Jehovah and Judaism, although Nietzsche might have located it in Christianity.

Weininger contrasted this conception of God with a notion that he thought of as Aryan, probably from Chamberlain. But the conception of God itself was a part of the religious tradition, for example, in Jakob Böhme and Meister Eckehart. It was belief in God in the traditional Western sense that Weininger was attacking, but he obscured this argument by emphasizing the opposition between Judaism and Christianity. Weininger actually intensified the existing tensions within the Western tradition by arguing that Judaism arose out of the split in the Hebrew tradition: "[T]he old Israel divided itself into Jews and Christians. The Jew as we know him, as I have described him, arose simultaneously with the Christian" (439). But Weininger was also arguing that Christianity and Judaism were two possibilities within Hebrew religious tradition and that the religious significance of Jesus must be understood in this context: "Christ is the human being who overcomes the most powerful negation, Judaism, in himself, and thereby creates the strongest position, Christianity, as the one most opposed to Judaism" (439).

Weininger argued that Western monotheism had become the basis for scientific materialism. The impiety that Weininger was worried about was not an ancient religious tradition but modern science, a way of seeing the world, which he thought derived from this religious tradition. Weininger's argument is a critique of modernity and its roots in Jewish tradition, which is in many ways analogous to Heidegger's critique of Greek tradition and the way it continued to determine the metaphysics of modernity.[100] Weininger believed that the literal-minded religious view of God as a man who created the world had made the modern scientific view possible, and he regarded modern science as the drive "to see the world in a way that is as flat and ordinary as possible in order to generate a sterile matter-of-factness of the universe" (421n). He defined the Jew as "the human being without faith," or, put differently, the object of Weininger's critique was "the impious human being in the widest sense" (431–432). "All genuine inner culture requires piety, and no matter what a human being takes to be the truth, the fact that there is culture for him, that there is truth, that there are values, rests on the basis of faith" (432n).

Weininger emphasized an internal view of religious experience rather than an external view of objective reality or cosmology in which religion is simply a primitive form of science. The contrast between Judaism and Christianity in Weininger's argument amounts to the contrast between the scientific reduction of the world and the self-determining, self-legislating moral self. As Western culture moved to a scientific self-understanding, the view of the self as transcendental, not reducible to scientific categories and self-interest, was endangered. What is essential in Weininger's critique of Judaism is his resistance to modernity, science, capitalism, and the matter-of-fact acceptance of the empirical world. Weininger seems to have persuaded himself that his own tradition was peculiarly responsible for creating the conditions of modern life, despite the fact that the principal shapers of his intellectual world and his troubles—Friedrich Nietzsche and Ernst Mach—were not Jewish.[101] Weininger's conception of the religious was not Jewish, but Greek, although his notion of a religious founder came from the model of Jesus.[102] Classical Greek culture had a much more powerful impact on Weininger's intellectual development than the Hebrew tradition did, and Plato often seems to be what Weininger meant by Christianity. Weininger explains in a footnote that "the most pious people in the world were the Greeks, and thus their culture was the highest among all cultures down to the present. But there was certainly never an outstanding religious founder among the Greeks (because they did not need one)" (433). Central to Weininger's thought was the notion of setting for himself the maximally difficult task of overcoming nihilism, of confronting the meaninglessness and lack of value in modern life. And in this regard he took Jesus as his model: "[P]erhaps there still lies in Judaism today the possibility of bringing forth the Christian, perhaps the next founder of a religion must even go through Judaism first" (440). He believed that his own struggle with his lack of faith might be the basis for redeeming modern society: "The founder of a religion is that person who lives completely godlessly and nonetheless has fought his way through to the highest faith" (438).[103] He wanted to achieve individuality, to become a genius, a Christian, the founder of a religion; and he wanted, like Christ, to overcome Judaism and unbelief.[104] As in his argument about gender, Weininger insisted on a polar way of thinking: choosing between two halves of humanity rather than trying to balance them in some way. For Weininger, Judaism and Christianity were ideal types, two possible responses to human experience, and he emphasized the necessity of deciding between them:

> Again and again, humanity must make a choice between Judaism and Christianity, between business and culture, between female and male, between species and personality, between nonvalue and value, between the mundane and the higher life, between nothingness and divinity. (441)

Weininger was conscious of the divided nature of human beings, which is part of what is significant in his critique of scientific materialism. But he did not accept this divided nature: repeatedly, he would settle only for the divine.[105]

Weininger suffered from a perfectionism that did not support a human world. His nihilism lies in his effort to be rational and divine at the expense of his empirical humanity. The argument of *Geschlecht und Charakter* aims at death. There is no way to soften that. But it is important to see that it does so by way of the search for perfection. This search is also an attempt to find redemption from modern life and from the culture that emerged with science and industrial capitalism. Weininger displayed many of the qualities of the saint, struggling with his own sinfulness, but he also felt the responsibility to behave as a savior figure, saving the whole world by overcoming the evil within himself. For all the self-centeredness of his views, his high-mindedness kept him from even considering the possibility of accepting himself (or the world). His commitment to this extreme ethical dualism was no merely personal matter, and his experience suggests the limits of his own way of seeing the world. Weininger displays some of the destructive dynamics of post-Nietzschean philosophy (the extreme sense of the loss of value and the extreme sense of personal responsibility to overcome this predicament), despite his genuine (if idiosyncratic) confession of faith in Christianity and pre-Nietzschean metaphysics. He was continuous with Schopenhauer and Nietzsche in the structure of his thought, in the creativity of his mind, and in the character of his prejudices against women. Indeed, his nihilism was roughly what Nietzsche predicted that Schopenhauer and modern society would lead to for creative people. The sense of loss in Weininger about the Western tradition is not so much about gender and race as it is about the possibility that there is some coherent sense to reality and human experience—and that these are related through the mind. Sixty years after Weininger's death Heimito von Doderer characterized him as "a monument to the reality of the spirit [Geist]".[106]

What is central to Weininger's thought is not misogyny or anti-Semitism but rather a crisis of liberal rationalism and individualism in the face of modern society and two powerful intellectual challenges: philosophical irrationalism and scientific materialism. Weininger was an important early warning sign of the power of these challenges to liberal humanism, and he formulated his concerns in terms of gender and religion. He felt threatened by the scientific reduction of religious life and by the irrational in himself; he generally thought of the former as Jewish, and the latter, as feminine, although these typologies often overlapped. Weininger was aiming at the possibility of meaningful, ethical existence in a world dominated by inauthenticity and manipulation. Weininger's agenda of crisis anticipated Martin Heidegger in many respects. But Weininger's approach to human existence also made social life, and perhaps life of any kind, difficult to imagine.

Robert Calasso distinguishes Weininger from real anti-Semites, true enemies of women, and real haters of homosexuals and argues that Weininger was the opposite of all this: he himself was Jewish, he inspired Kraus to defend prostitutes, and he put the discussion of homosexuality on a new level. Calasso emphasizes that Weininger's significance lies not in some systematic scholarly achievement but rather in the fact that he was "the faithful and clear-sighted chronicler of his culture's fantasies [Phantasmen]." The offense felt by contemporary taste at much of what Weininger has to say about women or Jews was felt even at the turn of the century, but Calasso questions conventional perceptions: "How can he be standing in our way once again after three quarters of a century, this arrogant young fellow, this suicide? This student who brought so much rage to bear in order to malign women, homosexuals, and Jews?"[107]

On one level, Weininger is a symptom of the anti-Semitism and anti-feminism of liberal intellectual culture around 1900. More precisely, he constitutes an effort to come to terms with modern culture that focuses on a critique of Judaism and femininity, while actually attempting to overcome the racism and sexism of Central Europe around 1900.[108] And the connections between Weininger and political anti-Semitism are sometimes confusing. For example, Alexander Centraf's study of Weininger, published in Berlin in 1943, came to the defense of women against Weininger's individualism and sexual science in the name of National Socialism.[109] Despite Weininger's anti-Semitism, his views were roughly the opposite of National Socialism, and he challenged the notion that Christianity was an ideology of the family—let alone an ideology of reproduction. Moreover, Weininger argued that it was the Jew rather than the Aryan who is anti-Semitic.

Weininger had a conception of intellectual and spiritual life in which sexuality could only appear as a disturbing and destructive element. This is perhaps most painfully apparent in his posthumous work, in which he criticized and in part retracted his own ideas about the female and expressed a new understanding about the vanity of individualism:

> How finally, can I reproach women that they are waiting for the man? The man wants nothing but the woman. There is no man who would not be pleased to know that he exercised a sexual influence on a woman.
>
> The hatred against the woman is always only not yet overcome hatred against one's own sexuality.[110]

Weininger's retraction of his central argument in *Gender and Character* appears in *Über die letzten Dinge:* "The 'intelligible ego' is, however, only vanity, that is, the binding [Verknüpfung] of value to the person" (184). This is arguably not so much a retraction as the honorable and consequential extension of his ideas, as well as a confession of the impossibility of realizing the demands he had formulated. And his requirements went even further to an autonomic "hygiene and therapy" in which total solitude must be endured and overcome.[111] In this direction lay only ever higher ethical expectations on his own poor empirical *moi haissable,* which he was finally forced after long ethical warfare to kill.

Weininger's conception of inwardness could not take feelings into account, and in this respect he spoke in a caricatured way for a much broader spectrum of nineteenth-century masculine ways of thinking and professionalism. Weininger claimed masculine values and moral standards for everyone, but his own life suggests that human existence is not supportable on this basis alone. This implies a critique of the narrowness of masculine values and individualism and of the exclusion of women from the moral world. Karl Kraus agreed with Weininger's account of the masculine but not with the value he placed on it. For most writers in the generation of 1905, male meant rational consciousness and individuality but not an enhancing relationship to experience. Kraus agreed with Weininger's perceptions but turned his values around, reversing the valences to argue that the female is sexuality—and that sexuality is what is most important. Yet Kraus himself regarded women as entirely sexual, and he saw men as dependent on women for a connection to feelings and creativity. In different ways, both Weininger and Kraus pointed to femininity as a metaphor for heightened experience, but it was left to Musil to identify the arbitrariness of valuing one side of human nature at the expense of another or of taking the nomenclature of gender too literally.

Figure 5. Robert Musil (1880–1942)

CHAPTER THREE

LOVE AND HUMAN KNOWLEDGE

*R*obert Musil made the most important attempt of any twentieth-century thinker to come to terms with both modern scientific thinking and an irrationalist approach to the feelings. He completed his doctorate in experimental psychology and philosophy, and followed developments in physics and psychology throughout his life, but he also wanted to find a place again for soul, a notion that had dropped out of scientific thinking during the nineteenth century.[1] It was Ernst Mach who gave the young Musil a way of thinking about positivism and the tradition that grew out of scientific materialism.[2] Musil learned about the unconscious from Eduard von Hartmann, but his real mentors were Nietzsche, Emerson, and the poets of the late nineteenth century—from the French symbolists to Dostoevsky. Musil was one of the most conspicuously post-Nietzschean modern thinkers, and he was especially conscious of his debts to Emerson and Nietzsche. But Musil was less limited in his individualism than either Emerson or Nietzsche and more nuanced in his understanding of sexuality and gender. He was also more at home with science and the modern world, and his scientific education was an important factor in giving him a way of writing and thinking that was clearly different from these two nineteenth-century mentors. Musil understood his work as a continuation of Nietzsche but also as an attempt to do for the realm of the feelings what modern science had done for the physical world. In this sense he might be seen as the ultimate positivist, applying intellect to the realm of the feelings. But he believed that the writer had to proceed differently from the scientist, not looking for laws and regularities but understanding emotional experience in a more individual way that relies on metaphor rather than laws. He wanted to bring the irrational sources of ethics and imagination into relation with the practical reality of the modern world, to achieve a spirituality commensurate with life in modern civilization.

Musil's view of modern life emphasized that rationalism and irrationalism were the poles of the age, and his thought was a sophisticated way of coming to terms with both, particularly by exploring his culture's understandings of sexuality and gender.[3] In Weininger's work, what seemed merely to be judgments about Jews and women turned out to be a powerful reaction against modern science and against the importance of sexuality and the unconscious in modern understandings of human experience. Weininger regarded science as the fundamental obstacle to spiritual life (as the rationalization of the feminine view of the world), whereas Musil accepted science as the fundamental given of spiritual life, as the reality of modern life and civilization.[4] Musil thought of science as practical and, therefore, masculine in the culture's terms: men displayed a good-natured lack of comprehension toward women, religion, feelings, and similar matters that were reserved for special occasions but had nothing to do with a sensible man's efforts to master the world. In *The Man without Qualities*, which he worked on from 1924 until his death in 1942, Musil portrayed Austrian social and intellectual elites in the year before the First World War as a special case of the ideological and cultural difficulties of Europe in the twentieth century. Through his protagonist, Ulrich (an engineer and mathematician), Musil attempted to bring the conceptually strong person, a type ordinarily associated with science or philosophy, into relation with the highly individualized experiences of literature—ethical experiences or experiences of feeling. In volume 2 of *The Man without Qualities* Ulrich meets his forgotten sister, Agathe, and together they explore the possibilities for balance between masculine and feminine, thinking and feeling.

Musil was preoccupied throughout his life with balancing what he understood to be the masculine and feminine within the personality and working out a new understanding of the relationship between thinking and feeling and between the normal relationship to experience and an enhanced relationship to the world. When he was twenty-five, he published his first novel, *Die Verwirrungen des Zöglings Törless* [Young Törless] (1906), a story about adolescent homosexuality and sadism in an Austrian military academy.[5] His second volume of fiction, *Vereinigungen* [Unions], appeared five years later and brought together two novellas that were written from the perspectives of women.[6] More than a decade later he published *Drei Frauen*, three love stories with male protagonists, and his plays of the 1920s dramatized romantic relationships between men and women.[7] *Der Mann ohne Eigenschaften* (1930–1933) portrayed Austrian elites as if each were half a human being still engaged in the search described by Aristophanes in Plato's *Symposium*. For Musil, conventional understandings of gender in the early twentieth century offered the most available metaphor for the confused relations in European culture between thinking and feeling.[8] He employed the metaphor of gender to describe two different kinds of knowledge, two different relations to experience, and the balance between thinking and feeling in the personality and in the culture. I begin with an account of Musil's understanding of himself as a writer within the intellectual world of Central Europe in the early twentieth century, and then turn to his view of sexuality and gender, especially in the fiction and essays he wrote before the war. In the last two sections I discuss the significance of Musil's critique of ideology in his essays of the 1920s and the role of gender in *The Man without Qualities*.

Science and the Writer

Musil believed that the characteristic predicament of Europeans in the early twentieth century had been the successful creation of a practical civilization and the widespread feeling of impotence in the realm of the spiritual. Despite great scientific successes, it was apparent by the end of the nineteenth century that intellectuals outside the natural sciences felt helpless by comparison—despairing about lost worldviews and yearning for intuition and emotional escapes from the facts. What we now call the Second Industrial Revolution had come into view by the 1890s: the importance of steel, electricity, chemicals, oil, the internal combustion engine, automobiles, airplanes, trade unions, assembly lines, and cinema.[9] It was also around this time that doubts about the vitality of Western culture became widespread—expressed most eloquently in Nietzsche's formula of the death of God. Musil was critical of humanistic intellectuals who blamed the cultural crisis and spiritual uncertainty of the time on science and intellect: "In the physical realm we have found an accommodation (the concept of function). In the spiritual realm we are completely helpless. Intellectuality leaves us in the lurch. But not because intellect is shallow (as if everything else had not left us in the lurch as well!) but because we have not worked at it."[10] For Musil, this new situation was not a decline but a challenge to the creation of a new culture.

Musil's own location in the intellectual world of the early twentieth century placed him between literary people complaining about reason and scientists who had no understanding of the important questions of life. He repeatedly emphasized the need for greater balance between scientific and humanistic education, which was central to what he called intellectual and spiritual organization. And he refused to set science and literature in opposition to one another as many German writers did in the generation of 1905—including Oswald Spengler, Martin Heidegger, and Ludwig Klages:

> [The] essential organizing function of society, however, rests in our time exclusively with the sciences, in the realm of pure intellect; in the humanistic area not even creative people recognize the need for it. On the contrary, precisely in humanistic circles . . . there exists no more stubborn prejudice than the belief that civilization's entire misdirection, and above all its spiritual dissolution, can be blamed on the scientific spirit our society panders to. . . . what one invariably means is that science gradually dissolves values that were previously accepted as integral and emotionally safe. But science can only have this effect where these values already have cracks in their emotional premises. The cause lies not in its nature, but in theirs![11]

This is the most important attitude that separated Musil from Weininger and Doderer, from German expressionism and from most German intellectuals of the early twentieth century.[12] Musil's resistance to this conventional dichotomy of German culture in his generation derived at least in part from his Austrian background and education, although Musil preferred to understate what he regarded as a provincial perspective. The strength of the Austrian tradition in the human sciences and philosophy was that it was at home with the changes in the picture of the world that came from the natural sciences in the late nineteenth century; and it was generally more sympathetic to empiricism than it was to dogmatic theorizing. In some respects Musil might be regarded as part of the Austrian tradition, entering the debate against German culture in the narrower sense. But he did not think in these terms.

Musil was born in Klagenfurt, Austria, in 1880 and grew up in Steyr (near Linz) and Brno (in Moravia). Whereas Weininger attended a classical gymnasium, which concentrated on history, literature, and languages but placed little emphasis on science and mathematics, Musil's education was roughly the opposite. He was never really comfortable in a foreign language, and he received his education in *Realschulen*, military academies, and technical institutes, exposed to a curriculum that emphasized science and mathematics rather than classical languages. At the turn of the century, he went to Germany to pursue his university work, first in mechanical engineering in Stuttgart and then in philosophy and experimental psychology in Berlin between 1903 and 1908.[13] In philosophy he trained with Carl Stumpf, who (like Freud and Edmund Husserl) had studied with Franz Brentano. Musil wrote his dissertation on Mach's view of causality and function, and he considered an academic position with Alexius Meinong in Graz, but his own experimental work was closer to Gestalt psychology.[14] Musil belonged to the hard edge of modern science, positivism, and empiricism, although he was less preoccupied than Rudolf Carnap, Moritz Schlick, and the Vienna Circle with logic and the attack on metaphysics. Indeed, he regarded the intellectual atmosphere of the Stumpf lab as more sober and scientific than the Vienna Circle, and he saw his education not as specifically Austrian but as part of the broad enthusiasm for science in the late nineteenth century.[15]

Musil's cultural heritage was the Austrian Enlightenment, Josephinism, and high liberal culture; and yet he also developed a critique of the limitations of this tradition in relation to feelings, religion, and ethics. His father, Alfred Musil, belonged to the scientific rationalism of the university tradition and to its practical applications in the late nineteenth century. Robert Musil believed that the rationalism of this tradition was threatened—justly insofar as it was narrow and exclusively instrumental, and wrongly insofar as "rationalism" was unfairly made into a term of abuse by people who were bad at mathematics and angry about modern civilization. He distinguished between the confidence of the Enlightenment's attempt to break with tradition and the narrow, hackneyed clichés that were despised as positivism by the late nineteenth century.[16] Musil's sophisticated appreciation of modern science (grounded in Mach and Nietzsche as well as his own study and research) was decisive in his empirical, relativist approach to gender as well as race; more than anything it was this understanding of science that set him apart from both Weininger and Doderer.

The writers who shaped Musil's thought were broadly European. There was almost nothing locally Austrian about Musil's mind, except perhaps the point of intersection of international ideas: French, Scandinavian, German, Russian, American, and most of all, scientific.[17] Nonetheless, he spent most of his life in Austria, and he chose Vienna in 1913 as the situation in which to think out and portray his understanding of modern culture. The setting of *The Man without Qualities* will always associate his name with the dual monarchy, or "Kakania," as he called it. Kakania was Musil's playful nickname for the *Kaiserlich und königlich* (imperial and royal) state, an institution he memorialized with breathtaking descriptions in his novel:

> The inhabitants of this Imperial and Royal Imperial-Royal Dual Monarchy
> had a serious problem: they were supposed to feel like Imperial and Royal
> Austro-Hungarian patriots, while at the same time being Royal Hungarian
> or Imperial Royal Austrian patriots. . . . Nor was there an Austria. Its two

components, Hungary and Austria, made a match like a red-white-and-green jacket with black-and-yellow trousers. The jacket was a jacket, but the trousers were the relic of an extinct black-and-yellow outfit that had been ripped apart in the year 1867.[18]

Musil's novel was concerned mainly with the trousers and hardly at all with the jacket. And, although his novel takes place in Vienna, Musil was not attempting a nostalgic historical novel to rehabilitate a lost empire.[19] Even beyond his satirical vision of Kakania in *The Man without Qualities*, Musil's attitude toward his Austrian identity was irritating to many Austrians, since he was not attracted to notions such as Austrian culture or Austrian literature. As he put it after the First World War and the collapse of the multinational Empire:

> The Austrian countenance smiled because it no longer had any muscles in its face. There is no need to deny that in this way something elegant, gentle, measured, skeptical, and so forth came into the Viennese sphere; but it was bought at too great a price. If there were nothing but this "Viennese culture" with its *esprit de finesse,* which degenerated more and more into *feuilletonism,* nothing but this elegance that could no longer separate energy from brutality: then it would be enough to wish it would drown in Germany's tumult.[20]

In his portrayal of Kakania in *The Man without Qualities*, he was concerned not so much with a particular traditional empire as with general qualities of modernity.

Musil saw himself as a German writer who had no desire to recover his lost Austria, however much he may have respected the accomplishments of the Josephinist bureaucracy before 1867. He appreciated the degree to which Cisleithanian Austria had behaved more intelligently toward its national minorities than the Magyars had in Hungary, and he respected how much room for individual freedom there had been for a person living in Vienna before 1914 and how permissive Austria had been toward its most impassioned critics during the war.[21] But he was convinced that the Austrian state had failed to develop a sufficient sense of purpose to make cooperation and political community possible, and he was perfectly content after 1918 to be annexed to Germany. Although the Anschluss of Austria did not take place until 1938 (under very different circumstances), the shift of cultural power had already occurred. By the last years of the Weimar Republic, Musil observed that so many Viennese lived in Berlin that there were not always enough creative people who remained at home.[22] Berlin had supplanted Vienna as the capital of German culture even before 1914, and Musil moved between Vienna and Berlin during the prewar decade, which arguably was the golden age of Central European culture.[23] He defined his generation as those who were between twenty-five and forty-five when the First World War began: those who made "a first attempt to move beyond traditional liberal culture to forge a genuinely modern culture, appropriate to life in modern, technological civilization." Older intellectuals who had participated in the creation of liberal political institutions in Austria during the 1860s and 1870s were inclined to perceive the 1890s in terms of morbidity and decadence, as the fin de siècle, "but to be young and culturally aware at the turn of the century meant a sense of standing at the beginning of something new and exciting in every area of the arts." For the intellectuals of the generation of 1905, "art took up the central position as a wellspring of the ethical and the source of transforming power and vision."[24]

> Recall one fact above all: around 1900 (the last spiritual and intellectual movement of great vital force in Germany), people believed in the future. In a social future. In a new art. The *fin de siècle* gave the period a veneer of morbidity and decadence: but both these negative definitions were only contingent expressions for the will to be different, to do things differently from the way people had done them in the past.

Musil found it hard to understand "how so much genuine ability and accomplishment could be concealed for so long beneath the illusion of decadence."[25] Reflecting in the 1920s on the significance of the novel he was writing about the spiritual situation of European culture before the First World War, he argued that the next generation would have to begin again where his had left off in 1914 and fill the "intellectual vacuum" that remained after the war.[26]

Before 1914, Musil's view of European culture emphasized the optimism and internationalism of his generation of intellectuals and the ethical and aesthetic possibilities that were being opened up precisely by the disintegration of traditional society. His account of modern culture underscored its relationship to the transformative energies of modern industrial capitalism:

> [I]n large states that have a backdrop of world trade and worldwide connections, something new has developed, a paradox: a nonintellectual but cracked soil in whose fissures, despite its barren inauspiciousness, culture is now settling better than ever on what are, for it, barely suitable surfaces. Today culture no longer realizes its goals through the state, as it once did in

Athens and Rome, but utilizes instead of the perfection of the whole (which does not permit much enhancement) its imperfections, its gaps, its inability to encompass each and every individual. Dissolving in the incalculable number is what constitutes the fundamental cultural difference between this and any other age, the loneliness and anonymity of the individual in an ever-increasing crowd, and this brings with it a new intellectual disposition whose consequences are still unfathomable. The clearest example we can already see today is the small amount of serious art we have. Its inability to be good and please many at the same time is actually unprecedented, and apparently indicates far beyond being a kind of aesthetic quarrel, the beginning of a new function for art.[27]

The picture of culture Musil offered was decentered, arising precisely out of the dominant culture's incapacity to create a whole, a disharmony that was even more apparent in multinational Austria than it was in Imperial Germany. But Musil explained that the "real precondition" of modern culture was the bourgeoisie, by which he did not mean the nineteenth-century bourgeoisie of most European cities, but something more modern—not a stable social stratum but a home for loneliness, gaps, and the lack of a firm culture. He argued that this "kind of bourgeoisie does not exist in Austria," although it was beginning to emerge to the North, thanks to the greater energy and dynamism of life in imperial Germany.

Musil's view of aesthetics was grounded in this problematic situation of modern culture, and he emphasized modern culture's formlessness as it emerged in the early twentieth century. Contemplating "the great inner disorder" of contemporary life, it seemed to him that "such an illogical disorder of life, such an unraveling of once-binding cultural energies and ideals, would have to be fertile soil for a great logician of spiritual values."[28] His idea was to set out from the social chaos and moral contradictions of modern life to "consciously become even bolder." He wanted to "examine all the inner possibilities once again, invent them anew, and finally transfer the virtues of an unbiased laboratory technique from natural science to morality." Given the inadequacies of traditional forms for giving shape and meaning to inwardness, and in the absence of a secure, coherent worldview, Musil's impulse was to turn the apparently negative into the basis for new possibilities.

For what is more precious in art today, I ask myself, than that freedom of movement of the feelings, which we owe to a loosening of moral prohibitions and aesthetic uniformity, in the last analysis here also to the too-great number of human beings? This makes possible that extraordinary flexibility of perspective that allows us to recognize good in evil and the ugly in the beautiful.[29]

His own generation's efforts to create a new spiritual culture, a new relation between thinking and feeling, and a new understanding of sexuality and gender were interrupted by the First World War. Much of Musil's mature work was an attempt to reflect on his own experience before 1914 and on the sense of excitement he saw in his generation of creative people.

Although he regarded science as the basis of any approach to knowledge or civilization in the modern world, Musil was convinced that the ways of thinking that had emerged out of the Enlightenment and the scientific revolution could not adequately address the concerns of art and ethics.[30] He believed that the scientific way of thinking had been the basis for a more universal solidarity than had been achieved by any church, and he thought it understandable that human beings had attempted to carry over this way of thinking from science to morality.

> In accord with its prescriptive nature, morality is tied to experiences that can be replicated, and these are precisely what characterize rationality as well, for a concept can only take hold where explicitness and, figuratively speaking, replicability obtain. Thus there exists a profound connection between the civilizing character of morality and of the scientific spirit, whereas the truly ethical experience, such as love, introspection, or humility, is, even where it is of a social nature, something difficult to transmit, something quite personal and almost antisocial. . . . What passes for ethics in our current literature is for the most part a narrow foundation of real ethics, with a skyscraper of morality above it.[31]

Musil's distinction between morality and ethics corresponded to two forms of knowledge, one in which laws are possible and one in which they are not.

Musil thought of literature as the whole of the spiritual endowment of a given period.[32] The task of the writer was to explore the variations, the departures from the norm, the individuality of the human being's experience in the world, especially experiences of a heightened relation to self and others. Musil believed that this project did not contradict the scientific understanding of the self or reality, and he refused to oppose the way of thinking of the writer or the essayist to the ("mere") rationality of the scientist. Instead, he valued the writer's method as a different way of using the intellect, one that depended on metaphor as a way of opening up new relations among things.[33] As early as 1912 Musil argued for another kind of rationality, not the sort that was ordinarily associated with verified knowledge and practical mastery, but a kind of reason "that would strive to discover and systematize truths giving new and bold directions to the feelings, . . . a rationality, in other words, for which thinking would exist only to give an intellectual armature to some still problematic way of being human: such a rationality is incomprehensible today even as a need."[34] In "The Mathematical Man" (1913), Musil distinguished between a thinking that limits itself "to the exclusively rational and scientific" and a thinking that "lays hold of the feelings." He called the latter "spirit." His contemporaries in the natural sciences might not know how "to transfer their intellectual level to the level on which they live," but they did "have some idea of what [was] beneath their notice."[35] Musil's aim was to raise literature to the intellectual level of science but in a way that was appropriate to literature: "Scientific reason . . . does in an area of secondary interest what we ought to be doing with the basic questions of life."[36] This was still Musil's project when he was writing *The Man without Qualities* twenty years later.

After the war, Musil continued to refine this distinction between the scientist's search for laws and regularities, or the "ratioid," and the writer's attempt to understand individual experiences of feeling, or the "nonratioid." "Ratioid" is Musil's word for the field of knowledge in which facts allow themselves to be organized under laws; this realm is characterized by dependable regularity and unambiguous communicability. In his "Sketch of What the Writer Knows" of 1918, Musil summarized his understanding of "this ratioid territory" and contrasted it to the nonratioid, to the view of the writer he had begun to develop before the war:

> If the ratioid is the area of the domination of the "rule with exceptions," the
> nonratioid area is that of the dominance of the exceptions over the rule. . . .
> In this region facts do not submit, laws are sieves, events do not repeat
> themselves but are infinitely variable and individual. There is no better way
> to characterize this region than to point out that it is the realm of the indi-
> vidual's reactivity to the world and other individuals, the realm of values
> and valuations, of ethical and aesthetic relationships, the realm of the idea.[37]

The unambiguous communication of science is not possible in the nonratioid realm; "science has eyes only for events that recur in changing situations, and not for unique, isolated events that happen just once."[38] At the same time, Musil was convinced that there was "no emotional *knowledge* or other, second kind of knowledge that could exist in opposition to science. . . . There is only *one* knowledge, but to esteem in the gathering of knowledge only the achievements of reason is merely a historical convention."[39]

The ratioid method has a tendency to reduce new experience to what is already known and thus to lose track of what is individual in people and events. This is what makes it the enemy of art and ethics. The writer moves into territory that has not been conquered by science (or by the rigidities of morality) and resists creating a bad science or metaphysics that is itself just a rational skeleton of ideas.[40] Musil opposed attempts to carry the rigidity of scientific laws over into the realm of ethics, whose task it is to be faithful to the immediacy and individuality of human experience. He emphasized that in the nonratioid, contradictory world of ethical experience it is difficult to fit things into neat patterns; facts and their relationships "are infinite and incalculable."

> This is the territory of the writer, the realm in which his reason reigns. While his counterpart [the scientist] seeks the solid and fixed, and is content when he can establish for his computations as many equations as he finds unknowns, there is in the writer's territory from the start no end of unknowns, of equations, and of possible solutions. The task is to discover ever new solutions, connections, constellations, variables, to set up prototypes of an order of events, appealing models of how one can be human, to *invent* the inner person.[41]

This ethical or nonratioid realm is suited to the type of the creative person, which includes the writer:

> One can describe this type as the person in whom the irredeemable solitude of the self in the world and among people comes most forcefully to mind; as the sensitive person who is never given his due; whose emotions react more to imponderable reasons than to compelling ones; who despises people of strong character with the anxious superiority a child has over an adult who will die half a lifetime before he will; who feels even in friendship and love that breath of antipathy that keeps every being distant from others and constitutes the painful, nihilistic secret of individuality; who is even able to hate his own ideals because they appear to him not as goals but as the products of the decay of his idealism.[42]

Musil defended both the search for scientific laws and the special tasks of intellect in the nonratioid realm; but he was also sensitive to the problem of the ethos created by modern science, characterized by "the existence of powerful, specialized brains in the souls of children." Musil's description of the scientist in "Political Confessions" (1913) anticipated his portrayal of scientists and practical men in *The Man without Qualities*: modern experts "come as young people from the most disparate areas of human society, equipped with the most diverse customs, demands, and aspirations in life" and continue "in ignorance of any other culture, the life of the spiritual hamlet from which they happen to have come."[43] But this also meant that the men who ran this practical civilization of facts were gullible and helpless outside the realm of the profane—the realm of their own technological or professional expertise.

In a prewar essay on Catholic modernism, Musil described the conflict between Roman Catholicism and the state as

> a struggle that began with the church allowing itself to be misled into wanting to rule the state in the state's way, and ended with the church being dominated by the state in the church's way, that of invisible spiritual penetration. . . . Indeed, it is impossible to enumerate how thoroughly Catholicism today is saturated by middle-class reasonableness; one need only recall how even baptism—once the most powerful expression of the church's opposition to the state, a symbol of entry into a spiritual countercommunity, a mystical adoption . . . is bound up today with middle-class record-keeping.[44]

He described the church's resistance to middle-class reason and the modern state, arguing that, "while holding fast to a spirituality opposed to this sort of rationality," the church did so "in senile fashion, merely spelling out dogmas by rote; but for the longest time it has had no understanding of the enormous, still-unlived value of its own unreason" (22).

> Only once did the church demonstrate, in Scholasticism, that it could construct an intellectual system of this sort—the kind that makes man the goal of metaphysics—whatever else this system may be. (25)

Musil argued that the system collapsed simply because it was built on Aristotle, whose "teachings had developed dry rot after two thousand years of service" (23).[45] Catholicism might have continued to speak to modern experience if it had not settled for a fixed scholasticism and a bureaucracy like the state.

In an essay he wrote a year later on secular religiosity, Musil generalized this argument to his culture as a whole:

> In a world so at home with the mundane, so busied with the this-worldly, there is easily something good-naturedly defenseless in relation to the pur-

veyors of holy teaching. They enjoy the irresponsible position of house chaplain in the castle of the robber barons.[46]

Two decades later Musil returned to this theme in *The Man without Qualities:*

[A]ll those energetic up-to-the-minute characters who wouldn't dream of driving a car more than five years old, or letting a disease be treated by methods that had been the best ten years ago, and who further give all their time, willy-nilly, to promoting the latest inventions and fervently believe in rationalizing everything in their domain . . . these people nevertheless abandon questions of beauty, justice, love, and faith—that is, all the questions of humanity—as long as their business interests are not involved, preferably to their wives or, where their wives are not quite up to it, to a subspecies of men given to intoning thousand-year-old phrases about the chalice and sword of life, to whom they listen casually, irritably, and skeptically, without believing any of it but also without considering the possibility that it might be done some other way.[47]

Musil believed that the task of the writer was to do in his realm what the scientist had already done in his, but he was also conscious of what he described after the war as "the current disparity between the accomplishments of the nonratiod realm and the purely rational accomplishments of science."[48]

SEXUALITY AND ETHICS

A dealer and promoter might exhibit works of Japanese wood-carvers in which several couples tangle in monstrous embraces like clusters of grapes with limbs groping like feelers across the ground or winding back into themselves like corkscrews in the unutterable loneliness of the subsequent let-down, eyes hanging like trembling, whirling bubbles over vacantly staring breasts.

Musil, "The Obscene and Pathological in Art" (1911)

The portrayal of sexual experience was central to Musil's development as a writer—from *Young Törless*, which appeared while he was a doctoral student in Berlin, to the love stories of *Drei Frauen*, his last major work of fiction before *The Man without Qualities*. In 1924, his friend Robert Müller characterized him in the *Prager Presse* as "the most erotic writer."[49] Musil set out to explore sexuality because it belongs to what we do not know, and *Törless*, *Vereinigungen*, and his prewar essays were the highpoint of his emphasis on sexual themes. In *Törless* (1906) Musil portrayed adolescent homosexuality, prostitution, and the erotic tensions between a mother and a son; in the novellas of 1911 he wrote about the infidelity of a married woman as a deeper union with her husband and about a woman's sexual fantasies; and in his early essays that appeared in expressionist journals he offered new ways of thinking about women, sexuality, and ethics. In the early twentieth century, the portrayal of sexuality was threatening to many people but intellectually interesting for the writer, and it was an ideal context for exploring the complex interactions between thinking and feeling that characterize the nonratioid realm.[50] From early in his intellectual development Musil wanted to reconcile intellectual life with the erotic connections between men and women and, more generally, to overcome the separation in the culture between intellect and feeling. From *Törless* to *Drei Frauen*, the sexual other in Musil stands in for the irrational givenness of the world but also for ecstatic states, and he believed that in this respect sexual excitement is like art. The author of *The Man without Qualities* began as an almost lyrical writer, concerned with sexuality, feelings, inwardness, and love; the erotic-spiritual mood of his prewar work and his emphasis on a creative morality continued to shape his mature fiction after the war.

Musil wrote *Young Törless* between 1902 and 1905 as he was making the transition from engineering in Brno (Moravia) and Stuttgart to philosophy in Berlin and acquiring a gymnasium education that would allow him to attend university.[51] His first novel portrays the harsh realities of the Austrian military academies where he spent his adolescence, and it captures his family's legacy of military and professional service to the Habsburg monarchy. The military academy represented both the male world of mastery (of violence and knowledge) and the social world to which Musil was expected to accommodate. *Young Törless* is a novel about the military, violence, and power but also about the line that seems to run right through people—about the unconscious and the way thoughts and feelings rise up from this unlit area or state of being.[52] What interested Musil in *Törless* was not only the material of homosexuality and sadism but other, inner processes that were easier to see in a sixteen-year-old. Weininger rather than Freud influenced Musil's way of thinking in his first novel, although Musil was receptive to most of the intellectual currents Weininger had rejected.[53] Törless discovers that sexuality is something inside himself—something that is related to the prostitute Bozena, to his classmate Basini, and to his mother. Sexuality appears as a dark side that is invisible in the daylight world but also related to everything that is not acknowledged in the apparently stable, secure world of the adults. Sexuality is only part of Törless's confusion, like Basini's theft or Beineberg's ideas about Indian mysticism or the place of irrational numbers in mathematics. This is what Törless is trying to sort out: "'I was interested in something going on in my own mind, something I don't know much about even now, in spite of everything—something that makes all that I think about the whole thing seem quite unimportant.'"[54] His interest is "concentrated on the growth of [his] own soul, or personality [des Geistes], or whatever one may call the thing within us that every now and then increases by the addition of some idea picked up between the lines of a book or which speaks to us in the silent language of a painting."[55]

As a young man Musil regarded himself not as a representative of Viennese decadence but as part of the Berlin avant-garde and of a broadly European modernism. He lived in Berlin between 1903 and 1910, and he was close to Berlin expressionism—historically and structurally. Expressionism was an art of emotional expression that was generally closer to lyric poetry and painting—especially for stylistic reasons, such as the emphasis on colors—and more likely to wish for revolution and a radical break with bourgeois society. Its assumptions were largely continuous with modernism in general and with the impressionism of the turn of the century.[56] Musil thought of himself in the decade before the war as moving away from the trivial experience studied by science to what we do not know, to the complex interactions between thinking and feeling that lie behind narrative events, what he envisioned as ethical experiences or understandings of feeling. He was particularly interested in the "zone between emotions and rational understandings in which the real blossoming of the soul takes place. An interweaving of the intellectual and the emotional."[57] For Musil, the portrayal of souls that is sometimes regarded as psychology in literature was really only "freer ethical thinking—people will say this is an immoral art, and yet it alone is a moral art."[58] The concentration on inwardness and soul connected Musil to expressionism, but he resisted a one-sided emphasis on emotion.

Despite his generational affinities with German expressionism, Musil did not identify personally with expressionism as a literary ideology, because he believed that it had too little respect for reality and intellect.[59] He was critical of the enthusiasm for feelings and ideals in German literature, and he emphasized the role of intellect in emotional life: "Soul is a complex interpenetration of feeling and intellect. What sort of interpenetration is a question that belongs to psychology. But no one should mistake the fact that the element of growth in this coupling lies in the intellect."[60] Musil belonged to the expressionist movement through journals such as *Die Aktion* and *Pan* and through his friendships with the liberal critic, Alfred Kerr, and with Paul Cassirer, the principal cultural entrepreneur of the period in both art and literature. Musil was also close to Franz Blei and Albert Paris von Gütersloh, two of the leading figures of Austrian expressionism. It was in these circles that Musil met Martha Marcovaldi during the grim denouement of his relationship with Herma Dietz. Martha (née Heimann) was the daughter of a Jewish businessman from the Berlin *Gründerzeit* and a student of the impressionist painter Lovis Corinth. In 1911 Musil married Martha (her third marriage) and returned to Austria to work in 1911, but he continued to publish essays in Berlin, where he became an editor of the *Neue Rundschau* just before the war began. Meeting Martha turned Musil's creativity toward thinking more carefully about a woman's experience of sexuality and coming to terms with his own sexual feelings and experiences. Martha seems to have been decisive in helping Musil to become himself and to sustain his creativity. Certainly her life was a permanent point of reference for his fiction, and she symbolized the importance of Berlin modernism in his life.[61]

In 1911 Musil published two novellas under the title *Vereinigungen* [Unions]; these meticulous, highly metaphorical love stories deal with sexual triangles and unconventional sexual behaviors. Musil was interested in portraying the experience of love rather than the social conventions on the surface, and these stories are as unconventional in form as they are in substance. In both regards this was Musil's most extreme moment, and nowhere is his text more resistant to interpretation. In her account of the internalization of the novel from Schopenhauer to Virginia Woolf and of the attempts of European writers to portray inner experience, Dorrit Cohn characterizes "The Perfecting of a Love" as "one of the most remarkable, and least remarked, early experiments in 'stream of consciousness' fiction" and argues that Musil's use of similes gives his account of Claudine's experience "an anti-narrative, nearly stationary quality, making it one of the most 'unreadable' stories ever written."[62] Musil himself wondered if these stories were "formed by disgust with storytelling." He thought of both the external events in a story and the psychological processes underlying them as impersonal, since psychology is "the nonindividual component of the personality," and he wanted to portray the way "egoism . . . leaves traces of polygamy" in every love. He was interested in "the more profound degree of 'empathy' that makes unfaithfulness a palpably coexisting element even in love."[63] What to a conventional view might seem to be the unraveling of a love appears in Musil's novella as the perfecting of a love. These stories represent a crucial stage in Musil's thinking about the relationship between thinking and feeling as he attempted to integrate his research in Gestalt psychology and perception with his interest in ethics, in the context of his portrayals of sexuality. In an unpublished fragment Musil discussed Claudine's experience and underscored the connection between romantic love and a broader understanding of ideology.

> She recognizes that happiness is an emotional balance, a quality of gestalt.
> A complicated, balanced-out object of a higher order. If one loses this
> tension for a moment, it goes into endless holes. One defends oneself
> against the world in that one spans it with this other world. Each spans a
> different world, and the world of each is for every other an abyss. Love
> means having a companion on this dangerous path.[64]

In the same year, Musil published an essay on the literary representation of sexuality. In "The Obscene and Pathological in Art" he addressed moral and political attitudes toward the portrayal of sexuality. A series of articles in *Pan* on the influx of French art (including a German translation of Flaubert's Egyptian diaries from the 1840s) provided the occasion when Paul Traugott von Jagow, the chief of the Berlin police and censor in Berlin, confiscated issues of the magazine.[65] Musil argued that "art ought to be permitted not only to depict the immoral and the completely reprehensible, but also to love them" and to transform them into something that is no longer obscene or sick. Indeed, he contended that the need to represent something artistically implies that the artist does not have a pressing need to gratify an impulse directly. The artist is interested in a hundred different connections, and the motivation is no more directly obscene than the impulse of the physician who wears "the glittering savior's mask." Like science, "[a]rt too seeks knowledge; it represents the obscene and the pathological by means of their relation to the decent and healthy, which is to say: art expands its knowledge of the decent and the healthy."[66]

Musil contended that "there is no perversity or immorality that would not have, as it were, a correlative health and morality. This assumes that all the elements of which perversity or immorality is composed have their analogy in the healthy soul that is fit for social life." He rejected "the chubby-cheeked standpoint of 'healthy-at-any-price' German art":

> Dangers are not to be denied. There are half desires that do not reach as far
> as daring to be realized in life yet attempt this in art, and there can be people
> who use life as well as art for this purpose. But in doing so they either suffer

this energy-transforming effect (and then it does not matter in the least whether the people involved incidentally happen to be sick as well), or there really can be no talk of art.

He conceded that art "achieves its effect in more dynamic, less disciplined inwardnesses than science does." Nonetheless, what is done for science must be done for art: "accepting undesirable side effects for the sake of the main goal. . . . In everyday life people will have to learn to think differently in order to understand art."[67] He also meant that people will have to learn to think differently in art in order to understand life. In his "Profile of a Program" in 1912 Musil distinguished between two kinds of art: an art that "makes one empathetic and thoughtful" but also isolated, and another that is decorative, exaggerated, pathetic, "that can stampede a hall full of people who are otherwise indifferent or offensive to each other into a dervish of applause, or produce by means of a book an epidemic of enthusiasm which is followed a year later by a yawn."[68] This aesthetic distinction also expressed Musil's preference for a more inward, thoughtful way of dealing with important issues, whether in politics or art.

In 1913 he satirized himself from the point of view of his critics, one of whom argues that Musil's early books "'simply do not have the slightest connection with the true forces of our age.'"

> "They appeal to a small circle of hypersensitive people who no longer have any feeling for reality, not even perverse feeling, but only literary conceptions of it. It's a matter of an artificially nourished art, which becomes barren and obscure out of weakness and plays itself out as pretension. Indeed, . . . the twentieth century is raining events like cats and dogs, and this person has nothing decisive to report about what's going on in life or the life of what's going on!"[69]

This was Musil's way of defending his style of literary modernism against his earnestly realistic critics. He believed that the intellectual has another task: to create the spiritual and intellectual resources on which politicians depend. Musil was interested in the internal structure of motivation and meaning rather than great events with no sense, and he refused to simply dismiss as evil an interest in what did not conform to conventional morality. He explored sexuality and the conditions of ethics together, creating space for more authentic ways of thinking that resisted automatic social conventions. This made him critical of art that refused to take seriously either sexuality or the solitude and ambiguity of ethical life.

As he did twenty years later in *The Man without Qualities*, Musil was already restraining the impulse to neatly sort out the mentally ill: he believed that "the boundary between mental health and illness, morality and immorality" was ordinarily sought "in a much too coarse and geometric way."[70] He wanted to diminish the moralistic dimension in the way we regard human action and to increase the ability to understand both ends of any emotional connection. In "Moral Fruitfulness" (1913) he challenged conventional oppositions between egoism and altruism, arguing that "[o]nly complete emotional deafness, an automatism without accompanying consciousness, would be purely egoistic." Ordinarily, however, altruistic and egoistic motives mix in every action: "What always turns up in practice when we investigate instances of egoism is an emotional relation to the environment, a relation between 'I' and 'Thou' that is difficult at both ends." As he put it, in a formulation that anticipated his portrayal of Moosbrugger in *The Man without Qualities*, "[e]ven a sex-murderer is, in some cranny of his soul, full of inner hurt and hidden appeals. . . . In the criminal there is both a vulnerability and a resistance against the world, and both are present in every person who has a powerful moral destiny. Before we destroy such a person—however despicable he may be—we ought to accept and preserve what was resistance in him and was degraded by his vulnerability."[71]

In Musil's view, a firm morality of judgment depends largely on the inability to imagine another person's point of view or the contradictions in one's own morality and behavior; for Musil, ethics was imagination. His point was not that "to understand all is to forgive all," although, for those who want a rigid, either/or morality, this is the obvious inference to draw from his approach. He wanted a way of thinking that took both the individuality of the person and the complexity of reality into account, to create a more flexible response to human experience and a larger number of permissible side roads. For Musil, altruism and egoism were simply two of the countless ways of expressing "moral imagination." Drawing on both Nietzsche and Mach, he distanced himself from the primitive, polar way of thinking that shaped moral discourse in his culture: "Diametrical opposition between good and evil corresponds to an earlier stage of thought that expected everything from the dichotomy; in any case this opposition is not very scientific," even if there is a legitimate argument for distinguishing between what should be supported and what should be opposed.[72] In place of conventional moralistic oppositions between good and evil, Musil suggested the more neutral and empirical language of "ego-petal" and "ego-fugal" in order to emphasize that all moral life goes out from its centers in the emotional balance of individuals.[73] The connection between sexuality and ethics is the solitary reality he portrayed in

Törless and *Vereinigungen,* and this personal, inward quality of ethics carries through all of Musil's writing, from Törless and Claudine to Ulrich and Agathe in *The Man without Qualities*—the loneliness and isolation of the individual even in love. In the 1920s Musil noted that his friend Béla Balázs had come close to characterizing his artistic intention:

> [T]his soul of which Musil makes us aware signifies the absolute solitude of the human being. But the struggle of the soul with its isolated solitude is actually nothing other than its outrage against the false connections among human beings in our society.[74]

Musil believed that the incommunicable nature of ethical life and the isolation of the self are precisely the reasons why most people require a morality of good and evil—a stable, either/or approach to experience and emotional life. The nonratioid reality of inwardness makes people look for something firmer and more dependable, but Musil wanted to portray the moment that makes ethics possible at all.

> [M]orality actually begins only in the solitude that separates each person from every other. That which is incommunicable, the encapsulation in the self, is what makes people need good and evil. Good and evil, duty and violation of duty, are forms in which the individual establishes an emotional balance between himself and the world.[75]

In an unpublished essay he wrote after the war, Musil gave a somewhat quirky example of his empirical morality and his view of how change and reform take place. It bears on his view of sexuality in his culture but also on the thinking that lay behind "The Perfecting of a Love" and some of his early essays:

> [L]et us attempt to construct from an ex[ample] what the beginning of a new epoch might be like. There are a great many secret polygamists among us, but officially, even before their own consciences, many of them are in favor of monogamy (according to the motto of the rule with tolerated exceptions, which dominates our whole morality). This is already an unstable condition, and it is conceivable that (in a situation that would weaken the conservative parties and the churches) the propaganda of a few determined reformers against marriage could suddenly lead to changes in the law from which, presumably, the most profound spiritual innovations might be expected.[76]

Musil was not so much advocating polygamy as he was arguing (like Schopenhauer, Marx, and Engels) for the recognition of polygamy as a given of European erotic life. He considered the possibility that people might some day "wean themselves away from the soul and develop constitutions suited to this life. Love would then become procreation with the help of an irritation of the skin that was just impersonal, like freezing or burning. I have no interest in getting too excited about this future possibility, but it is a fact that we suffer from its being something that is not real, but nonetheless possible!"[77]

Writing about Austrian politics in 1912, Musil drew on the dynamics of sexuality as a way to understand the nature of feelings. He compared the conflicting nationalisms of Austrian politics to "shallow lovers, who are constantly overcoming separations and obstacles because they sense that the moment these obstacles are overcome they will have no idea what to do with one another. Like passion, simply a pretext for not having feelings." In the same essay he described the German of the empire to the north as standing "in relation to his ideals like those unbearably devoted wives who are glued to their husbands like a wet bathing suit." Here there is the germ of his later critique of what passed for idealism in German culture and politics; but his metaphor certainly leaves the impression that he wanted to say something about the stereotype of the German wife.[78] His real interests were repeatedly private rather than public, and he had trouble taking politics seriously, especially in Austria. After the war Musil wrote important analyses of Central European politics, but his more basic intention was to work for an unpolitical thinking and feeling.[79] Sexuality and ethics continued to be major themes in his postwar fiction—in the stories of *Drei Frauen*, the lyric poem "Isis und Osiris," *Die Schwärmer, Vinzenz*, and his early experiments with what became *The Man without Qualities*. But by the early 1920s Musil had already begun to move away from emphasizing the explicitly sexual to a more general understanding of the relationship between ideology and soul, between the forms of human experience and the formlessness of human feeling.

Before the First World War, Musil wrote not only about sexuality but also about gender difference—at the height of classical feminism and the women's suffrage movement in Europe.[80] For Musil the important process in the early twentieth century was not the conspicuous public struggle for women's suffrage but the changing relations between men and women. Although it was understandable that the feminist movement had begun by concentrating on basic needs such as the right to work and political action, he believed that internal changes could be even more striking. In an essay named after Penthesilea, the Amazonian warrior-queen who encountered Achilles in armed combat, Musil argued that the historical forms of more manly women, of women as "a more lordly, stronger type" were inaccessible to most men of his day, except perhaps in a zoo, or when a man "is frightened by a Great Dane and does not forget that it is a female."[81]

> And so, when finally eroticism—which today is actually in opposition to the commonality and degenerates under a cowardly feeling of shame—allows the limits to fall away, rejects every artificial feeling of shame, in order again to seek for something more inward and personal, when the reliance of the ego on conquest requires no locked and protected places of retreat, the inclusion of all human relations in the sexual will be possible.[82]

Here Musil announced a kind of manifesto: a resexualization of human experience that was grounded in a more inward eroticism and a more erotic inwardness. He characterized attitudes toward sexuality and gender in his society as a narrowing of his culture's spiritual inheritance: "[W]hole countries of the soul have been lost and submerged."[83] He believed that the task of his generation was to rethink gender identity and conventions, a project that had not been undertaken since the Middle Ages. For Musil, the fundamental importance of the changing role of women lay "not in the realm of the emancipation of the woman but, rather, in the emancipation of the man from traditional styles of eroticism; and the path sketched by ideology runs from the passive enfranchisement of women to sensuousness and from there to a refined humanity."[84] The other side of the liberation of the male from traditional styles of eroticism was the liberation of both men and women from conventional assumptions about gender.

Musil believed that a day would come of sexual camaraderie between men and women. Even before the First World War, he imagined a time when the uniform of gender would become less standardized so that clothing would no longer express the impersonal distinction of gender but the thousandfold variations of personality.[85]

> It is already a pleasure not to be the exclusive thought of a woman, but a central element in her interests. . . . A time could come when . . . the bipolar erotic would seem a sin or a weakness, almost as mindless as obliviousness toward the loved one in unfaithfulness.[86]

Looking back seventeen years later at prewar sexuality and women's emancipation, Musil displayed his playful attitude toward historical changes in the lives of women and in the relations between the sexes in an essay on the new woman. He began "Woman Yesterday and Tomorrow" by describing the extravagance hidden in the sexual imagination of the male and the way in which the education of the male imagination about women tended to an excess, much like records in sports.[87] Musil caricatured the madness in this idealization of the woman and came to the defense of the woman who no longer wished to be the screen for male projections but rather to invent her own ideals.

> I am not on the side of those who complain about the matter-of-factness of young women. The human body cannot in the long run experience itself only as the receiver of sense stimuli; it always turns to becoming the portrayer, the actor of itself in all the relationships it enters. (213)

From the vantage point of 1929, the "folded, puffed, frilled, and layered masses of clothes" that women had worn before 1914 appeared as "an uncannily artificial enlargement of the erotic surface." Musil wondered whether there really was a new woman, whose reality seemed to lie largely in a change of fashion.

> The dress of the old-fashioned woman, like her morality, had the task of capturing and dispersing the urgent desire of the male. It distributed the simple beam of this desire over a great surface (and morally over a hundred difficulties). . . . according to the law that gives desire and will a special place among human powers (since obstacles increase rather than diminish them), this dress multiplied desire to an absolutely ridiculous degree, so that acts of undressing that don't strike us at all were for earlier people shattering adventures.[88]

Musil gave an account of the change since the late nineteenth century from the ideal of "the knight who seeks and finds his lady."

> [T]he original Christian-chivalric ideal had distributed itself in such a way that the chivalric attainments fell to the man and the Christian ones to the woman. This concept of love, which hardly ever existed in real life, although life continued to follow it, is presumably now over. With it disappears the limitation of the age of love for women to the brief span between their seventeenth and thirty-fourth years, which is today already almost incomprehensible.[89]

After the changes of fashion in the 1920s, these traditional conceptions of romantic love survived mainly in "the form of an almost senseless rigidity."

> It was the war that liberated the mass of women from their deference to masculine ideals, and thus from the ideal of the woman as well. The decisive battle was in the last analysis fought not by the pioneers of emancipation but by the tailors. (212)

Much of *The Man without Qualities* is a satire of the outmoded forms of sexual love and the conventions of European men and women in this realm.

There is great continuity in the evolution of Musil's fiction: from his ideas for a surgeon of the soul in the diaries at the turn of the century to Ulrich in *The Man without Qualities*. *Die Schwärmer* [The Enthusiasts or The Visionaries], a drama that Musil began in 1908, did not appear until 1921, and his relationship with Herma Dietz around the turn of the century provided the material for a story in *Drei Frauen* two decades later. His portrayals of erotic life before the war established his postwar theme of the creative person who is sensitive to the fluidity of values and the isolation of the individual in the world.[90] But whatever the countless levels of continuity in Musil's thought and fiction, the significance of 1914 as the decisive break must be underscored: "The pressures of the coming scientific, objective age of civilization, when all people will be wise and moderate, already weighed on this generation, whose last flight was sexuality and war."[91] August 1914 and the war itself were ruptures that occurred within the context of the empires in Austria-Hungary and Germany—before the dissolution of the empires in 1918 and the emergence of republics in Vienna and Berlin. The First World War drew Musil back into the realities of the Habsburg monarchy and the limitations of this multinational empire in an age of nationalism.[92]

For Musil's generation, the First World War dramatically interrupted its attempt to come to terms with the rigidification of European civilization. Musil experienced the outbreak of war as an editor in Berlin, and he felt a mystical sense of the solidarity of Germans across state boundaries. As an officer on the Italian front, he came to know the helplessness of being part of a mass and the senselessness of nationalism and irredentism, next to which the old monarchy looked appealing. He saw the years before 1914 as a moment in which the possibilities and contradictions of his age had become visible for his generation. His descriptions of late imperial Germany and Austria in *The Man without Qualities* implied the First World War and the political events of the interwar years, but he preferred to stay with this old-fashioned setting of Vienna 1913. "When the War broke out the church failed, socialism failed, both under the pressure of an either-or ideology that was a superstition."[93] For Musil the political task of the 1920s was to find a way beyond "the blind alley of national imperialism to a new possibility of world order."[94] Before

1914 Musil emphasized the freedom of the feelings and the disintegration of old forms; after 1918 he emphasized the goal of giving form to the feelings while staying flexible and open. He believed that the task of the writer was to give shape and direction to experience, but he believed that the principles available within his culture were not adequate to modern life.

IDEOLOGY AND SOUL

> Ideology is: intellectual ordering of the feelings; an objective connection among them that makes the subjective connection easier. It can be philosophical or religious or a traditional mixture of both. . . . An order of the feelings is conceivable, a harmonious organization of the spiritual life—which Nietzsche sometimes advocated—on the basis of tradition and instinct, but without a supporting intellectual system. Here I would also call this an ideology, although it would no longer be one. But experience teaches that such ways of organizing life never exist without "teaching."
>
> Musil, "The German as Symptom" (1923)

Musil's essays on theory and culture in the 1920s constitute his most important work between the early fiction and *The Man without Qualities;* they are important both for his critique of all forms of ideology and for his emphasis on understanding the feelings and emotional experiences that lie at the basis of ideologies.[95] These essays belong to a modern tradition of thinking about the role of ideology in human life—from Marx to Nietzsche to Freud to Weber. "The German as Symptom," Musil's most nearly systematic attempt to state his view, was written in 1923 but not published until after he died. It was a major work of synthesis, however fragmentary and incomplete. During the early 1920s he also published important essays on Spengler, on the European situation after the First World War, and on German nationalism. "Toward a New Aesthetics" (1925), his most finished statement of his aesthetic theory, describes his distinction between the practical relationship to reality and the heightened relation to experience, which he called "the other condition." By the late 1920s, the novel he had been working on since before the war had moved toward a less direct emphasis on sexuality to concentrate on a critique of the rigidified forms of thinking and feeling in his culture.

The revolutions of 1918–1919 in Austria and Germany brought a wave of excitement and enthusiasm to Central Europeans that was comparable to 1914, but this euphoria quickly collapsed into exhaustion and a more conservative mentality. The decisive fact about the state that emerged in Austria after the First World War was that almost no one wanted it. Only when military defeat was certain did a separate German-Austrian Republic emerge, which immediately declared itself "a constituent part of the German Republic" that had been proclaimed the day before in Berlin. A few months later, annexation to Germany was blocked by article 88 of the Treaty of Saint-Germain, and Austria was left with a tiny state of six and a half million people that was not viable economically or militarily.[96] The collapse of the multinational monarchy in Austria was suited to Musil's style of gentle irony and to his critique of what was old-fashioned in the cultural and intellectual life of the interwar years. Ideological conflicts were sharper in Germany, but Musil also believed that the real battles were going to be fought in Germany, and he favored Anschluss, as did most Socialists and members of the German camp in Austria. Although he spent most of the 1920s writing a novel about the Habsburg monarchy in 1913, he watched the German political situation carefully whether he was in Vienna or Berlin.

Musil emphasized the inability of Europeans to take in the experiences of war and revolution: "[W]e were lacking the concepts with which to absorb what we experienced; or perhaps lacking the feelings whose magnetism sets the concepts in motion."[97] He believed that the malleability of human nature had allowed good Europeans to do terrible things during the war, while the breakdown of traditional ideologies had left an intellectual vacuum and a lack of adequate ideologies to give order to this flood of new experience:

> Popular philosophy and topical discussion are either content with the liberal scraps of an unfounded faith in reason and progress, or invent the familiar fetishes of epoch, nation, race, Catholicism, the intuitive man—all of which share negatively a predilection for sentimental carping at the intellect and, positively, a need to seek a foothold, to find gigantic skeletons, however ethereal, on which to hang the impressions that constituted our one remaining bit of substance. (127)

Musil believed that the war had "erupted like a disease in this social organism" (128). He thought of this as an instance of the periodic breakdown of a dominant ideology and mentality, in this case "that of the bourgeoisie" (130). He underscored the intellectual fragmentation of the age, and he saw the war as an expression of an explosive inner force in human beings: a revolt of the soul against order that corresponded to the failure and breakdown of ideologies (130).

After the war, Musil tried to understand how Europeans had lost track of a feeling of optimism, of the conviction that human beings are in a position

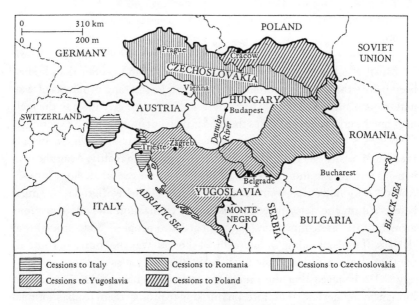

Figure 6. The disintegration of Austria-Hungary after the First World War. Austria and Hungary became separate states, while Czechoslovakia, Yugoslavia, and Poland emerged and parts of the old monarchy were integrated into Italy and Romania.

to create their own world and to determine their own fate.[98] Although he lived mainly in Vienna, even serving as a consultant for Austria's postwar reform of the army during the coalition government of Socialists and Catholics, Musil wrote for Weimar intellectuals and thought of himself as part of a wider German culture that was centered in Berlin. The immediate postwar years were a particularly creative period for German thought, especially for conservative thinkers such as Oswald Spengler, Martin Heidegger, and Ernst Jünger. Musil absorbed this atmosphere, while resisting ideologies of political antirationalism, racism, nationalism, and historicism. He rejected theories of inevitability or hidden essence, and he emphasized the openness of historical situations. For Musil, the decisive feature of Weimar culture was the antirationalism of a German idea of spirit that was cut off from intellect; he associated this attitude with despair, conservatism, and a yearning for great ideological superstructures. And he believed that the expressionist reaction to the scraps of the liberal ideology of reason and progress was "not much more than a charade" (127):

> Naturalism offered reality without spirit, Expressionism spirit without
> reality: both are nonspirit. On the other hand, however, a certain dried-fish

rationality has come among us, and the two opponents are worthy of each other.[99]

Musil was less focused on themes of sexuality and gender than he had been before the war and more interested in understanding problems of war, nationalism, and ideology. He was interested in how to give form to the feelings, and he criticized ideologies that had grown out of touch with experience. He wanted something more empirical, whether in sexuality, religion, or politics—a more flexible morality that came to terms with reality. After the war, Musil's writing was more sobered, taking a larger canvass of ideology into account. "A morality that wants to be more than a patchwork today . . . must be erected on the deformity that European civilization and the enormous growth of its interconnections have imparted to people."[100] He argued that the lack of understanding in the realm of the soul was the source of contemporary suffering, although he regarded soul as only a special case of ideology.[101] He believed that the important feelings remain the same and that human beings depend, therefore, on thinking to protect them from emotional rigidity and to keep them in touch with the realities of changing experience. His intellectual goal was a flexibility of thinking and feeling that allowed for a complex, nuanced view of reality and for a heightened relation to experience. He argued that the genuinely religious and ethical task of the writer was to free the human being from rigidity, whether intellectual or emotional, to recover his own experience and motivation. The challenge for Musil was to sustain the emotional meaning of the world in the right relation to undiminished intelligence without pretending that there was a mysterious logic of inevitability hidden in history or race.

In a postwar essay on the ideal of the nation, Musil criticized the idealistic ethics of his time:

> We stabilize our ideals like Platonic-Pythagorean ideas, immovable and unalterable, and when reality does not conform to them we are in a position to regard this very fact, that reality is only their "impure" realization, as characteristic of their ideality. We strive to conform the incalculable curve of being to the rigid polygon that passes through our fixed moral points by breaking the rectitude of our principles into ever new angles, but still without ever achieving the curve. It may be that the inner life has the same need for fixed connecting points that thought does; but as ideals these have led us to a point where things can hardly go any further, since—as everyone knows—in order to approximate it to reality we must burden each ideal with so many limitations and disclaimers that hardly anything is left.[102]

In his account of the German nation in 1921 Musil criticized the tendency for Germans to identify race with nation, even though "everyone knows nations are racial mixtures"; instead, people "make use of 'race' as if it were as straightforward as the concept of a cube."[103] More than a decade before Hitler came to power in Weimar Germany, Musil puzzled over the idea of "race," which already seemed to constitute most of what passed for national idealism:

> People say [that this idea of race comes from] anti-Semitism, but that is almost just another word for the phenomenon itself. The essential thing is that behind the phenomenon there lurks a genuine idealism. This is a typical case of the regressive need to refer every idea back to older, eternal ideas that are considered sublime, instead of trying to think it through: in short precisely what in this country counts as idealism. This produces the person who has fixed recipes and sublimely simple rules for everything, who puts himself above spiritual experience: the Pharisee. (107)

Musil resisted firm definitions of identity—whether individual or national. A nation for him was not a race but at most a language community for solving practical problems. Just as he wanted a human science rather than a national science, he wanted a literature that built on human rather than national truth. Ten years later in an unpublished essay, he suggested that the method that drew together the elements of racial theory 'is roughly this, that one could base a Weltanschauung equally well on the inferiority of women or the beauty of the stars."[104] In 1923 he argued that the German case—"this moral situation that no longer finds a point of reference in itself, but looks for one in the past (race, nation, religion, old-fashioned simplicity and strength, uncorrupted goodness)"—was already "the latent spiritual situation of Europe as a whole."[105] Musil wanted "to create an organization that protects the possibilities" for developing new ways of thinking and feeling while getting beyond "the half-witted ideologies of state and nation."[106] His own description of the nation took into account the formlessness and shapelessness of this new civilization and the human beings who remained after the war. He characterized the nation as an "enormous, heterogeneous mass, on which nothing can quite make an impression, which cannot quite express itself, whose composition changes every day as much as the stimuli that act upon it," and he argued that "this mass, nonmass, that oscillates between solid and fluid, this nothing without firm feelings, ideas, or resolution" was the really sustaining substance of the nation's life" (111).

Musil believed that the "need for the unequivocal, repeatable, and fixed is satisfied in the realm of the soul by violence. And a special form of this violence, shockingly flexible, highly developed, and creative in many respects is capitalism" (182). He accepted capitalism as the way the world is held together in our time, and he regarded the "ordered selfishness" of capitalism as "the most powerful and elastic form of organization that human beings have so far devised" (180). He also believed that it was "nonsense to think that selfishness would be abolished along with capitalism," but he was equally prepared to characterize capitalism in the early 1920s as "unspeakably cruel."[107] Nonetheless, he saw the addictions ("dominated and ruled by those involving money") as a satanic corrective to bureaucracy and the state, and he regarded Marxism as, "all in all, half true."[108] He believed that the "sulking intellectuals, just like those who have fled into the church of communism," were betraying their responsibilities (152).[109] Repeatedly Musil found himself defending intellect against the antirationalism and intuitionism of his fellow intellectuals. While outlining his understanding of philosophical irrationalism in an essay from 1921, Musil wrote about Oswald Spengler in a way that anticipated the dangers of antirationalism in politics:

> A person is not only intellect, but also will, feeling, lack of awareness, and often mere actuality, like the drifting of clouds in the sky. But those who see in people only what is not achieved by reason would finally have to seek the ideal in an anthill or beehive state, against whose mythos, harmony, and intuitive certainty of rhythm everything human presumably amounts to nothing.[110]

Musil especially emphasized the problematic role of the word "intuition" in Weimar antirationalism. He saw the 1920s as an age that was "softened by immoderate, advanced addiction to intuition," and he argued that "the entire substance of intuition amounts to the fact that one cannot say or treat what is most important"; these experiences are locked in a chest, "the cistern of intuition. One should finally open it and see what's in it. It may be a new world."[111]

For Musil, ideology was a way to help people to guide and form the soul, to allow them to connect the practical realities of their lives to "a very personal state of excitement."[112] He believed that the average person in the 1920s was "a far more involved metaphysician than he is usually willing to concede."

> A dull, persistent feeling of his strange cosmic situation seldom leaves him. Death, the tininess of the earth, the dubious illusion of the self, the senselessness of existence, which becomes more pressing with the years: these are

questions at which the average person scoffs, but which he nonetheless feels surrounding him all his life like the walls of a dark room.[113]

Life is made bearable for most people by "social bonds," by a set of assumptions that save and store energy—and give shape to the human being:

> Principles, guidelines, models, and limitations are storehouses of energy. To see how shapeless a person would be without them, think for a moment of a process like love; it is only the actual seizing of the little woman that is determined by this notion, whereas the whole complex we call love, with all its gradations, types, perversions, and subcategories is determined by social conventions (even if only in opposition to them). Even our feelings form like fluids in containers that generations have formed, and these containers receive our shapelessness.[114]

Musil argued that the great world religions had their origins in the same immediacy of experience, which it was the task of the writer to achieve and portray. The problem with religions and other ideologies was that they evolved into rational skeletons and theoretical structures that were no different from science except that they were less adequate accounts of the realities they claimed to describe. In the early 1920s Musil's view of theology and religion was in some respects close to Heidegger's identification at that time with Protestant mysticism after Luther—"not theology, but 'renewal of the entire human being.'"[115]

> This is the protest of our feelings, our will, our vital and changeable faculties, all our innate humanity setting itself off against calcified, rigid theological "knowledge." Moreover, stripped of all theological connections and their related specializations, this protest has always been the mainstream of all mysticism. All those words such as love, contemplation, awakening, and the like describe in their profound vagueness and tender plentitude nothing but a deeper embedding of thought in the emotional sphere, a more personal relation to the experiencing subject.[116]

Musil was interested in that nameless power of concentration and heightened feeling that appears in the history of religion and world literature, and he believed that at the core of art "is another attitude toward the world."[117] Musil's clearest statement of his view appeared in 1925 in his "Toward a New Aesthetic":

> It seems . . . that a bifurcation runs throughout the whole of human history, dividing it into two spiritual conditions, which even though they have influenced each other in many ways and entered into compromises, have nonetheless never properly mixed with one another. One of the two is familiar as the normal condition of our relationship to the world, to people, and to ourselves. (198)

The other condition "has been called the condition of love, of goodness, of renunciation of the world, of contemplation, of vision, of approach to God, of entrancement, of will-lessness, of meditation, and many other aspects of a fundamental experience that recurs in the religion, mysticism, and ethics of all historical peoples as universally as it has, remarkably, remained undeveloped."[118] Musil argued that the temptation of modern art, especially in expressionism, had been to pursue the other condition in a way that set feelings in opposition to thinking, but he believed that this was a misunderstanding of the true opposition: "In contrast to facts, actions, business, the politics of force . . . stand love and poetry. These are conditions that rise above the transactions of the world."[119] He saw no fundamental distinction between religion and literature, except with regard to organization and the degree of subordination of the individual.[120] He identified the religious element in secular life with soul: "Irreligious times like the Enlightenment, which lack this element, are unbearably Philistine."[121]

Musil rejected the positivist assumption that human beings had evolved beyond a primitive stage of consciousness that was reflected in the history of myth, the notion that dream and imagination are simply vestiges of some primitive, now overcome stage of human development. He argued that art, religion, and dreams were not simply bad science (or imperfect attempts to master practical reality) or even symptoms of neurosis or some pathological or undesirable state but, rather, expressions of a suppressed side of the self. He saw no reason why the "countless remainders of the dreams of humanity, which were overcome by waking thought and shattered," could not "be made again into a whole" and "set off again into something new." Musil believed that such heightened conditions of being lay at the basis of all the world's religions but also that these forms had grown hard, corrupt, and pathological. He regarded modern art as an attempt to gain access to this other relation to the world: "The world in which we live and participate every day, this world of authorized conditions of intellect and soul, is only a makeshift substitute for another world to which our true relationship has been lost."[122]

Musil believed that moral life was endangered both by an excess of the real and the literal-minded and by an excess of dream and feeling in the midst of solving real practical problems. He believed that these two sides of life, reality and dream, had never been brought together in the right way. This split in modern consciousness was often associated with prejudices about the nature of masculinity and femininity, and the goal of Musil's reflections on gender was to achieve a more balanced understanding of these human qualities.[123]

> [The] spiritual double existence that we lead between a state of conscious-
> ness that is too unlyrical and one that is too lyrical, which is no longer
> bound to the truth of reality, is one of the reasons why the arts are felt to
> be so artificial and life so mechanical; that is, neither state of consciousness
> connects to the full needs of the human soul.[124]

For Musil, talk about gender was a way of discussing this issue, which he believed was more basic than gender difference.

In "The German as Symptom, " Musil argued that the very distinction between objectivity and subjectivity (the fantastical) arises out of the normal relationship to the world. This is the basis for the scientific attitude toward things, which amounts to seeing things without love.

> It is a well-known fact that a person is completely transformed depending
> on whether one observes him sympathetically or unsympathetically, and
> our science may be characterized as observation without sympathy, for that
> is an important essence of the demand that it not be fantastical. People will
> of course ask if even lifeless things actually change, depending on whether
> we observe them with or without love, and I would answer yes.[125]

For Musil, eros is like art because it focuses attention; it abstracts, hypnotizes, and changes states of being in an attempt to affect the world in magical ways. The task of art is to liberate the human being from entrapment in the ego and the normal total experience of the world, from the customary existence that is dominated by the formulaic organization of thought and feeling. Musil believed that an age of science and capitalism had lost track of this suppressed side of the self: "We may say that [the other condition] is just as much a de-reification of the self as of the world." The normal condition is keyed to what is useful, the other condition to what is enhancing.[126]

The normal condition gives the only firm ground for practical mastery, systematic thought, social status, sexual prowess, "real" achievement, and the like. Thus, thinking in love and other experiences of a different relation to the world are at a disadvantage morally and intellectually. What is at stake is a host of private relations, qualities, states of being, and purposes, which have some claim to be the real substance of life. Of these, sexual intercourse is only the most obvious example and, apparently, the easiest to grasp for people whose understanding functions better with public realities. Musil wanted to assert the validity of these claims, especially for art, but also for life; yet he also wanted to avoid anti-intellectualism, sentimentality, the resentment that arises from failed life struggle, or the underestimation of the real value of practical mastery, science, and technology.

The Man without Qualities has sometimes been perceived as a historical novel, and certainly it is strongly marked by social satire and takes into account most of the important ideologies of the early twentieth century in Europe. There has seemed to be a contrast between the later Musil, who wrote on politics and ideology, and the early Musil, who wrote on sexuality and love but also between the apparently political themes of volume 1 and the love story in volume 2. In the framework Musil finally decided on, the patriotic campaign to redeem Austria parallels a similar campaign in Germany, also designed to celebrate the anniversary of the emperor in 1918. The pseudoplot of the novel foreshadows the outbreak of the war and the demise of the two Central European empires, but Musil characterizes the Austrian "Parallel Campaign" as "pseudoreality" (*Seinesgleichen geschieht*). The Parallel Campaign, led by Ulrich's beautiful cousin Diotima, was senseless, because "world history undoubtedly comes into being like all the other stories. Authors can never think of anything new, and they all copy from each other."[127] In this sense history is an imitation of authentic being. Still worse, it has no author at all: "For the most part . . . history is made without authors. It evolves not from some inner center but from the periphery" (391). Here Musil took issue with Hegel, Marx, Spengler, and their many journalistic emulators in Weimar Germany. Musil's point is that history has no sense; but he regarded this as an optimistic view, which emphasized that human beings are free to invent their own lives, their own history. What worries Ulrich is that human beings seem to take history seriously only in times of crisis. Most people think of history not as their own lives, but as a far-off sound from an orchestra over which they have no influence. They are perfectly content to drift until there is an emergency, which usually comes from a disturbance in this far-off orchestra. Musil's point is not that reality is unimportant but that it is locked in clichés and not thoughtfully challenged by literature and the imagination.

Musil began to conceive earlier versions of *The Man without Qualities* even before 1914, but the First World War came to define the structure of his magnum opus and required him to order his material within that frame, even when he was writing about events in the 1930s. By the time he turned to volume 2, his emphasis on inward themes seemed to conflict with his commentaries in his essays and diaries on Hitler, Stalin, and the Second World War.[128] This historical situation has tended to sharpen distinctions between politics and mysticism in interpretations of Musil's work and to concentrate scholarly attention on the puzzle of how Musil had intended to complete his novel, if at all: with the war, with the mystical union of the siblings, or with sexual union and the collapse of the love affair. But what is certain is that most of volume 2 is devoted to a love story between Ulrich and his sister Agathe. This was not accidental but central to Musil's intellectual preoccupations. The relationship between Ulrich and Agathe is both a utopian possibility and an exploration of masculine and feminine qualities in the person and the ways in which these gendered qualities shaped ethical life and human feeling.

This novel, which is often described as a social and political analysis of the Habsburg monarchy in decline, turns out to be a love story. Although *The Man without Qualities* seems at first to be about Austrian elites undertaking a patriotic campaign and about the pluralism of modern political and cultural life, the theme of gender is established in volume 1 and becomes central to volume 2 and to Musil's portrayal of the structure of human experience. Musil's approach to his characters in volume 1 of *The Man without Qualities* was ironic and playful. In the midst of the novel's apparent emphasis on political themes, Ulrich searches for the bases of motivated action, and he eventually concludes that motivated action is not possible in his society. In volume 2 of the novel he withdraws with his sister Agathe to attempt an experiment—to try to gain access to the genuine sources of ethical motivation on the assumption that his culture has divided the human being into masculine and feminine fragments that need to be brought into the right relation to one another. This story is not told ironically. Ulrich and Agathe explore the possibilities of recovering the other condition and of finding ways to connect it to practical social life. This allows Musil to develop a distinctive (and ungrounded) view of ethics that is closely tied to his understandings of sexuality and gender. Volume 2 of *The Man without Qualities* centers on Ulrich's relationship to his sister Agathe, whose name is the feminine form for the Greek word for the "good":

> "I shall have to make Agathe see that morality is the subordination of every momentary state in our life to one enduring one!" . . . As always when he thought of her, he felt that he had shown himself in her company in a different frame of mind than usual. And he knew, too, that he was longing passionately to get back into that frame of mind.[129]

Volume 1 of *Der Mann ohne Eigenschaften* was enthusiastically received by Weimar intellectuals when it appeared at the end of 1930, and Musil moved from Vienna to Berlin, publishing a truncated volume 2 just as Hitler came to power in 1933. Musil and Martha returned to Austria, which quickly moved in 1934 to a Catholic authoritarianism that was barely tolerable to liberal intellectuals. Musil spoke in Vienna, Basel, and Paris on the fascist era, but he was marginalized as a liberal intellectual who was neither fascist nor communist. When Germany annexed Austria, Musil left for Switzerland, where he died in 1942 with his novel unfinished. Thomas Mann and others had tried unsuccessfully to arrange for him to come to the United States, but his work did not become familiar there until fifty years later.

Gender and the Other Condition

"The essence of morality virtually hinges on the important feelings remaining constant," Ulrich thought, "and all the individual has to do is act in accord with them."

Musil, *The Man without Qualities*

The theme of gender is central to *The Man without Qualities* and to Musil's portrayal of the ethical significance of the other condition. One could imagine Musil writing a novel that concentrated on male figures. It would then be a novel about an intellectual (Ulrich), a great German industrialist (Arnheim), a psychotic murderer (Moosbrugger), a Wagnerian (Walter), an Austrian bureaucrat (Tuzzi), a general (Stumm von Bordwehr), a young nationalist (Hans Sepp), a Jewish banker (Fischel), a philosopher of vitalism (Meingast), an educator (Hagauer), a minister (Lindner), an aristocrat or two (Leinsdorf and Stallburg), and so forth. But Musil did not write that novel, and attentive readers will not be surprised to find that volume 2 does not concentrate on politics. Apparent to every reader of volume 1 is the prominence of Ulrich's actual or potential lovers: Leona (who mainly eats a great deal), Bonadea (the nymphomaniac), Diotima (Tuzzi's frustrated wife), Gerda (Fischel's daughter), and Clarisse (Walter's wife). From the outset of the novel Musil works out a complicated process of pairing male and female characters: Diotima with Tuzzi, but also with Arnheim and Ulrich, as well as the marvelous General Stumm; Agathe with Ulrich, but also with her first husband, as well as with Lindner and her second husband, Hagauer—and with Stumm.

Gender appears in *The Man without Qualities* as a metaphor both for reconciling thinking and feeling and for the duality of force and love in human affairs. The latter formulation is closer to the distinction between the normal condition and the other condition—and to the distinctive qualities of Musil's argument. For Musil, male and female also represent other dualities in his culture: knowledge and love, evil and good. He regarded conventional discussions of gender as simplified ways of thinking about complex feelings and realities, but in general he was concerned with bringing these so-called opposites into relationship with one another in more complex and intelligent ways. He believed that Europeans were at a very early stage of understanding relations between thinking and feeling and between the normal condition and the other condition, and that his own efforts had to work against rigid feelings, which had long been repressed or unexpressed. Musil thought that an alliance between men and women was an important place to begin.

The Man without Qualities was intended as an intellectual and spiritual adventure and as a contribution to the search for more intelligent ways of living—to the larger process of anonymous ethical activity at work in modern culture. *The Man without Qualities* is a critique of taking the ego seriously in the way that was simply assumed by liberal and haut bourgeois elites in the early twentieth century, an ego that Musil sometimes associated with the masculine ethic of achievement.[130] The novel and Musil's protagonist offer perhaps the most complete and consequential critique of nineteenth-century liberalism's understanding of the firm self or ego—a critique that appears in related forms in Schopenhauer, Nietzsche, Freud, Mach, and Hofmannsthal. Musil emphasizes Ulrich's inclination to "abolish reality" and the underdevelopment in him of that "sense of having firm ground underfoot and a firm skin all around, which appears so natural to most people." This is what separated him from Diotima, who, like Arnheim, felt confidence in her identity stitched on her underwear. Ulrich is characterized negatively by his boyhood friend Walter as "'a man without qualities,'" "'the human type produced by our time!'"[131] Musil portrays Ulrich as a soldier, an engineer, and a mathematician—and as a man who gave women "the illusion of a reliable virility."[132] An important dimension of this man without qualities is precisely his maleness, as opposed to Heidegger's apparently genderless *Dasein*. Ulrich had been acculturated to the conventional roles of his class and gender both in his identity as sexual predator and in his capacity to lose his sanity in the affair with the major's wife.

Ulrich explores contemporary ways of thinking about sexuality through conversations with his mistress, Bonadea, and his idealistic cousin, Diotima. Bonadea, the good goddess, decides to contribute to Diotima's inquiries into the revolution of the age. Diotima had felt torn between body and soul until she "was surprised to find plenty of advice in the books of the *zeitgeist*, once she had decided to deal with her fate from the physical angle, as represented by her husband."

> She had not known that our time, which has presumably distanced itself from the concept of passionate love because it is more of a religious than a sexual concept, regards love contemptuously as being too childish to still bother about, devoting all its energies instead to marriage, the bodily operations of which in all their variants it investigates with zestful specificity. There was already at that time a spate of books that discussed the "sexual revolution" with the clean-mindedness of a gym-teacher, and whose aim was to help people be happy though married. . . . In these books man or wife were referred to only as 'male and female procreators,' and the boredom they were supposed to exorcize by all manner of mental and physical diversions was labeled "the sexual problem."[133]

Musil believed that sexual interactions between men and women in his culture had become so stereotypical as to be emptied of motivation and meaning. As Ulrich puts it in a conversation with his sister:

> "Love is basically a simple urge to come close, to grab at something that has been split in two poles, lady and gentleman, with incredible tensions, frustrations, spasms, and perversions arising in between them. We've now had enough of this inflated ideology; it's become nearly as ridiculous as a science of eating. I'm convinced that most people would be glad if this connection between an epidermic itch and the entire personality could be revoked. And sooner or later there will be an era of simple sexual companionship in which boy and girl will stand in perfectly tuned incomprehension, staring at a heap of broken springs that used to be Man and Woman."[134]

On one level, Musil was concerned about the loss of the primacy of simple human liking. He was also concerned about the reduction of everything human to genital sexuality, mainly because this interfered with the feelings sexuality tried to express, and partly because modern science can take such a sober view of reproduction and epidermal friction.

> With a certain amount of goodwill on both sides that happens, unfortunately, all too easily. From the moment they first began to think about it, a man and a woman find a ready-made matrix of feelings, acts, and complications to take them in charge, and beneath this matrix the process takes its

course in reverse; the stream no longer flows from the spring; the last things
to happen push their way to the front of consciousness; the pure pleasure
two people have in each other, this simplest and deepest of all feelings in
love, and the natural source of all the rest, disappears completely in this
psychic reversal.[135]

The decisive problem for Musil was the division in his culture between
male and female roles and qualities, which determined the tendency for each
human being to be half of a self. This was, above all, an obstacle to balancing
thinking and feeling, to bringing the other condition into the right relation
with the normal, average condition of experience. Here Musil connects to
Weininger but also to a tradition that Ulrich describes to his sister as a
broader phenomenon than Plato's "myth of the human being divided in two;
we could also mention Pygmalion, the Hermaphrodite, or Isis and Osiris—
all different forms of the same theme."

> It's the ancient longing for a *doppelgänger* of the opposite sex, for a lover
> who will be the same as yourself and yet someone else, a magical figure that
> is oneself and yet remains magical, with the advantage over something we
> merely imagine of having the breath of autonomy and independence.[136]

The vision Ulrich characterizes for Agathe is both Musil's utopia of a possible
relationship between a man and a woman and Ulrich's answer to Agathe's
question about "that myth Plato tells, following some ancient source, that the
gods divided the original human being into two halves, male and female."[137]
Ulrich and Agathe decide that as siblings they have a certain advantage over
most of the human halves, who run around in the world without knowing
which person is the missing half. "In this way human beings keep 'halving'
themselves physiologically, while the ideal of oneness remains as far away as
the moon outside the bedroom window."[138] Ulrich and Agathe decide to think
of themselves as twins, but they leave each other free in matters of sexuality.
They are more concerned with states of feeling, particularly ethical states.

Ulrich, who has developed his intellectual qualities to an impressive level,
needs an ally in order to begin to apply values of freedom to the realm of the
feelings—to undertake the project Musil identified before the war of exploring the new freedom of the feelings that emerged with the cracking and
breaking up of traditional culture.

> [Ulrich] felt what his sister meant to him. It was to her that he had revealed
> that curious and unlimited, incredible, and unforgettable state of mind in

which everything is an affirmation: the condition in which one is incapable
of any spiritual movement except a moral one, therefore the only state in
which there exists a morality without interruption, even though it may
only consist in all actions floating ungrounded within it. And all Agathe had
done was to stretch out her hand toward it.[139]

Ulrich's description of a moral state of mind is what is most important to
Musil in his exploration of the problem of gender, of the problem of sexual/
romantic attraction, and the presence of force and love in the world. Musil
wanted to sustain an ethical state out of which one acts, even if there are no
firm principles or ideologies to depend on. What is interesting is that Musil
apparently believed that such a condition was possible (and real, in that
sense). He argued that the enduring challenges of morality are to achieve this
state and to bring it into the right relationship with practical reality and the
requirements of social life. He regarded Nietzsche as the greatest moralist of
the nineteenth century because he was gifted at gaining access to this state
and offered a brilliant critique of the rigidified forms that block connection to
it; but Musil was more interested than Nietzsche in thinking about the connections to practical, social reality.

Musil regarded the "erotic transformation of consciousness" in love as "a
special instance of something more general: for an evening at the theater, a
concert, a church service, all such manifestations of the inner life today are
similar, quickly dissolving islands of a second state of consciousness that is
sometimes interpolated into the ordinary one."[140] In chapter 32 of volume 1,
he distinguishes between the inner and the outer man, between "a gentle,
dark inwardness" and "the hectoring tones of mathematics or scientific
language."[141]

> No doubt that regrettably absurd affair of the major's wife was his only at-
> tempt to reach a full development on this gentle shadow side of his life; it
> was also the beginning of a recoil that had never stopped. . . . His develop-
> ment had evidently split into two tracks, one running on the surface in day-
> light, the other in the dark below and closed to traffic, so that the state of
> moral arrest that had oppressed him for a long time . . . might simply be the
> result of his failure to bring these two tracks together.[142]

Musil wanted to bring erotic energy into the right connection with thinking.
In his account of sexual experience, Ulrich begins by distinguishing "first
of all a physical experience, to be classed with other irritations of the skin,

a purely sensory indulgence without any requisite moral or emotional accessories."

> Second, emotions are usually involved, which become intensely associated with the physical experience, but in such a way that with slight variations they are the same for everyone; so that even the compulsory sameness of love's climax belongs on the physical-mechanical level rather than on that of the soul. Finally, there is also the real spiritual experience of love, which doesn't necessarily have anything to do with the other two. One can love God, one can love the world; perhaps one can only love God or the world. Anyway, it's not necessary to love a person. But if one does, the physical element takes over the whole world, so that it turns everything upside down, as it were.[143]

Ulrich continues to explain that love is an exception, which cannot be a model for everyday life, that love is a shadowy doubling of the self "in the other's opposite nature. I'm a man, you're a woman; it's widely believed that every person bears within him the shadowy or repressed opposite inclination; at least each of us has this longing, unless he's disgustingly self-satisfied." Musil wondered if it was possible to let feelings be impersonal in the way we sometimes let intellect be, rather than experiencing feelings and love as something ego-centered, particularistic, and possessive. Ulrich wants to experiment with a way of thinking that takes the self less personally—for the sake of the value of feeling and love. But Ulrich was also concerned with personal happiness, with the embedding of emotional and ethical experience in a more personal sphere, something less mechanical and lifeless than the ethics of achievement.

Musil believed that activity and rest, violence and love, were fundamental polarities in nature that his culture arbitrarily identified with men and women rather than acknowledging that violence and love are powers within each individual, as close together as the wings of a great, silent bird.[144] Musil did not aim at eliminating force from the world but at combining force and love in a way that made social life possible. Everything in Ulrich "that inclined him toward nihilism and hardness was implied in the word 'violence,' whatever flowed from every kind of skeptical, factual, conscious behavior; a certain hard, cold aggressiveness had even entered into his choice of career, so that an undercurrent of cruelty might have led to his becoming a mathematician." He thought of love in the sense that we "are moved by the word to long for a condition profoundly different . . . from the poverty of lovelessness . . . when we feel that we can lay claim to every quality as naturally as to none; or when it seems to us that what happens is only semblances prevailing, because life—bursting with conceit over its here-and-now but really a most uncertain, even a downright unreal condition—pours itself headlong into the few dozen cake molds of which reality consists."[145]

The brother-sister conversations are intended as part of a search for the true sources of ethical motivation—the other condition.

> Look, there's so much in life that we understand without agreeing with it; that's why accepting someone from the beginning, before understanding him, is pure mindless magic, like water in spring running down all the hillsides to the valley!"
>
> . . . And what he thought was: "Whenever I succeed in shedding all my selfish and egocentric feelings toward Agathe, and every single hateful feeling of indifference too, she draws the qualities out of me the way the Magnetic Mountain draws the nails out of a ship. She leaves me morally dissolved into a primary atomic state, one in which I am neither myself nor her. Could this be bliss?"[146]

Musil believed that marriage was ordinarily "egoism by twos," and he wanted something else—something that acknowledged the end of the ego and worked for more connection to the sources of ethical motivation—and more selfless qualities. Even romanticism was based on the principle "be mine." The narrator describes Agathe as Ulrich meets his twenty-seven-year-old sister for the first time in five years; the siblings were dressed so nearly alike as to seem like twins in Pierrot costumes, and Agathe seems neither "emancipated nor bohemian," but there is "something hermaphroditic" about her.[147]

Ulrich is still masculine enough that he seems to be unable to develop his feminine side without projecting it onto a woman, albeit his sister, a kind of twin or double. It was a considerable departure from the norm in Musil's generation for a man not only to embrace feminine values as positive but to take them as values for men. This is very different from either Weininger or Kraus, both of whom were trying to decide whether it was male or female qualities that were valuable. Musil represents an androgynous balance of gender qualities in the mind.[148] Although Ulrich cannot be said to embody this, his choice of Agathe as a partner and their attempt to cooperate in the ethical life point beyond traditional conventions of masculinity, even though their relationship as siblings is similar to the typical bourgeois marriage. Musil's characters are generally not androgynous; for the most part, qualities his culture regards as masculine are embodied by men, while feminine qualities are embodied by women. Thus, Tuzzi is the epitome of realism, sobriety, and male sexuality, while Diotima is idealism, feelings, and advocacy of a new, feminine sexuality.[149] What is androgynous, however, is Musil's imagination—especially his ability to portray women throughout his life, from Claudine to Agathe. Agathe's masculine qualities are emphasized, but there is nothing very new on this level in the novel. Agathe is "boyish" (and in this sense reflects the ideals of the 1920s) but not more "masculine" than Ulrich. Musil wants to explore these qualities—masculine and feminine—more or less experimentally, but he is interested in something beyond sexuality and gender: the feeling of love.[150]

Musil wanted to bring practical reality and dream into the right relationship to one another, and he often employed the polarity between masculine and feminine as a metaphor for this. But Musil believed that what was essential was not sexuality or gender, much less the institutions and conventions that form and organize them for social purposes. As he once put it, ideologies change, but the important feelings remain the same. He was looking for the right relationship between the two halves of the divided self, and the relationship between Ulrich and Agathe allowed him to concentrate on this. He wanted to ironize the culture's conception of the male but also the conventions of male-female relationships. Musil emphasized the rigidification of conventional manliness and the importance of human variety rather than the static preoccupation with the gender difference. "After Hitler, the bankruptcy of the male idea, a matriarchy will follow. America."[151]

Musil emerged out of a culture of Austrian elites but had only a modest influence on them. He did not have the deep resonance and penetration within his society that Doderer did.[152] There is an abstract quality to Musil's thinking and writing that was quite uncongenial to Doderer, who emphasized the historical, the narrative, the particular, and visible. These qualities made Doderer a better storyteller than Musil, closer to history and Spengler, to Heidegger and the impulse to break with liberal civilization and modernity. Musil's way of thinking, especially his affinity for intellect and science, was part of what Doderer disliked about liberal civilization as a young man and part of what motivated his anti-Semitism in the interwar years, although Doderer moved closer to Musil's empiricism and irony in his mature work. Musil emphasized the need for more balance between intellectual and emotional capacities in the human being and for a more discriminating and individual application of intellect to the realm of the feelings. He believed that the simple exchange, "I love you!" is capable of bringing the world into order: "For the soul, for contentment, for self-consciousness, and for the 'enclosed-

ness' of the world as well as human beings, it is not a matter of knowledge."
On the other hand, Musil knew that after a while the human being was al-
ways eager again to be offered the apple of knowledge. After a time, "even the
'I love you' becomes intolerable. So then knowledge begins again."[153]

What is most important about Musil's thought is how unfixed his ideas
remained—how resistant to ideologies and programs, while remaining in
touch with the creative sources of ethics and imagination.[154] And yet there
are tendencies and directions within this openness. Musil was a resigned advocate of science and modern civilization—and, in a more qualified way, of
capitalism, at least as a practical form of organizing human beings. Although
he criticized the intellectual narrowness and rigidity of late nineteenth-
century liberalism, it is right to see him as an attempt to preserve what was
most valuable in this tradition in the midst of war, ideological polarization,
and the fascist era. In relation to sexuality, he resisted any specific ideology or
social program, but his commitments were clearly to flexibility, pluralism,
variety, and not to bourgeois conventions about marriage and the family. But
Musil was close to Wittgenstein's view that what is most important cannot
be said. His task as a writer was to explore what we do not know—to invent
the inner person—and in his generation this project was often close to
themes of sexuality and gender.

Figure 7. Heimito von Doderer (1896–1966)

Chapter Four

Sexuality and the Politics of the Fascist Era

Heimito von Doderer was a more typical representative of Austrian culture than either Weininger or Musil, if one may say this of a man of high social status whose life was powerfully shaped by gender and social class. Although Doderer thought of himself as an outsider, he learned to be the voice of his social milieu and he was comfortable with all the nuances of social life in Vienna. He was an authentic storyteller about his world and eventually a thoughtful person about the neuroses that plagued him. He might be regarded as a kind of literary successor to Freud in the sense that he was interested in the moral and psychological consequences of repression for the individual personality, and he was conscious of the importance of Freud, Weininger, and Musil for his thought and imagination. Doderer studied history and psychology at the University of Vienna, but his scientific background was not comparable to Freud's or Musil's and he was not part of the psychoanalytic movement. His teachers were Weininger's friend, Hermann Swoboda, and Musil's friend, Albert Paris Gütersloh. Doderer identified more strongly than Musil with the Habsburg monarchy and with the theme of Austrian culture, and he became a member of the Austrian National Socialist Party in the 1930s. Yet no Austrian writer did more than Doderer to shape Austrian ideology away from the Habsburg monarchy and toward the reality of the Second Republic in the 1950s. What liberated Doderer from his attachment to the Austrian Empire during the interwar years was his own *grossdeutsch* ideology, but he came to think of his experience with National Socialism as a typical instance of the more general phenomenon of ideology.

Doderer's *The Demons,* which appeared in Vienna in 1956, was in some respects the great novel of Austrian social realism that was never written in the nineteenth century. It is a compelling account of Vienna as a city in which the elites of the high *Bürgertum* appear not at their height in the 1860s but in 1927, at a moment of radical social crisis and breakdown, when the polarized political camps of interwar Austria collided in a disastrous way. The workers of Vienna shut down the city in something very like Sorel's vision of the general strike, and the Palace of Justice was destroyed in a huge fire that dominated the city and the violent events of the day. This confrontation between Red Vienna and the conservative Austrian state on July 15, 1927, set the terms for the end of the First Republic, as well as the Austrian Civil War of 1934 and the defeat of Austrian Socialism. The victory of Catholic authoritarianism in the 1930s was a prelude to Austria's annexation by Germany in 1938. Doderer's novel grew out of his experience in Vienna in the 1920s, although he seems to have paid little attention to Austrian politics at the time. From 1930 to 1936 he wrote the initial version of part 1, and from 1933 to 1938 he was a member of the National Socialist Party in Austria. Between 1938 and 1955, he found his way beyond National Socialism and matured as a prose writer. His thinking about eros and apperception was central in these years, both in the diary he kept during the Second World War and in his first two Vienna novels, which appeared in 1951, as he turned to the revision of *The Demons.*[1]

In *The Demons* (his third novel about Vienna), Doderer intended to write a historical novel, a social history, and an account of real political events, and he took reality more seriously and more literally than Musil did. But Doderer also wrote his novel after modernism in literature and the arts, after expressionism, after Schopenhauer and Nietzsche, after the liberal certainties of scientific objectivity, and after National Socialism and the ideological polarization of the interwar years. He spoke for a conservative age in the 1950s, for a time of exhaustion and ideological disillusionment, and he represented a point of view that is close to the dangers of conservative apology—of justifying the special interests of a little Austria and its German-speaking elites. He was perceived as the great conservative writer of postwar Austria, and critics in the 1950s welcomed him as a master of storytelling, language, and metaphor. Doderer framed his own work as a critique of ideology and as an attempt to approach the world as nearly as possible without prejudice, and in the 1970s German critics emphasized the conservatism of his view of art and the impossibility of seeing the world without presuppositions.[2]

The dangers of Doderer's critique of ideology are particularly apparent in light of his anti-Semitism and National Socialism in the 1930s, his service as a captain in the German Air Force in the Second World War, and his role as the advocate of a conservative Austrian ideology in the 1950s. And yet his Jewish friends—Hilde Spiel, Hans Weigel, Friedrich Torberg, and Paul Elbogen—emphasized the absurdity of reducing him to anti-Semitism and National Socialism. If Musil represents Austrian culture at its most resistant to the blandishments of modern racism and nationalism, Doderer represents the passage of Austrian liberalism to German nationalism, anti-Semitism, and political antirationalism, as well as the recoil from ideology and from the experience of National Socialism. His resistance to modernity brought with it considerable ideological and political dangers, but he gradually developed a distinctive view of sexuality and human experience. Throughout his life he regarded sexuality as the decisive test case for human experience, from his personal obsessions and stories of the 1920s and 1930s to his mature theory and novels of the 1950s.

The War and the Writer

The First World War and its aftermath provided the formative experiences of Doderer's adult life and the context for his mature work. In Austria, as in most European countries, generational identity among creative people seems to have been divided between a group that reached creative maturity before 1914 and one that reached maturity after the war.[3] Doderer's generation of intellectuals was old enough to fight in the war but lacked adult experience in the years before 1914. This generation's political understanding was largely defined by the Great War, and the younger front-generation was active in the politics of the 1930s and influential after the Second World War in the creation of the Second Austrian Republic. Although Doderer had a child's memory of the years before 1914, he was defined by the war and by his prisoner-of-war experience in Russia. In Siberia he received the intellectual imprint of a slightly older generation of expressionist writers and artists, and he came to see the war as the undigested reality of his generation. Like many veterans of the Great War, his defining experience was not so much of war as of imprisonment. For Doderer and many other intellectuals of his generation, the dramatic events of 1927 crystallized their experience of politics during the interwar years. If the war and Siberia defined Doderer as a person and as a writer, it was July 15, 1927, that came to be the center of his adult awareness of politics.[4]

Doderer was born west of Vienna in Weidlingau (now Hadersdorf) on September 5, 1896; as an heir to the Viennese high *Bürgertum*, he was destined to belong to the professional elite of the Habsburg monarchy. He came from a wealthy Protestant professional family that had emigrated from Germany in the nineteenth century and had belonged to the lower nobility for two generations. His grandfathers were both architects, and his father was a successful construction engineer and builder whose social status was elevated enough to allow him an audience with Kaiser Franz Joseph.[5] As the youngest of six children, Heimito had to cope with the weight of family history and expectations as he was growing up, but he also benefited from an economically and socially privileged life. The models of gender he encountered as a child seem to have been divided between an angry, authoritarian father with high expectations in every respect and a doting, accommodating mother.[6] As a teenager, he displayed a talent for music (cello), but he was not an intellectual or even a particularly good student (except at German). Elegant, cultivated, and athletic, Heimo was preoccupied with sexual adventures (including both men and women), and he engaged in voyeurism from the windows of his parents' house. The women he was involved with were often prostitutes, while the men were ordinarily from his own social stratum, beginning with Albrecht Reif, an older student who was Doderer's tutor in gymnasium. Reif spent the summer of 1911 at Riegelhof, the Doderers' summer home in Prein an der Rax; he gave Heimito a copy of Plato's *Symposium* and set the norms for Doderer's impression that men smell better than women—at least better than prostitutes and cooks.[7] On the eve of the First World War, Doderer completed the Landstrasser Gymnasium in the Third District and began to study law at the University of Vienna. He interrupted his studies at the age of nineteen to join the prestigious Dragoner Regiment No. 3. As a cavalry officer, he defended the Habsburg monarchy in Galicia, in the northeastern corner of the empire, where he was taken prisoner in 1916 and deported to a Russian prisoner-of-war camp in Siberia.

Doderer regarded his experience as a prisoner of war in a positive light, and he remembered the camp in Krasnaia-Rjetschka on the border with China as "an island of the blessed."[8] His four years in Russia marked the beginning of his self-understanding as a writer, and his attempts to draw on the "wintry clarity" of Siberia and on his memories of Vienna anticipated much of his later work. As a prisoner of war, he enjoyed a reasonably comfortable and highly intellectual milieu; he was able to correspond with his family in Austria, and he received the packages that were sent to him. Because he was an officer, he lived more or less as he wished in the prison world of libraries, coffeehouses, soccer, handball, and chess. One of his early, unpublished pieces captures the impact that his imprisonment in Siberia had on him: "Our conscience and the consciousness of our negligence will forever bind us to these years and to this place. Only the lowlifes, who have no respect for themselves or God, will be able to lightly leave both behind because it has an unbeautiful name: prisoner-of-war camp."[9] Doderer's return to Vienna was delayed by the revolution and the civil war in Russia and by uncertainty in the ideological camps of the postwar years about how these officers and troops might behave upon release in Russia or in the successor states of the Habsburg monarchy. In the spring of 1919 he was transferred east to Krasnoiarsk, a White camp in the area occupied by anti-Bolshevik forces. Although conditions there were worse, he was allowed enough independence to work as a lumberjack, and he made connections in the intellectual world of Vienna, including the publisher Rudolf Haybach (1886–1983) and the painter Erwin Lang (1886–1962). A year later, Doderer escaped with other officers—walking and finding what transportation he could, he made his way through the Kirghiz steppe and returned to Vienna on August 14, 1920. He arrived in Vienna just as the postwar coalition government of Christian Socials and Socialists was coming to an end, beginning the slide of Austrian politics from cooperation to polarization over the course of the decade.[10]

In the 1920s Doderer returned to his father's house, where he experienced the frustration of financial dependence as well as his father's own financial problems and poor health after the war. There was apparent agreement for a time between his father's expectation of a professional career and Doderer's wish to continue his education, but Doderer was conscious of the tension between the world of academic learning and his real intellectual and personal life.[11] His life in Vienna continued the excitement and creativity of the years in Russia: his studies at the University of Vienna between 1921 and 1925 were followed by the years that he came to see as the center of his experience in Vienna.[12] Taking up more systematically the intellectual life he had begun in Siberia, Doderer chose history and psychology as the ideal scholarly fields to prepare a prose narrator for his life's work, "two sciences that concern themselves immediately with life!"[13] He studied medieval history, completing his doctorate under Oswald Redlich (1858–1944) in 1925 with a dissertation on historical writing in the fifteenth century.[14] His work in psychology as a secondary field with Hermann Swoboda (1873–1962) permanently influenced his ideas, particularly by encouraging his interest in Otto Weininger.[15] Despite the appeal of history and psychology for Doderer as a writer, he read much more widely. He was conscious of his lack of intellectual background but clear about the people he needed to read, especially "Goethe, Kant, Schopenhauer, Schiller, Weininger."[16] He was powerfully influenced by Nietzsche, Spengler, and Dostoevsky but especially by Schopenhauer, whom he characterized as a "truly European writer" who had won him over immediately simply by "his diction and his whole attitude."[17] Doderer's thinking as a young man was shaped by philosophical irrationalism, and he was close to expressionist literary currents of the postwar years that hoped for a radical break with bourgeois society.[18]

As a young man Doderer was tormented by his sexuality. He had already established some of his sexual preferences and patterns as a teenager, but his military experience and the long imprisonment seem to have made him even more complex. He suffered as well from anger and depression. His diaries from the 1920s are strongly marked by the sexual obsessions that dominated his personal life and provided much of the material for his early fictional work: "As histor[ical] source my diary will hardly be useful in the future— (at most for the histor[ical] psychologist of a later time)—for I concern myself here, as it just struck me, exclusively with my own dirt."[19] Doderer experienced a wide variety of the sexualities available to him in his culture, from the most conventional to the least, with men and women and alone, with all classes and body types and degrees of sublimation. Considering how much time he devoted to writing fiction and how concerned he was with making the most of his time, Doderer's pedantically detailed accounts of his activities in this realm are staggering. He had an enormous appetite for sexual experience in all its varieties and he would jeopardize the most important relationships in his life to pursue these adventures; but he had very little understanding of his feelings.

At the center of his personal life in the 1920s was Gusti Hasterlik, a woman from a Jewish family (although Gusti and her parents were Catholics), whom he met shortly after his return from Russia. They met through Ernst Pentlarz, Doderer's friend from the cavalry, who appears as a key figure in Doderer's recovery of his past as E. P. in *Die Strudlhofstiege* [The Strudlhof Steps]. By 1921 Doderer and Gusti already seemed like a married couple, but he was uncomfortable with this. He experienced the tensions between his family's social world and the milieu of the Jewish high *Bürgertum* to which Gusti introduced him. He felt that his bohemian life was threatened by the expectations of Gusti's family, but in fact their relationship was worn down by his own impossibility as a person. His main issue with Gusti was his resistance to what he took to be the woman's need for security, but he also criticized her for her "Jewish intellectualism."[20] Meanwhile, one of his sisters, Astri, immediately disliked Gusti for anti-Semitic reasons. Certainly Doderer was not yet confident enough to take his life into his own hands in this social arena or sexually stable enough to build a world on the passion he and Gusti shared in the early 1920s. Gusti and her mother laughed at Doderer's inner life as if he were "a fool estranged from the world" (80), and Doderer felt pressure from Gusti's mother to become something more conventional like a banker. He saw Gusti's wish for marriage as bourgeois convention even though she simply loved him, and he finally married her in 1930, when the relationship was virtually over. Gusti was his most intense experience of romantic love with an equal, but many other women, including his sisters, played important roles in his life. His friendship during the interwar years with Countess Lotte Paumgarten led him to the character of Quapp in *The Demons*. The women closest to him, from Gusti Hasterlik in the 1920s to his second wife, Emma Maria Thoma von Doderer in the 1950s, displayed a high degree of tolerance toward his sexual adventures.[21] The intellectual legacy of Weininger helped Doderer to shape his reception of the norms of Viennese culture and his sexual cynicism about women, especially his emphasis on the centrality of the Weiningerian female [das Weib] in every healthy woman (59).

Doderer's first prose work, *Die Bresche* [The Breach], appeared in 1924.[22] This short novel, written in 1921 just after he returned from Russia, indirectly captured the mood of the war and imprisonment in Siberia; it portrays three main characters in an urban setting: a woman, a sadistic businessman, and a sage. Magdalena Güllich is herself the owner of a small business, but she is here primarily as the victim of Jan Herzka's violence; although she is not the principal character, Doderer portrays her sympathetically and from her own point of view. For Herzka, the central figure in the story, his violent outburst breaks through the walls of his well-ordered bourgeois world, but also through the walls of his own personality. This pathological moment reveals itself in the course of the story as a liberation from the rigidity of his own character and from *bürgerlich* routine. The moment of breach proves to be an opportunity for self-knowledge and growth. Something dark and brutal—very like Schopenhauer's Will—breaks through the walls of his routine bourgeois life, and he discovers that he does not know himself, indeed is not a self, that his earlier goodness was not his own, not real goodness but conventionality. The creative moment for growth in this experience is elicited by the Russian composer, S. A. Slobedeff, through whom Herzka becomes aware of his own conformity and the unmotivated routine of his life. Jan Herzka appears again thirty years later as an important figure in *The Demons*, still struggling with his sadistic fantasies.

At about the time he finished *Die Bresche*, Doderer began to write "Jutta Bamberger," a story about a lesbian, which was not published until 1962. This portrayal of a woman's emotional development is a fascinating work and a remarkable accomplishment for a young man in the 1920s.[23] Jutta was an imaginary figure, whom Doderer saw one day in 1923 after he had invented her, and his account was almost certainly inspired by Weininger's discussion of gender and spiritual orthopedics. He thought of this portrayal of a young woman's sexual and social development as part of understanding his own experience growing up in the high *Bürgertum*. Here Doderer also began to experiment with characters who appeared later in *The Demons*, including Laura Konterhonz, the officer's daughter and the image of conventional femininity, and Hans (or René) Schlaggenberg, based more or less on himself as a teenager.

During the late 1920s and the early 1930s Doderer began to make his way as a journalist and writer. This was the period of his friendships in Döbling (a fashionable suburban district inhabited by artists' colonies), the strong influence of Gütersloh, and Doderer's painful extrication from his relationship with Gusti by way of marriage and divorce. In 1928 Doderer finally moved out of his parents' house to live in Döbling, where many of his friends were former soldiers and people he had met in Siberia.[24] There is a break in his diary between 1927 and 1930, and in the early 1930s the balance in his diary begins to shift from biographical detail toward the writer's workshop. We lose track of much that happened in these years, especially his political reactions and the immediate agony of the end of his relationship with Gusti. Doderer came to distinguish between his experience as a young man (primarily in Siberia and at the University of Vienna, as well as the experience of falling in love with Gusti) and the more problematic person who emerged in the late 1920s and early 1930s.

During the 1920s Doderer seems to have felt powerfully the contrast between the simplicity of his life in Siberia and the inauthenticity of the life he found when he returned to Vienna. He disliked the triviality of bourgeois life, and Russia had had an enormous impact on him—from tea to Dostoevsky. Like many Central Europeans, Doderer felt himself between two world historical forces, Russia and the United States, and his imagination faced East rather than West:

> Here we are then—here in Central Europe [Mitteleuropa]—we are between two fires, or between fire and water, life and death. For a long time I thought that Europe would simply become the battlefield on which the two world powers of today (someday) would have their decisive encounter: East and West, becoming and being (to use the language of Spengler!) . . . finite civilization and infinite life . . . but I no longer believe this today.[25]

About the time he moved to Döbling, Doderer wrote a novel about his experience in Siberia during the Russian Civil War, *The Secret of the Empire*,

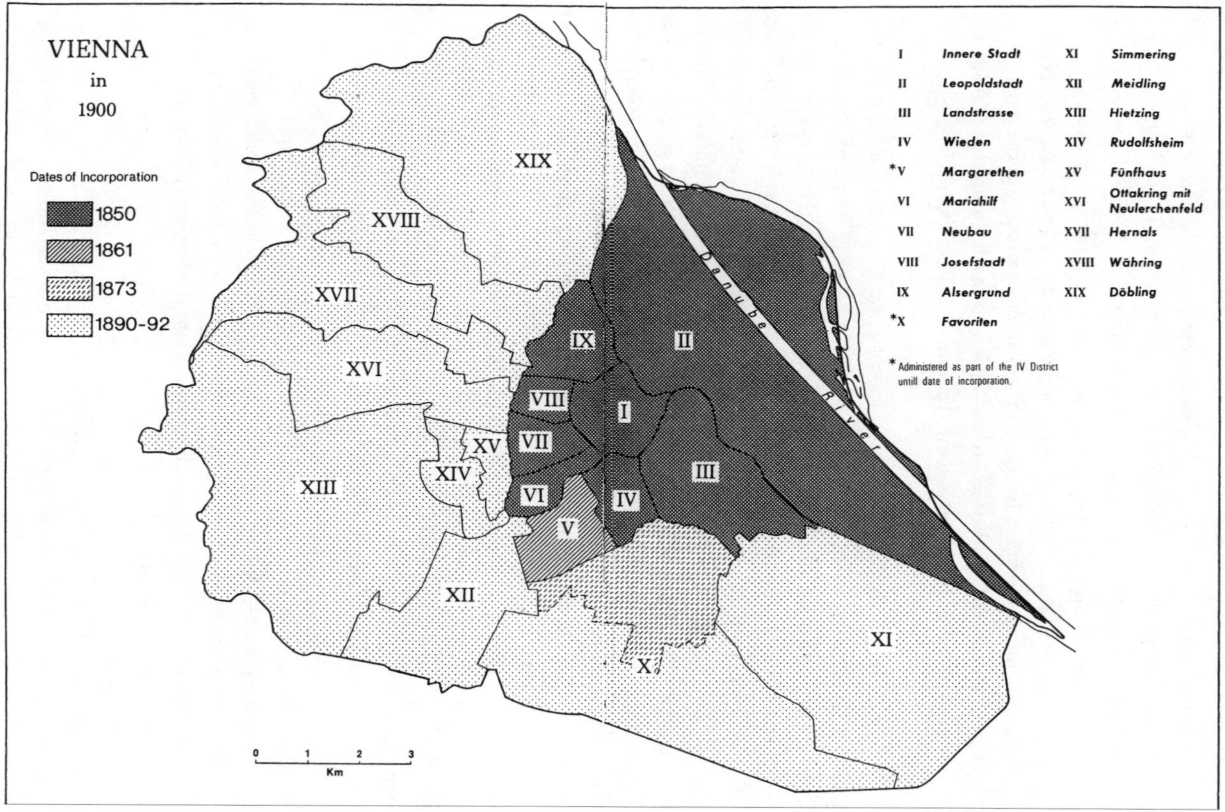

Figure 8. Vienna and its districts

VIENNA
in
1900

Dates of Incorporation

1850
1861
1873
1890-92

I	Innere Stadt	XI	Simmering
II	Leopoldstadt	XII	Meidling
III	Landstrasse	XIII	Hietzing
IV	Wieden	XIV	Rudolfsheim
*v	Margarethen	XV	Fünfhaus
VI	Mariahilf	XVI	Ottakring mit Neulerchenfeld
VII	Neubau	XVII	Hernals
VIII	Josefstadt	XVIII	Währing
IX	Alsergrund	XIX	Döbling
*x	Favoriten		

* Administered as part of the IV District until date of incorporation.

Danube River

0 1 2 3
Km

and his account of "the secret" is perceptive for someone writing in 1930, especially for a writer who is often described as unpolitical:

> What does it mean that the Reds triumphed despite every reasonable expectation and chased the foreigners out of their country, what does it mean that this communism, which is of highly western intellectual heritage, in the end fulfilled the task of closing Russia off from the West for the longest time; and what does it mean that the much-announced "World Revolution," on which the entire communist idea depends in the last analysis— this end stage of the "Dictatorship of the Proletariat"—never occurred? Was Lenin, the internationalist, freethinker, and atheist perhaps just the most faithful servant of Holy Russia, so loyal that he himself was unable to realize it, something that would become clear only at a later date???[26]

The Secret of the Empire begins in a strongly expressionist style that seems disconnected from reality but settles into an account of the Russian Civil War and three friends, Austrian officers who find themselves in a Siberian prisoner-of-war camp: Jan Alwersik, Dorian, and René Stangeler. Stangeler became a central autobiographical figure in Doderer's later novels, but in this story the main character is Alwersik, who improvises his way through the Siberian prison camp and the Russian Civil War playing a role in the Red Army and, unintentionally, in the death of his lover, Katia.[27] The free play of the story is allowed by the freedom of officers even while they are imprisoned; some of them are actually living outside the camp during the Civil War—whether as lumberjacks or as Red soldiers. Despite the problematic relationships among the three friends and Katia, Doderer keeps his moralizing to a minimum and emphasizes the degree to which everyone was living by his wits in the Russian Civil War just to stay alive. Katia is portrayed from her own point of view, like Magdalena in *Die Bresche*, but she also foreshadows the dreams and fires at the end of *The Demons* twenty-five years later:

> Something frightful was coming, she knew it realistically as if it had already happened—much more terrible than anything a human could possibly bear, steam rollers, landslides of horror, terror, such that one could only howl and scream, oh, she was being thrown into the fire, everything was burning all around. (107)

What comes is the White Terror, and eventually the Red Terror, which takes her life because of the complicated and corrupt human links between the Left and Right in the Siberia of 1920. The repetition of the vision that the horizon is burning provides a link between subjective dream and objective brutality that recapitulates the contrasts between subjective inwardness and the objective vastness of Russia and its political conflicts.

Doderer shows no partiality to reaction in *The Secret of the Empire*, and he remembered the Czech Legions as especially brutal. He mainly liked the Russians, including the Reds as the political group that came to represent the Russians best in this period, and he gives a sympathetic account of Trotsky and what Doderer took to be the real forces of Russian nationalism. Doderer's account of Trotsky's heroic mistake describes the experiences that shaped Doderer's understanding of political irrationalism:

> Basically invisible to him and his "comrades" was the gigantic, dark, shadowy something which mutely shoved in behind all the rational and understandable, accepted and convincing, theoretical and practical, beneficent and futuristic machinations of the party. . . . Thus Trotsky served—deceived by his exalted destiny in an exalted way—thus, he, the non-Russian, the international, the intellectual, the ideologue, served in the end, despite all the programmatic noise in the foreground, the slow, dim destiny that only now, in the midst of all that busyness began to sleepily raise its heavy eyelids, then awakened in those millions unversed in reading and writing . . . (120)

This is the "secret of the empire" Doderer has in mind. For Doderer, the real destiny of Russia was to drive out the foreigners (the Entente), to usher in a new age and restore the integrity of Russia. But this "was only recognized as such when the so-called world revolution failed to occur."

> And it seems to have been symbolically terminated by the expulsion of Leo Trotsky from the territories of the Soviet Union, which was like someone unbuckling his sword. He was the last real Communist in Russia and it was said of him at that time that "A righteous man is departing." (121)

Doderer was working on *The Secret of the Empire* when he agreed to write about Gütersloh, a major figure of prewar expressionism whose *Die tänzende Törin* [The Dancing Fool; Berlin, 1911] Doderer had read in Siberia in 1919. Gütersloh offered a model for moving the criterion of value from talent and works "much further inward," to what Doderer calls "the realm of the physiognomic in the highest sense," in contrast to the pathetic liberal "'without respect for the person.'"[28] *Der Fall Gütersloh: Ein Schicksal und seine Deutung* [The Case of Gütersloh: A Destiny and Its Meaning] is much like Nietzsche's *Schopenhauer as Educator* in the sense that Doderer took the figure of

Gütersloh as an occasion to reflect on the nature of the creative person. Doderer explains that he chose to write about a phenomenon that was more evident in someone who was both a writer and a painter, which allowed him to raise the question of the sources of creativity in a more generic way.[29] Central to Der Fall Gütersloh is the distinction between the type of the "spiritually creative person" (38) who continues to explore the chaos of the world like a baby and the type who accepts preformed pictures of the world from parents and other adults. Doderer believed that left to ourselves most of us would invent the worldview of an idiot, so that it is usually best that adults intervene and short-circuit the process. Thus, most people take "the short way to the dubious property," to the name and not the essence (12). The young creative person feels defined before the fact by the preset types given in the world of social forms; the key is to avoid achieving form too quickly—the dead forms of the others—but rather to form the self and the world in one's own way (25). Gütersloh became Doderer's mentor (Kyrill Scolander in The Demons) and an important figure in his personal life. Indeed, Doderer's admiration for Gütersloh seems to have been his politics at this time. But even in his Gütersloh book, Doderer's politics is only vaguely present. Gütersloh not only influenced Doderer's conception of the writer and the creative person but also encouraged his tendency toward aristocratic elitism and, along with his friends from Siberia, seems to have played an important role in his decision to join the National Socialist Party in 1933.[30]

It is not always possible to determine just how Doderer's ideas developed from the late 1920s to the early 1930s because of the gaps in his diaries for this period. In 1930, listening to a reading on the radio by Robert Musil, Doderer described the older writer as "an exalted island in today's sea of trash." But when the first volume of Der Mann ohne Eigenschaften appeared a few weeks later, Doderer expressed a negative reaction in anti-Semitic and anti-intellectual terms. He found himself unable to read beyond the first four hundred pages, and he judged that the author lacked "even the very minimum of forming power." This "boring book" seemed to Doderer a catastrophe that would lead to "an epidemic among the coffeehouse intellectuals." The "Jew-boys" and intellectuals would all claim to have read every word (and even a second time), even if they had never managed to read any further than Doderer had.[31] At this time, Doderer regarded the whole liberal way of thinking about politics and knowledge as shallow and bankrupt—and he described Musil in his diary as both typically Jewish and as "a guaranteed goy!"[32] When Der Fall Gütersloh appeared in 1930 Doderer was thirty-four, and he did not publish another book for eight years.

The First Republic never recovered from the dramatic polarization of political forces in 1927. For the years 1927–1933, we know very little about Doderer's political thoughts and motivations in a specific way, but his trajectory in these years probably followed the tendencies of professionals as the First Republic broke down. Austria's slide toward authoritarian government took place under Engelbert Dollfuss between 1932 and 1934, largely because of the continuing economic crisis but also because of the increasing popularity of National Socialism and the inability of the three leading parties—Christian Social, German Nationalist, and Social Democratic—to work together. What is sometimes called Austro-fascism was not a mass movement but rather an attempt to protect traditional elites that was less characterized by terror, propaganda, and mobilization than fascism. However, it functioned as a transition to Austria's absorption into Hitler's Reich in March 1938.[33] The authoritarian regime in Austria between 1934 and 1938 was fascist in the sense that it brutally defeated Socialism in February 1934 and in the sense that it grew out of an alliance between the conservative state and the *Heimwehr*, or home guard, but it also defeated internal Nazism a few months later, and the Socialists and the Nazis sometimes worked together against authoritarian rule. In these years Doderer seems to have mirrored broader tendencies of Austrian society and politics, given the crisis of legitimacy of the First Republic and the emotional and economic appeal of union with the German Reich. From 1933 to 1938 Doderer was a Nazi, and in 1936 he moved to Germany in order to be able to draw on his mother's German funds but also to look for political and publishing connections. His friend Gabriele Murad found him an apartment near Munich in Dachau, where he lived for the next two years.[34] The novel Doderer began to write in the 1930s and his relationship to National Socialism are so central to his significance that these years of apparent failure as a writer take on importance.

The Novel and National Socialism

About the time he finished *The Secret of the Empire* and *The Case of Gütersloh*, Doderer began a novel that was based on his own preoccupations with generously proportioned women. He initially called it "Dicke Damen" or Fat Ladies (also Chronique Scandaleuse) but renamed it *Die Dämonen* after the German title of Dostoevsky's *The Possessed*. He was discouraged by the end of his relationship with Gusti and by the economic situation in Austria, and the story he told was entangled with his own anti-Semitism and with the failure of his marriage. In 1933, after he joined the National Socialist Party in Austria, Doderer changed the title of his novel to "Die Dämonen von Ostmark," and his plans for the second part took on the strongly ideological theme of a division of Viennese society along racial lines, between Aryans and Jews. When he moved to Germany in 1936, he made a point of emphasizing the congruence between his novel and National Socialism. The novel was to portray the Jewish world: eros, the press, banks.[35]

> Around the turn of the year 1930–31 I began to write the novel "The Demons (of Ostmark)," a very comprehensively conceived work. I had recognized—from an unusual wealth of private, social, and professional experience—that Judaism in Austria and especially in Vienna must assume an overwhelming importance as a result of decisions whose approach one already sensed at that time.[36]

Doderer saw himself as the first "purely German author" to write about "contemporary Judaism in Austria" (820), and his perceptions were shaped by his own resentments against Jewish political, economic, and cultural influence in Vienna. He thought of this material as the basis for part 2 of his novel, "An der Wasserscheide"; *Wasserscheide* is sometimes rendered in English as "watershed," but Doderer meant it in the sense of the line that divides two neighboring river systems from one another—in the sense of a parting of the ways or a polarization. Part 2 was to have culminated in the burning of the Palace of Justice in July 1927, while the third part was to have covered 1927 to 1932. He wrote this account for a friend in 1936, and he also used it to present himself to the Reich Chamber of Literature when he moved to Germany.[37]

In the early 1930s National Socialism looked to many bourgeois intellectuals in Austria like the obvious alternative to the polarization of ideological camps between Socialists and Catholics and to the failure of parliamentarism and the First Republic. Many Austrians, including German-speaking professionals, wished for union with Germany as an alternative to the failure of the Christian Socials to master the problems of the depression. Given his background and experience, it is certainly not surprising that Doderer moved toward the right of the political spectrum, but the nuances of his thinking were not always explicit. Doderer's anti-Semitism seems to have been of a fairly conventionally Austrian sort—antiliberal, antirational, and intensified by his personal economic difficulties and the deepening depression.[38] But he was also strongly influenced by the ideology of anti-Semitic spirituality best articulated by Weininger and by an additive of generational rebellion in alliance with his sister Astri against the world of high liberalism, which he identified with his parents and with Jews. He looked to Germany politically and personally, but he also hoped for a break with bourgeois rigidity. His sympathy for the idea of Anschluss (often with an element of idealism about the idea of the German Reich), combined with the economic crisis and the collapse of the national camp in Austria, eventually led him to National Socialism.[39] For Doderer, the main content of joining the Austrian National Socialist Party seems to have been a rejection of Catholic authoritarianism and parochialism and an extension of his concerns as a writer to be a part of the German nation and to have a better opportunity for economic success in a healthier, larger economy. He apparently reached the high point of his Nazism in 1936, when he was marketing himself in Germany, but this was also the year he moved to Germany and began to see for himself. His comments about his work at this time show how close his thinking was to National Socialism, but his experience in Germany seems to have begun to move him away from National Socialism, though mainly for conservative, elitist reasons.

In the mid-1930s Doderer apparently thought that National Socialism could save Germany and Austria, both economically and spiritually, from a nebulous disease of the age, which included mass culture and the centrality of social and economic issues. He described the novel he was writing this way: "Here in Vienna all social communication was and is penetrated by Jewish elements, and this society—stitched together superficially and unselectively in the Liberalism of the 1880s from the most varied materials by financial interests in the accelerated economic life—this society (if you want to call it that)" was confronted by sharp divisions, and Doderer regarded himself as sensitive to them because of "the purity of his blood."[40] When he lived in Germany between 1936 and 1938, however, Doderer began to regard the new age as suffering from the typical problems of modern mass culture. He also started to come to the view that National Socialism was not the solution (that perhaps no political solution was possible) and that Jews were not the essence of what was wrong. His manuscript for the first part of *The Demons* in 1937 is already not obviously Nazi but also not the book he would write twenty years later, and his anti-Semitism was close to being his way of dealing with the painful end of a ten-year relationship with Gusti Hasterlik. Through his friend Haybach, Doderer found a publisher in Germany, C. H. Beck, and considered publishing volume 1 of "Die Dämonen von Ostmark." He completed this volume in 1936 but decided in 1937 not to publish it; and, from the time he arrived in Munich in 1936, he postponed working on volume 2 *of The Demons of Ostmark* in order to write *Ein Mord den jeder begeht* [Every Man a Murderer], which appeared in October 1938. Although he published very little in these years, he wrote a great deal, including short historical pieces set in the Middle Ages and the early modern period.[41] Yet this period is more important for his creativity than is often appreciated: he conceived *The De-*

mons and wrote five hundred typescript pages that are still available to us, and he published his first mature novel.[42]

The Demons began as a novel about the end of Doderer's relationship with Gusti and his own development as a human being. His descriptions of the novel for the Reich Ministry say more about his desire for success as a writer in the new Reich than about the content of the manuscript. Despite his efforts at self-propaganda, the novel he had written by 1936 did not have much to do with the themes he emphasized. By 1937, Doderer had seventeen typescript chapters—his *magnum opus in nucleo*—which later became the basis for part 1 of the novel he published in 1956. Doderer conceived of the idea of a figural narrator, Sektionsrat Geyrenhoff, who is named after G—ff, the narrator in Dostoevsky's *The Possessed*. The novel Doderer wrote was an attempt to understand himself: central to it were three autobiographical characters (Stangeler, Schlaggenberg, and Geyrenhoff), all of whom contribute to the chronicle, as do other more minor figures.

In the overture, Geyrenhoff (a retired Austrian civil servant) explains that two other writers have actually helped him with his chronicle: René von Stangeler (the Ensign) and Kajetan von Schlaggenberg. These three aristocratic characters are based on Doderer's own experience in the 1920s and 1930s.[43] Gusti Hasterlik was the model for two of the main figures: Grete Siebenschein (Gusti in the early 1920s) and Camy Schlaggenberg (Katejan's wife, based on Gusti in the 1930s). Doderer's friend Lotte Paumgarten became the young violinist Charlotte Schlaggenberg (known as Quapp, which is an abbreviation of *Kaulquappe* or tadpole).[44] Quapp counts as what Simone de Beauvoir would call an "honorary man," but she is also an aristocrat and a creative person who embodies the agony of creativity. In 1937 Doderer's story was enclosed on a circle of friends and mainly extended into the wider world through a detective story: the machinations of Herr Lévielle, Frau Ruthmayr's financial counselor. But this plot also involves the portrayal of the Siebenschein family and their friends. Young René Stangeler is caught between these two worlds by his romance with Grete Siebenschein.

The central character, however, is Katejan Schlaggenberg, who is trying to find his way beyond his relationship with his first wife, Camy. His story parallels the account of the younger René Stangeler's love affair with Grete Siebenschein and, to a lesser extent, the story of Neuberg's relationship with his fiancée, Angelika Trapp. The theme of the division in society is present but in a subtle and not very political way. The friends live near each other in Döbling and frequently get together to drink and dine and talk. They share in the masculinist values of the front-generation and experience the frustrations of working in the journalistic world of capitalist publishing. The 1937 version of *The Demons* is very much a male novel, despite the special status of Quapp and Frau Ruthmayr. The novel began as a kind of day-to-day autobiography or chronicle, and the events Doderer wrote about were very immediate for him. He was particularly concerned about the late 1920s and early 1930s, although he located part 1 more specifically in the mid-1920s, at a time when he had begun to conceive the novel. This also allowed Doderer to aim his story toward the dramatic events of 1927. Schlaggenberg provides a fairly good impression of how disordered Doderer was in the early 1930s, while Geyrenhoff is Doderer's own authorial capacity for self-observation and distance; the two friends, Schlaggenberg and Geyrenhoff, stand in judgment of the younger man's relationship with Camy. Schlaggenberg is dealing with the failure of his relationship with Camy, often by talking with Geyrenhoff, Eulenfeld, and Stangeler. In this way Doderer was able to explore the problem of being a creative person without a dependable income and what this meant for a woman of a higher type who loved him (meaning Camy); but Schlaggenberg and Camy faded considerably in importance in the later version of the novel.

Doderer's typescript of 1937 began just as his novel did in 1956—with an overture written by Geyrenhoff. Part 1 of the original version, which consumes the rest of the nearly five-hundred-page manuscript, concentrates on the portrayal of Geyrenhoff's friends; and, in this regard as well, the typescript is close to part 1 of the published version. The changes Doderer later made to part 1 were in some respects very minor and hardly affect the portrayal of this group of friends and Schlaggenberg's interest in the ladies in the café by the Danube. Important characters and themes from 1937 remained to establish the undertone of the later version. In "The Demons of Ostmark" Doderer's interest is in friendship, relationships, and the development of personality, and, despite his masculinist values, he is not idealizing war and violence. Geyrenhoff put it this way when he sat down to write the overture in 1935 in the same words Doderer used twenty years later:

> Terrible things took place in my native land and in this, my native city, at
> a time long after the grave and lighthearted stories I wish to relate here had
> come to an end. And one thing that lay curled among the amorphous and
> germinal within the events that I must recount, emerged dripping blood,
> took on a name, became visible to the eye which had been almost blinded by
> the vortex of events, shot forth, and was, even in its beginnings, recogniz-
> able—gruesomely inconspicuous and yet distinctly recognizable for what
> it was.[45]

Figure 9. Gusti Hasterlik and Heimito von Doderer. The couple was the basis for Grete Siebenschein and René von Stangeler in *The Demons,* but also for the more painful relationship between Camy and Katejan von Schlaggenberg.

What seems to have been new in Doderer's writing by the late 1930s was a greater concern with establishing a connection between the individual and external social reality: "[T]he 'free invention' of the writer corresponds exactly to the lack of congruence between the inner world and the outer world, that is, the lack of reality of an age."[46] Doderer was coming to believe that this unreality was especially marked in Germany in the 1930s. By 1936 he was already convinced that "the real novel is *always* a social novel!" and that the novelist is *"the real writer of contemporary history of his age"*; but rather than an abstract, conceptual history that takes place on a podium, he wanted to write a history that takes place "in the brains, hearts, and nerves of *individual human beings."*[47] By 1937 Doderer's novel had begun to move away from the theme of racial division [Wasserscheide] toward the form the novel took twenty years later.

In 1938 Doderer published *Ein Mord den jeder begeht* rather than the larger novel he had been working on since 1930. *Ein Mord* is, of course, just a story, but it is one of our best sources for understanding Doderer's thinking as he was, by his own account, finding his way beyond National Socialism. *Ein Mord* is Doderer's most finished work of fiction from the 1930s, and it is a very personal book, in a sense the male equivalent of his "Jutta Bamberger." It can be viewed either as a symptom of this period of personal and political crisis or as the germ of his mature fiction. The novel is set in Germany, and it is an eerily German book that can be read as an oblique critique of the new age. Like most of Doderer's early fiction, the novel is monographic, centered on a single figure and themes of fate, character, love, and death. The novel is not so much a detective story as a Sophoclean exploration of the protagonist's own guilt that is strongly autobiographical. In *Every Man a Murderer*, Conrad Castiletz decides to find the murderer of his sister-in-law (who is also in his fantasy the woman he loves) and learns that he was himself her murderer years before—unwittingly but in a way that was connected to his limitations of character. His death follows—not as a suicide, but in a way that links the recovery of his youthful relation to the world to his accidental death, which is to say that accident, fate, and character are all somehow linked. For Doderer the task of becoming a person, the task of humanization, begins with overcoming character.[48] This is the sense of the opening lines of the novel: "Everyone's childhood is dumped over his head like a bucket. The contents of this bucket are at first unknown. But throughout life, the stuff drips down on him slowly—and there's no changing clothes or costume, for the dripping will continue."[49] Only when Conrad begins to respect this is he able to overcome his own fate and character to become a person. Some commentators have emphasized the "oppressive Gestapo-atmosphere" of the novel.[50] Certainly this is a strange book from the author of the Vienna trilogy, and a discussion about secret police and inquisitions near the beginning of part three is quite remarkable for a book published in Germany in 1938:

> "I've always thought how dreadful it must have been to live in such a time, in Spain, I mean, when the Inquisition was active there," Conrad said. "The slightest suspicion, or a denunciation, was enough to put a man in line for horrible tortures. How could anyone have enjoyed his life or taken up any interests . . ."[51] (203–204)

Although Doderer emphasized the continuity of his work as a writer, he saw *Ein Mord* as the beginning of his true corpus.

Doderer seems justified in this claim, in response to those (including Doderer himself at times) who emphasize a break in his work around 1938.[52] But this also makes him vulnerable to arguments that he never really changed after the 1930s. Such arguments usually focus on conservative prejudice and superstition, National Socialism, and anti-Semitism. Doderer was always a bit conservative, aristocratic, and uncomfortable with the modern world, and he tended toward a tolerance for the magical, for physiognomy, and for ways of thinking that are not satisfying to a scientific mind. He seems to have moved away from his sympathy for National Socialism at least by 1937 or 1938, and this is probably the reason he stopped working on "Die Daemonen" and turned to *Every Man a Murderer*. At the end of 1938, Doderer returned to Vienna. His own life had run aground along with the political and intellectual life of Austria as a whole.

Eros and Apperception, 1938–1955

From 1938 to 1955 Doderer withdrew into a process that allowed his mature capacities as a novelist to emerge. These were the years between the Anschluss and the independence of the Second Austrian Republic, when Doderer found his way back to *The Demons* and to his rehabilitation and success as a writer. Doderer thought of himself after 1938 as no longer a Nazi, although he did nothing to dramatize this except for stopping his membership dues and, in 1940, converting to Catholicism. During the Second World War he served in the German Luftwaffe on the French and Russian fronts and in Norway. He was a good officer, preoccupied mainly with protecting the soldiers under his command, and even in the midst of the war he moved still further away from Germany and National Socialism toward Austria, Catholicism, and the private world of the writer. In 1945, for the second time in his life, he was a prisoner of war, now with the British in Austria, and he went through the experience of de-Nazification and gradual rehabilitation in the late 1940s. The deprivations of the hunger years from 1946 to 1948 were especially difficult, but, living mainly on cigarettes, he was able to finish *Die Strudlhofstiege* in 1948. For two years he resumed his studies at the Austrian Institute for Historical Research, waiting until he was allowed to publish once again. As the Second Austrian Republic came into being in the decade after 1945, Doderer completed three fictional works, which have come to be known as his Vienna novels. *Die erleuchteten Fenster* and *Die Strudlhofstiege* appeared in 1951, and the 1937 typescript of "Die Daemonen von Ostmark" became the basis for part 1 of *The Demons* as Doderer began to work on the novel again in 1951.

During the war, Doderer's work on *The Demons* moved into his diaries,

Figure 10. The Anschluss

where he also developed ideas for *Die Strudlhofstiege* as a way to break out of his creative impasse. The fictional path to *The Demons* was *The Strudlhof Steps,* but the intellectual path was his diary, which has been published as *Tangenten: Tagebuch eines Schriftstellers, 1940–1950.* This is the best source for understanding Doderer's ideas about human experience at this point in his life.[53] In these years Doderer became increasingly convinced that there was a connection between the two most problematic dimensions of his life:

his sexual obsessions and his political ideology. He came to believe that sexual obsessions and political ideologies were both forms of diminished reality, of a failure to be open to the world. Common to Doderer's conceptions of political and sexual ideologies was the attempt to impose a preconceived picture on the world. For Doderer, the sexual situation was the purest type of the situation but also an ideal location for neurosis and obsession, and he described his own process of coming to terms with his ideological and personal confusions during the 1940s as his most significant contribution: "To discover the basic evil of one's age collected together in oneself and to seek to overcome it: that means to be truly contemporary and really to achieve something for one's time" (741).

The central theme of these years of isolation and transition was the idea of apperception, of heightened perception and awareness, and Doderer took the sexual situation as the model for what he had in mind. In his Vienna novels and in the diaries and essays of these years, Doderer worked out his view of the similarities between his sexual obsessiveness and total ideologies—and argued that apperception was the path to overcoming both. He emphasized the senses in his use of "apperception" (689), but he also applied this word to reflexive knowledge of the self, to the ability to be aware of the obsessiveness and encapsulation of the self. His understanding of apperception, then, referred to internal as well as to external reality, since the ability to see external reality is a function of the ability to see internal reality. Doderer thought of the human being's relationship to the world in apperception as "an inward penetration between us and the world of objects," and he regarded unconscious thought as "the ground of resonance of that complex apperception" (265). But "apperception" was also an ethical ideal of experience with a minimum of preconceptions: "An apperception that is no longer inhibited by any sort of preconception must gain the upper hand with us and, in this way, break out of the ring of entrapment—our prison—the place where we ourselves once stood" (765). He had begun to develop his distinctive way of thinking in the 1930s, but the elaboration of the idea of apperception was decisive for his maturation as a person and a writer during the 1940s. He came to regard writing as the highest form of apperception; both apperception and writing, he believed, were grounded in the irrational pole of intelligence, and writing was the process by which this nonverbalized awareness became fully conscious.

Although the word "apperception" appears in the tradition in both a psychological and a philosophical sense, it has broad affinities with the concern of German classical culture for *Bildung*, with the development and enhancement of the individual's inner powers and self-knowledge and of the individual's capacity to learn from the external world. Apperception as a concept de-rives from Leibniz, Kant, Weininger, and Johann Friedrich Herbart; the word is close in meaning to perception, but it ordinarily has the sense of conscious awareness or attention. In his "Principles of Nature and Grace" (1714), Leib-niz distinguished "between *perception*, which is the inner state of the Monad representing outer things, and *apperception*, which is *consciousness* or the reflective knowledge of this inner state, and which is not given to all souls nor to the same soul at all times."[54] In response to Locke's view of human under-standing, Leibniz made a similar distinction between "*perception* and being aware," between small, unconscious, or inadvertent perceptions and con-scious thought about perceptions.[55] Already apparent in Leibniz was the blur-ring of two definitions that were still important for Doderer two hundred years later: "consciousness, or conscious distinct conceiving" and "reflective cognition of our inner states."[56] The Herbartian view of apperception, which was influential in Austria during the nineteenth century, emphasized "the ef-fects of accumulated contents of the soul, acquired during the course of men-tal development."[57] These ideas seem to have come to Doderer mainly through Weininger and Swoboda.

In the fall of 1938, Doderer returned to Vienna to live with Gütersloh on Buchfeldgasse, where he began his systematic examination of lighted win-dows, observing naked women with a telescope along with his friend Edmund Schüller.[58] Begun in 1938 but published in 1951, *The Lighted Windows, or The Humanization of the Bureaucrat Julius Zihal* announces the themes of Doderer's mature work: apperception, sexuality, and ideology. His work on this novel inaugurates a new period in Doderer's life, which he thought of as his own process of humanization and coming to clarity about apperception. Here he came to terms with his own voyeurism and turned his obsessiveness into the capacity to see both external and internal reality. The satirical metaphor of the telescope also provides the fictional parallel to Doderer's thinking about apperception during the 1940s. Zihal's real perversity is not his voyeurism but his obsession with order, his determination to organize these experiences in a completely pedantic way (43).[59] The solution for Zi-hal—this former bureaucrat and retired fanatic of order—is to have a real re-lationship with a woman.

Doderer believed that the self-preoccupation of the neurotic in obsessive thinking had something in common with the refusal to respect reality that appears in thinking that is strongly committed to political ideology. He ar-gued that the total state arose from the flight into unreality "and the found-ing of a second reality next to this one," and he believed that he had "lived just like this."[60] He saw both neurosis and totalitarian ideology as obstacles to experiencing life directly and authentically, and he came to see the attempt to impose a personal order on life as problematic in much the same way that the political attempt to create a second reality fails to acknowledge the chaos and irrationality of experience. "Personal order is the way in which someone fills out his cavity in existence, his burrow in the world, and to be sure in a way that is suited to generating a constant illusion about the nature of life" (522). He had had a long career of obsessions and psychological unreality before he diverted himself briefly into the political, what Franz Blei called "the final and most evil flattening of the human being."[61] Doderer regretted his lapse into the political in the 1930s, but he characterized his involvement with politics as not his first or most intensive "step into the unreal" but simply the most objective (471). In the early 1940s it seems to have been precisely Doderer's identity as a writer that determined his passive attitude toward National Socialism. Even though he served throughout the war in the German Air Force, he later claimed that he had never doubted National Socialism's eventual defeat.[62] What looks like false consciousness in retrospect seemed to Doderer a form of imprisonment that was intimately tied to the writer's desire to retreat from the primacy of politics. This recalls Doderer's own view that "the most dangerous situations in life must be passed through in a condition of diminished lucidity of consciousness" (600). But he learned not to be too self-righteous about his earlier political mistakes. As he put it in 1946: "I no longer imagine to myself that nine years ago [1937] I migrated from pure error into pure reality" (469).

The importance of the erotic for apperception came into focus between 1948 and 1950 while Doderer was writing "Sexualität und totaler Staat" [Sexuality and Total State].[63] But even as early as 1944, Doderer had made clear that "existential apperception" is "a fusion, an erotic process" (267).[64] As a metaphor, eros had always been central to his argument: "Existential apperception requires surrender, conscious thought requires willpower" (267). Sexuality, then, is only the most obvious metaphor for the relation to experience in general and the nature of all situations. But, during the late 1940s, Doderer displayed an increasing commitment to the importance of the erotic for his understanding of apperception: The erotic "remains always the last and most extreme possibility" for human experience and apperception (816). Doderer defined reality as "the complete congruence between the inner world and the outer world" or, at the least, as "a certain minimum of congruence between inner and outer" (178) and unreality as "the complete absence of any congruence between inner and outer" (605). After his conversion to Catholicism and his discovery of Thomas Aquinas, Doderer referred to the congruence between inner and outer (subjective and objective) as the

Analogia entis or analogy of being. For Doderer it was beyond doubt that "in writing or thinking I am always only playing variations on the *Analogia entis* . . . that I am, as it were, a born Thomist, without the need—until now [1948]—to examine this, my foundation, critically" (616).[65]

Although he was only too well aware of the dangers of neurosis and obsession (what he called "pseudology") in the realm of sexuality, Doderer argued that "we must fight for sexuality in order to hold it in its maximal category and so that it will not be consumed by the pseudological" (643). And he pointed out that even in Greek mythology, the heroes never thought of doing anything so foolish as to make war on sexuality—as, of course, Weininger had. Doderer had been an expressionist and a sexual adventurer in the 1920s, but he had separated his world of sexual obsessions from the professional world of academic learning. This split was what he sought to overcome in order to become himself and to become a writer. He concluded that both academic writing and sexual obsessions had the typical faults of ideology and bourgeois culture: an excess of conscious intention. He wanted to move toward memory, smell, and the unconscious ground of apperception and intelligence.[66] Doderer goes so far as to say that sexuality is the clasp that holds the two realms of inner and outer together in the *Analogia entis*. This also accounts, of course, for the danger and power of the pseudological in the sexual realm; Doderer believed that he had put his greatest weakness (i.e., his sexual obsessions) precisely in the place where the solution lay. He spent most of his life during the interwar years hoping for a fundamental change in himself by way of intelligence in the narrow sense, but he eventually realized that this could be achieved only on the spiritual [geistigen] level, "on that of the erotic. Here, and nowhere else, is . . . the *Analogia entis* to be restored" (815). He came to the view that the erotic level *is* the spiritual level, that sexuality is the most important door of apperception. According to Doderer, apperception requires a sexuality that does not set itself against intelligence. "The most deadly danger of my life consisted in the fact that I exempted sexuality from apperception and thereby from intelligence and precisely thereby closed for myself the most important door of apperception" (752). He became convinced that any dichotomy between eros and spirit is barbaric (534). He wanted to overcome his neurotic preoccupation with sexuality but without devaluing the importance of eros. "The sexual wants to draw the human being, this deserter, into life" (746).

Doderer regarded "everything that we say or do in a space that is separated from the remainder of life and its requirements" as "pseudological" (628). Pseudological inwardness bears no relation to external reality except as a kind of parallelism that follows the patterns established by the healthy and automatic mechanisms of the mind. For Doderer, the antidote to unreality is always to endure reality, while "pseudology" is the false reality that is created by the refusal of apperception, a characteristic of neurotic thinking and also a typical feature of his own society. Writing in 1944, Doderer put it this way: "The astonishing fundamental fact of the age is the nonapperception of the objectively given. The way from not wanting to apperceive to no longer being able to apperceive seems to have been completed" (264). He thought of apperception as a "maximum of being open," and he regarded it as "the antidote against every pseudology" (697), against everything that keeps us from moving beyond the neurotic or pseudological condition that impairs sight. So central is the metaphor of seeing that Doderer recalls Aristotle's view in the *Metaphysics* that we would love to practice seeing, "even if it were good for nothing" (689).

> *"Cultivated Literature."* Educated people imagine that there is a parquet of the mind. They do not notice that what glistens there is the ice on which the donkey goes dancing, because he will never have the slightest notion of the depth of the water beneath and of the thinness of the layer above it. He is still fundamentally a half-educated person, this donkey, just like most educated people. And half-education is a birth defect, as I have already said, an irreparable one. (286–287)

The original appeal of National Socialism for Doderer seems to have been related to his expectation that this political movement would be an irrational break with the fixity and rigidity of bourgeois life. He advocated the unusual view that National Socialism constituted the consummation of the nineteenth-century's tendency to exaggerate the importance of conscious thought. It was not the irrationality of National Socialism that disappointed him but its continuity with bourgeois rationality and the excess of conscious purposes. His problem with the Third Reich was not that it was irrational but rather that it was unreal. He believed that an excess of conscious intention becomes apparent in the neurotic and the ideologue, although the classical historical form of this excess was the mainstream of *bürgerlich* culture as it developed in the German-speaking world in the nineteenth century. He argued that, just as the unconscious was beginning to receive attention from modern psychology, both ordinary life and writing were migrating in the direction of conscious thought.

Doderer believed that an excess of conscious intention was the mistake of the revolutionary and the *Bürger* alike, and of modern German culture in particular. Here his concerns were more or less the opposite of what had worried Weininger about the modern age of the unconscious. Doderer's emphasis on a connection between the willfulness of the *Bürger* and the revolutionary (whether communist or fascist) may seem puzzling to some, but the psychological encapsulation and the lack of respect for reality were central for Doderer, as well as the emphasis on consciousness: "[T]his fundamental act of the nineteenth century [the emphasis on consciousness in writing]— whose writing moved so specifically toward the direct extension of conscious thought, without any longer dipping into the swamps and detours of the unconscious—seems to me the root of the relatively incomparable events we have recently experienced" (454). In this sense, the nineteenth-century catastrophe of language was the loss of the sense of what religion and poetry are good for, what Musil had in mind when he referred to the writer's opposition to secular rationalism. Doderer wanted more swamps and detours. "Only when the process of rejecting deperception has reached to the level of the erotic and overrun it can the prison walls of stupidity open" (823). He regarded the erotic as the "most sensitive organ of apperception" (838), but also as the one most vulnerable to distortion and blindness; despite this, he believed that sexuality could be the path to apperception, individuality, and intelligence:

> The foundation of all apperception—as its most intensive case!—is sexuality, thus the lack of sexual prejudice. While a purely lateral sexuality sets itself apart from the rest of life and thus eludes apperception, memory, and thus also intelligence—establishing its own isolated continuum of sexual *mémoires*—the fundamental sexuality becomes . . . the continually ready, most intensive and most universal form of apperception and thus precisely the basis of intelligence. (752)

Doderer believed that the conditions of modern life required psychology as a preliminary to experiencing reality at all, as a way of clearing away the psychological obstacles to apperception (12–13). He came to the conclusion that what was crucial was always to keep one eye open, even under the worst pressures of pseudology, neurosis, psychological suffering, and self-preoccupation, to see all this stupidity and blindness as truly and objectively as possible. In effect, Doderer's insight into mental health is that one does not get well in order to be able to see clearly but, rather, one sees clearly in order to be able to get well. Very much in the spirit of Freud, Doderer argued that "all pathology lives only from repression" (178). Doderer was conscious that his discussion of the refusal of apperception touched closely on the achievements of Freud, that it was precisely here, in his account of repression, that Freud had shown his genius (172–173). Doderer's notion of apperception involves an awareness that not only allows unconscious thought to emerge into the lighted area but also allows external reality to penetrate the walls of the pseudological ego. Self-understanding comes not only through introspection but through "opening one's eyes," through seeing oneself and a situation (12–13).[67]

It is frequently apparent that Doderer is responding to Weininger: "The aversion of the human being to universal perception (thus, what Weininger associates with genius) could be explained by the fear that for this reason libido will no longer be felt: for this always requires, to be sure, a minimum of isolation for its object" (630). Doderer's view of universal apperception is grounded in an immediate understanding of experience, for it is always nothingness that "becomes visible when we do not act in accord with the nearest requirements of life" (185). Doderer's psychological counsel is always to stop and pay attention, to endure the situation (both inner and outer) just as it is, without resisting perception, but simply absorbing the full reality of the situation precisely as it is. He came to believe that what was decisive for him as a person and as a writer was to come to terms with his own real situation, and even as late as June 1945, he regarded himself as "an adept of apperception in the very earliest stages" (331). At the center of this process of coming to terms with himself was his idea for a novel that would take place before *The Demons* and connect the 1920s to the prewar years. This fictional realization of his thinking about apperception centered on a staircase near what he called "the Swoboda-Allers-Weininger Area" of Vienna.[68]

In the Ninth District of Vienna, not far from the university and from the Berggasse address where Freud lived, a public staircase on the Strudlhofgasse connects the Boltzmanngasse to an older residential district below. Building a novel around this staircase (and its *genius loci*) was Doderer's way of recovering the link between the interwar years and his experience as a young man before and during the war—a sense of the deeper structure of historical time and of the writer's memory. *The Strudlhof Steps, or Melzer and the Depth of the Years* portrayed some of the characters he had created for *The Demons*; he introduced Mary K. and developed the character of René Stangeler, but he also reached back into the prewar period, to "the depth of the years" and the monarchy.[69] Stangeler in *Die Strudlhofstiege* is roughly Doderer as he imagined himself had he stayed with Gusti and not been caught up in sexual obsessions and political ideology. For Stangeler the staircase represents his process of emerging from *Befangenheit* [entrapment, constraint] to acknowledge the reality of the external world.[70] For Doderer, *Die Strudlhofstiege* was the path beyond his inability to write *The Demons*; Melzer, the central figure in the novel, represents apperception as well as Doderer's own recovery of memory and the past.[71] Doderer tells the whole story of the novel in the first sentence and in parentheses: When Mary K. still "walked on two very beautiful legs (her right leg was run over by a trolley, not far from her apartment, on September 21, 1925)."

Doderer makes his understanding of apperception most explicit in the experience of Melzer and in the words of René Stangeler.[72] The two men discuss Grete Siebenschein, Stangeler's fiancée, near the end of the novel:

> "When you get married," [Stangeler] said, "you accept the person of the woman in question along with all the external and internal circumstances of your relationship to her, the damaging as well as the advantageous, all in all. Just as it is. Your wishes can no longer affect it. When you see what is lacking really clearly and truthfully, but do not revolt against it, but rather want to live with it, then it is no longer lacking because you have struck it at the center."

Stangeler should not be taken here to be an opponent of change. In a way that recalls Musil's essay on stupidity, Stangeler quotes one of Doderer's most problematic characters, Captain Eulenfeld, on this question: "The Captain

Figure 11. The Strudlhof Steps

once said to me that a stupid person, who is aware of his stupidity, is already thereby as good as very intelligent."[73] But Doderer is always sensitive to the metaphorical sense, in this case to the pleasure that "arises from the marriage of life with knowledge" (679). Seeing the world as it is without trying to change it allows René to marry Grete, which he was unable to do in the original plan for part 2 of "The Demons of Ostmark." In the final version of *The Demons*, Schlaggenberg comments on the process of getting past his refusal of apperception and his clouded sight:

> "Every real apperception is not only a contact and superficial mingling of inner and outer; it is an interpenetration of both—more than that, a chemical process, a compound, an 'alchemical marriage' between us and the world, in which we are playing the feminine role." (1076–1077)

In his attempt to express the interpenetration of subject and object, Doderer adopted the sexual situation as a model for the ethical relationship to the world, but it is also, of course, a view of what sexuality ought to be about. The erotic had special significance for Doderer because it was the pure type of the situation, the purest metaphor of the interpenetration of inner and outer, and the clearest instance of the irrational pole of intelligence. Here Doderer contrasts strikingly with his esteemed Weininger, not only in taking the sexual situation as his ethical model but in advocating the feminine role.

Doderer's ideal of an unconditional apperception with a minimum of preconceptions was consciously directed against political ideologies, and it is vulnerable to the charge that no view can be utterly free of prejudice—indeed, that the critique of ideology is itself an ideology.[74] Certainly Doderer's view of apperception did not provide him with a theory of objective knowledge or protect him from charges of conservative bias, and he was convinced that the "basic attitude of the apperceptive person is conservative, that is a spiritual-mechanical law" (597). But the significance of apperception for Doderer was primarily ethical and aesthetic rather than epistemological or political. He believed that the principal value of politics in his time was the fight to restore normal life, and his work is a protest on behalf of the ordinary person and the writer against politics. "The psychological primacy of politics" seemed questionable to him even in the midst of war, because it allows us to believe in the most honorable and rational way that there could nonetheless be "something more pressing to take care of than the most unconditional apperception" (11). Doderer believed that politics in the modern world had become a very thin concept that barely touched the reality of experience—except in times like National Socialism when a second reality (or pseudoreality) excluded the possibility of authentic experience almost entirely. For him, everyday life rather than politics was the primary form of historical life: "Normal times are the everyday life of history. Everyone knows that precisely everyday life is our severest test" (448).

In Doderer's view, National Socialism did not prove to be an irrational break with the nineteenth-century values he disliked but rather a leap into unreality that was much like his own neuroses. This experience turned Doderer away from trying to find political solutions for his problems and made him suspicious of the psychological disorders that underlie political ideology and the expectation that the state would transform life in fundamental ways. At every level, he believed, conscious intentionality continued to dominate modern life. As a writer he cast his vote against the psychological primacy of politics and for everyday life and a maximum of openness to perception. His mature view of politics was a retreat from the consequences of political antirationalism, but it was also a more general critique of totalitarianism and a rejection of the political. For Doderer, the writer's task was largely to overcome politics and history and to establish the possibility of real life. In an age of totalitarian societies, he devoted himself to the value of private existence, "the sublime work of saving the human person" (399); and he opposed "the primacy of politics and the dehumanization that is bound up with it" (398). He was convinced that insofar as a human being works his way beyond the merely psychological to the world of things, precisely then does he live primarily from the inside out. "For my part I am inclined to see the human being as living more from the inside out, that is, insofar as he is a human being and not what he frequently is today, primarily a psychological reaction mechanism" (430). For Doderer, prose was "the art of standing outside things" (763), but this was possible only when psychological *Befangenheit* had been overcome, and with it "the pseudological striving for security and fixation" (765).

For Doderer, the years from 1938 to 1955 meant reconciling himself to a Catholic-conservative tradition that he had opposed in the 1930s and working his way beyond the ideological polarization of the interwar years. This Protestant with German grandparents, this former anti-Semite and Nazi, who was entirely outside the Austrian establishment in the late 1940s while he was writing *Die Strudlhofstiege*, became the most famous Austrian writer of the 1950s, the voice of the Second Republic and of a Catholic, Austrian conservatism and realism. Between 1951 and 1955 Doderer wrote *The Demons*, beginning with the revision of his manuscript, "The Demons of Ostmark."[75] The appearance of *The Demons* in 1956 marked the highpoint of his accomplishments and his recognition as the greatest living Austrian writer. To

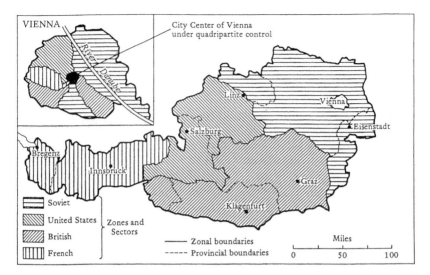

Figure 12. Austria, 1945–1955. Like Germany, Austria was divided into zones of military occupation after the Second World War. In Austria these zones were combined to form the Second Republic.

many intellectuals in the newly independent Austria, Doderer seemed to fit the conservative, Austrian ideology of the 1950s, and his work was to some extent accommodated to this reception in the atmosphere of the Cold War mid–twentieth century.[76] In this sense, Doderer came to represent the Austrian *Bürgertum*'s adaptation to modernity and the Second Republic: moving from polarization and civil war to cooperation and consociational democracy.[77] *The Demons* was Doderer's version of overcoming the past, of standing in for human freedom after the polarizations and simplifications of the fascist era. He came to see the intellectuals (including himself) as having contributed to what went wrong, and he criticized the failure of people in his society to absorb the experience of the First World War or to see where things were headed after 1927.[78]

Ideology and the Novel

The Demons is a strange masterpiece. The significance of this novel lies in the quality of Doderer's rendering of Vienna in the early twentieth century and in the overcoming of his problematic relation to his own sexuality and to National Socialism. Doderer wrote *The Demons* in two main phases that were separated by more than a decade, and the novel captures his life and its conflicts—the quality of his mind, steadily at work in the context of his own life.

The two stages of writing, however, are only imperfectly integrated, and ideological changes and shifts of thematic emphasis that took place in Doderer's mind during these years are often blurred or unspecified in the text. Doderer's entire life is in *The Demons* but in a fluid state rather than immediately autobiographical as it had been in the 1930s. Everything in the novel had significance for him, and nothing is there simply for the chatty superficiality his narrator sometimes lays claim to, so that even apparently trivial details are important for the plot and the characters.[79] In one sense, *The Demons* may be regarded as Doderer's attempt to write what is sometimes referred to as a total novel, a nonthematic rendering of the complexity of real life. In another sense, Doderer decided to allow himself a theme: second reality or deperception, which he regarded as the fundamental quality of his time, that is, the refusal to apperceive the objectively given.

This very long novel (more than 1,300 pages) culminates in the events of July 15, 1927, when Viennese workers demonstrated against class justice, and Austrian politics began to descend toward civil war. In the penultimate chapter of *The Demons*, Doderer portrays the events of July 15: a spontaneous strike of Viennese workers, who marched down the *Ringstrasse* in protest against the acquittal of right-wing paramilitary soldiers who had shot two socialist protesters (a war veteran and a little boy) in Schattendorf, a small town on the border with Hungary. This act of shutting down the city was on such a scale that no one was really in control of it, whether the socialist leadership (who did not call for the action) or the Viennese police. Eventually someone set fire to a building with the symbolic name of the Palace of Justice, and the police shot into the crowd. Eighty-nine people were killed, including four policemen, and there were more than a thousand casualties.[80] Although *The Demons* is a contemporary history and Doderer was fanatical about his sources and achieving a maximum of realistic detail, his concern was not primarily with the political events of July 15 but with human relationships and the relationships of human beings to the world, with the challenge of everyday life. His methodological point as a historian is that history is the "science of the future," the future as it appeared in 1927.[81] Then the world still seemed new and liberated from the diseases of the old world, but most characters in the novel are also oblivious to Schattendorf and to the approaching catastrophe.[82]

The Demons is a novelist's rendering of the history of Vienna from 1925 to 1927. Mary K.'s accident with the trolley at the end of *Die Strudlhofstiege* immediately precedes the events of the novel, and *The Demons* ends with the fire in Frau Mayrinker's kitchen. The substance of part 1 is largely as it had been in the 1930s, emphasizing Schlaggenberg and his friends, and the overture remained exactly as Doderer had written it in 1935; but Geyrenhoff's chronicle breaks off during the novel as Doderer takes over the work of narration himself. The crowd (*die Unsrigen* as in "Our Gang") is a fairly miscellaneous group of bourgeois intellectuals, some of whom are connected obscurely to right-wing political movements in Austria and Hungary. The friends who are mentioned most often in this political context are Dr. Körger (with "the unconscious bankroll at the back of his neck"), Captain Eulenfeld (who spends most of his time drinking and driving his sports car), and at times, Géza Orkay (a Hungarian diplomat who falls in love with Quapp) and Schlaggenberg himself. Imre von Gyurkicz, also a Hungarian and Quapp's lover for much of the novel, has a particularly ambiguous political identity (or lack of identity): he is connected to right-wing activists in Burgenland, but he dies as an advocate of the demonstrators at the Palace of Justice. Geyrenhoff is explicitly distanced from the more ideological aspects of the group, as is young René Stangeler. The narrative suspense is provided by a relatively banal story of identity and inheritance. The plot hangs by the battlefield testament that Captain Ruthmayr entrusted to Sergeant Gach and functions as a detective story: Can Sektionsrat Geyrenhoff bring to light the attempts of Financial Counsellor Levielle to conceal the existence of Captain Ruthmayr's will? This story had already been present in "Die Daemonen von Ostmark," but Doderer moved away from the earlier ideological content, and by 1940 the novel had grown into a conservative critique of ideology. Doderer added many new characters in the early 1950s and achieved a novel that is much more broadly conceived. In its final form, *The Demons* is held together by the original detective story, by the approach of July 15, 1927, and by the theme of second reality.

Anton Reininger argues that Doderer never quite found a way to make *The Demons* work in literary terms because the original version was built around Our Crowd and the theme of anti-Semitism.[83] Reininger contends that since Doderer found no way to develop this material, he simply added two stories from the outside: Schlaggenberg's preoccupation with fat ladies (developed in part 3, although this theme had been present from the beginning) and René's discovery of a late medieval manuscript on witch trials (introduced in part 2). Both of these subplots deal with problematic sexuality. Reininger's argument makes sense to some extent, insofar as we have sources to judge from at all, and Schlaggenberg's research on fat ladies and Ruodlieb von der Vläntsch's account of witch trials do become the principal examples of the way sexual ideologies function as forms of second reality. But this summary does not suggest the scale of the novel and the huge panoply of characters from the most varied social strata, from the most elegant elites to criminals from the underworld, such as Meisgeier, who rises from the sewers at the end of the novel—or the genuine power of the original story of Our Crowd and its problems with Levielle (Doderer slightly changed the earlier spelling). Moreover, Doderer added tremendously to the complexity of his original design, especially through new characters such as Mary K. and Leonhard Kakabsa, the central romantic figures; Dwight Williams and Fräulein Drobil, the characters who appear at the periphery in chapter 1 to give the novel a new course; and Frau Kapsreiter and Renata, who are connected to events in Schattendorf and to the two fires, the burning of the Palace of Justice and the fire in Frau Mayrinker's kitchen. These new characters establish the frame of reference for Doderer's climactic presentation of the events of July 15 in chapter 11 of part 3, "The Fire."[84]

As Doderer recast his novel in the 1950s, *The Demons* took the form of a conservative critique of modern society as it had emerged in the 1920s. A complex of characters—Hofrat von Gürtzner-Gontard, Sergeant Gach, Captain Ruthmayr, and Prince Croix (the master of apperception)—represent the aristocratic world of principle that had still been alive in 1914. Doderer portrays the transition from a more stable, hierarchical status society before 1914 to the more brittle class relationships of the 1920s and the starker polarizations between the working class, on the one hand, and business, industry, and police, on the other. He seems to have thought of "progress" as middle-class consumerism and as a wish for security that was oblivious to the war and to the people who fought it.[85] As a young man, Doderer associated these values especially with young women and Jews, that is, with Gusti Hasterlik. His earlier anti-Semitism seems to have been a matter of projecting onto Jews his generation's wish for progress and distraction in the 1920s. That he had such categories at all was, in part, his debt to Weininger—but, in a different sense, to his entire culture. But Weininger also helped Doderer to see what he (like Heidegger) took to be a real problem: the escape into progress, distraction, and egotism.[86] *The Demons* is critical of modern culture as it emerged in the 1920s, whether in its mania for cars or big capitalism.[87] But Doderer no longer identified these themes explicitly with Jews and women, and he moved away a bit from his extreme spiritualism toward individuality and reconciliation with modern life. A conservative, aristocratic tone remains, but the novel is not anti-Semitic, and it is opposed equally to fascism and to communism; and women play much more significant roles than in the earlier version.[88] Indeed, Doderer's critique of his own anti-Semitism appears early in the novel, when Geyrenhoff mentions Schlaggenberg's "allusion to his wife's racial stock. Here the ground dropped away from under my feet" (66). Geyrenhoff immediately changes the subject to one that comes to interest Schlaggenberg and his friends: fat ladies. For Doderer, this was a substitute for the anti-Semitic theme, although it had already been present earlier. Schlaggenberg proceeds to expatiate on his ideal woman: "Somewhere between a hundred and eighty and two hundred pounds" (67).

Schlaggenberg's ideology about women had given the novel its original title, "Dicke Damen." Schlaggenberg contends that the girls of the 1920s are "'unfit to become companions of anyone with aims going beyond bourgeois security,'" and he explains that these young women begin as intellectual companions but soon want only children and a good provider:

> "For what this generation between two wars needs is not the kind of girl who is waiting impatiently at the doors of life, waiting until the doors open and she catches sight of—the set dinner table. We are not concerned with these eternally demanding women who want to drag us off our path, force us to pursue their everlastingly monotonous ends." (259)

Schlaggenberg prefers the mature, stout woman who is no longer driven by reproductive commitments, the "massive, maternal type of woman . . . the well-stuffed woman" (261). He advocates the restoration of his generation's love for the motherly type of woman rather than the modern type of girl "whose resemblance to maleness introduces an almost homosexual element into love" (261). Geyrenhoff faults Schlaggenberg's typology as a pseudoscience, what the young Stangeler calls "second reality."

> "But I think your strategy is all wrong, because it is too mathematical. It smacks of the calculus of probability. It is one thing in life to be ready for an event which in the end you more or less bring about, conjure up, by your constant readiness. But what you are doing is virtually setting a trap for life—at least that is what your project sounds like. . . . You want to catch life in your nets, but I am afraid it is too tricky for that." (385)

This is also what is significant in Doderer's view of life that goes beyond politics or sexuality: his anti-ideological respect for reality. Geyrenhoff explains to his friend Katejan that he cannot control life, much less love (386). In his search for his sexual type, Schlaggenberg suffers from "a kind of secondary sexuality," searching for "a second and phantasmagoric reality" (684). He reaches out for experiences that can only come to a person.

Geyrenhoff presents Schlaggenberg's manuscript about the fat ladies in the cafés along the Danube as a typical instance of ideology and an attempt "to work reforms in a restricted but highly central field." This minor insanity appears as an instance of what all ideologies are like in their attempts to improve life: "For these ideologies all wear blinkers which blind them to the real constitution of the world. They are all as crazy as Kajetan's Theory of the Necessity of Fat Females to the Sex Life of the Superior Man Today" (857). All this typological excess is a "fanatical craving for the ordering of a sexuality turned inside out" (867).

> "For sex is the greatest window of our apperception, and if this window clouds, all the others will soon suffer from cataracts. Half blind, you will peer out at all things only through the narrow slit of some program or other, always anticipating what ought to be. And in the end you will call it an ideal." (1077)

Schlaggenberg's own instinct is that "'there is no explanation for the fact that emptiness can become substance—and yet it does'" (866). This is Doderer's theme and what he means by the demonic.

Doderer describes the demonic more generally in part 2: "[I]t is characteristic of all matters connected with the demonic that although they create a tremendous stir and a great deal of motion, they never leave anyone with anything substantial in his hands afterwards" (1024). The central new material in part 2 deals with the return of Jan Herzka from *Die Bresche* ("five" fictional years later) to a more intelligent version of his sadistic outburst in Doderer's first novel.[89] Herzka's mother had been a Baroness Neudegg, but Herzka is just a substantial middle-class businessman who discovers that he has inherited a castle. His assistant, Agnes Gebaur, seems to fit his fantasy, drawing fuel from his earlier experience with Magdalena Güllich. Here Doderer interpolates a story within the story, a document he actually wrote himself on the history of witch trials and their misuse for personal reasons by those without jurisdictional authority.[90] The story took place in 1464 and was written down in 1517 by the page, Ruodlieb von der Vläntsch, who had witnessed it. The events that took place at Neudegg turn out not to have been a tragedy but "a ridiculous farce of the passions" (744). As Stangeler studies this late medieval document, he becomes aware that Jan Herzka might be crazy. "Perhaps Herr Achaz of 1464 had likewise been insane. Jan and Achaz both. Each in the style of his age. Likewise Körger. Probably Schlaggenberg too." Stangeler comments, "[O]nly what comes along is first class. Everything aimed at and attainable by aiming at is second class'" (749). He decides that most of his friends would have belonged in this castle, as madmen holding the world at bay: "Suddenly Stangeler felt that his association with

Schlaggenberg, Eulenfeld, Orkay, Körger, was harming him all the time. The damage we derive from a friend is often as great as the benefit we derive from an enemy." Stangeler summarizes the story that is told in the manuscript:

> "And this was a torture chamber. In the adjoining room the victim was undressed and examined for the witches' mark, though not in every case. Then she was led out, tied by her wrists to the pillar, and scourged, sometimes, no doubt, only for form's sake, in order to intimidate her. Almost every interrogation began that way. Here, at this pillar, the widow of a mayor of Lienz was scourged—a beautiful woman, so it is said, though about fifty years old. And another woman also." (760–761)

This late medieval account of sexuality and ideology makes visible a more general experience that Doderer believed was characteristically modern, "the clash between a first and a second reality, between which no bridge exists" (1019). Herzka comes to realize (much like Julius Zihal in *The Lighted Windows*) that a real relationship with Agnes might have the power to lift him "from a second into a first reality" (1041), and Agnes is identified with feminine wisdom (1043), in contrast to "[p]rogrammed sexuality" (1049). As the young historian Stengeler, puts it,

> The question is, what are you going to do with it? Unfortunately I suspect that the ridiculous details in which this suddenly heightened reality of your life has been manifested are far more important to you than the heightening of reality itself. For which reason, my friend, you're going to go grubbing around in the details instead of so shaping your life that similar heightenings of reality—of a worthier sort—may enter it. (749)

The ideologue reaches out for experiences that have to come to a person. Here Doderer goes on to underscore the distinction between first and second reality and why sexual ideologies and political ideologies are similar. Stangeler summarizes Doderer's view of modern man and his critique of ideology as it emerged after 1938:

> "Achaz was an ideologue simply because he reached out his hand for experiences which—which can only be given to one. That's what all ideologues do. Reformers go out directly for a change of circumstances, instead of beginning with themselves; if they did the latter, a new reality would accrue to them, a reality of the first rank, not a phantom reality like Achaz's artificial, arranged sexual experiences. Achaz had a program. It's nonsense, of course,

to maintain that political programs are a form of sublimated sexuality, or an outgrowth of it. Ideology does not come from sexuality; it is no substitute for it. Still, it stands under the same pale phantasmal light as Achaz's *idées fixes*. That is why he was a modern man."[91]

Doderer thought it was important to start with oneself—a new reality would grow out of this, and he portrayed this above all in the figure of Leonhard Kakabsa, the most important character to be added after the 1937 typescript.

There are many stories in *The Demons*, but Leonhard's part of the novel is a *Bildungsroman* about a young man becoming a person through classical education and the crossing of the dialect divide via a Latin grammar, smells, and memory. Leonhard Kakabsa is a young man from the working-class district who embodies Doderer's view of the relationship between mind and eros. He is associated with the stream of life (the Danube) and the unconscious but also with the dislike for schools and socialism. He is a genius of apperception and seeing the world as it is. Doderer associates language, invention, and creativity with the critique of conscious intention and the emphasis on accident. Leonhard has two closely related passions: Latin and Fiedler's daughter Malva. Leonhard meets Malva Fiedler by accident, in front of her father's bookstore, as he catches the books that are slipping from her grasp. "Leonhard felt the girl's body with an almost unbelievable palpability; he stood pressed close against her, after all. He felt distinctly her soft compactness, the very curve of her abdomen" (141). Here Doderer portrays what he means when he speaks of the way in which eros draws this deserter into life. Leonhard remembered her smell; he had been caught, but he had also been enlightened and moved beyond the conceit of absolute independence. Leonhard's resistance to entanglement—whether in groups or relationships or ideologies—makes him an exemplar of the individual and the hard work of education and humanization:

> In a certain sense our Leonhard's biography might be everyone's. For with the perceptions that we have acquired from our early experiences, we proceed to hurl our original selves into whatever sets of circumstances the outside world happens to offer. It ought to surprise no one that we then find ourselves stuck somewhere where we do not belong. And in difficult situations these choices can scarcely be rescinded. (117)

Leonhard was added to the novel in the 1950s along with the working-class milieu in which he is portrayed as an outsider. He embodies the power of the Latinate tradition in Vienna as well as the ideal connection between humanistic learning and humane action.[92] Doderer wants to see history from the individual's point of view, from the perspective of everyday life, and Leonhard is Doderer's individualistic, anti-Marxist account of the working class coming to consciousness.

Doderer describes the working-class world as one in which any face that "betrayed signs of intelligence was sure to be on the receiving end of contemptuous and challenging looks" and argues that "it was intelligence itself that aroused their antagonism, not at all superior economic position, which at this time was no longer bound up with intelligence—quite the contrary" (123). But Doderer's account bears less on Social Democracy than on the consequences of the First World War:

> Intelligence had not been able to prevent the World War and its unfortunate conclusion. Intellectuals, with their gift for language, had done the talking for the inarticulate people. And they had spoken evilly, had preached madness. Afterwards a general hatred for every kind of authority erupted. (123)

Doderer criticizes the anti-intellectualism of his own generation, what had most set him in opposition to Musil. "Evidently they had never realized that real intelligence can only be the outward extension of inner strength, not its opposite—and that there is nothing rotten about such intelligence. . . . during those years, both in our own little circle and in wider spheres, only this utterly corrupt notion of 'intellect' prevailed" (327).

In Leonhard's world this anti-intellectualism attached especially to the working class elite who met in the taprooms, and Leonhard lived an inward-turned existence while he was learning Latin, walled off from external reality but in a way that was psychologically healthy. He was simultaneously learning that one enters the gates of thought on words and that Malva, who knew Latin and Greek, was "a planet prone to swift and icy storms" (162). He explains to Malva's father why he has no intention of leaving his work at the factory to advance in a career:

> "It must be proved that a worker is not an unfortunate, hopeless person who can only wait until conditions in the world improve, until which time there's nothing for him but his family, the movies, the saloon. . . . It remains to be proved that right now, right this minute, at this time, everything is open to a worker, without class struggle and the rest of it. It remains to be proved that he needs his work not only to maintain himself, not only to earn his livelihood, but actually as a counterweight to the rest, to make sure that the rest is genuine, not fake." (164)

Fielder, who "liked Leonhard Kakabsa very much," responds that Leonhard has already proved it (164). In this way Doderer defends the working-class movements of the late nineteenth century but argues a decline in the quality of socialism by the 1920s. "The possibilities for a personal turning of the road, for deliverance, . . . do not exist for the person who expects everything to come from a change of circumstances, and from a tremendous massed advance in which 10,000 men will simultaneously set one foot over the threshold of the earthly paradise" (523–524).

Doderer establishes the context for events on July 15, 1927, by diverting some of his characters to Burgenland in southeastern Austria, where he also explores the Socialist and anti-Socialist ideologies of the 1920s. On a visit to Burgenland, Leonhard and a friend meet Sergeant Gach, who had served with Captain Ruthmayr in the war. Gach tells wonderful stories about the battles at the beginning of the war, but he is very clear about what came after those first moments of glory: "[A]ll those long years, that was just one dreadful, really horrible misery; and there mustn't ever be anything like that again, under no circumstances, never again, and if your party can really stop war, then it has a reason to exist, but only then" (599). In his account of Hungarian reactionaries and their political activities along the border with Burgenland, Doderer expresses a more general, one might say Austrian, resistance to ideology and an emphasis on the complexity and openness to being in the world. The Hungarians who meet at a hut on the border of Burgenland had been part of Horthy's gang, the men who had done the dirty work of "liquidating the dictatorship of Béla Kuhn" (556). But Doderer also describes another group of politically active men (in this case, the socialists) as "suspended from some kind of wire which was not common hatred or common love, but rather a common cable of assured knowledge in which each had his certificated share, which answered every question for him, even the question of the meaning of life (which always ought to remain open), or of humanity, not to speak of humanity's history or development" (644–645). Doderer's critique of revolution finds its most forceful expression in Hofrat Gürtzner-Gontard, who emphasizes that generalizing is what makes a revolutionary. But Gürtzner-Gontard's real point is about the psychological bases of revolution: "A person who has not been able to endure himself becomes a revolutionary; then it is others who have to endure him." The revolutionary gives up on the concrete task of his own life and often finds himself with people who are essentially hostile to him, "who likewise have somewhere and at some time run away, after their own fashions, from their concrete immediacies" (491). Gürtzner-Gontard offers Geyrenhoff an explanation that is at once Burkean and psychological in a more twentieth-century way:

"Thus you might say that a priori abstraction is the mother of all revolutionaries. The revolutionary flees from what is hardest for him to bear, the aimless variety of life; he seeks perfection, which in the world of his trivialities can at best mean completeness." (493)

Gürtzner-Gontard's daughter, Renata, represents the rebellion of the children of the 1920s against the parental homes that "reek of the last century" (891).[93] Much like Leonhard, she embodies the turning away from political movements: "It was not yet known that everything would soon depend upon the individual and that it was incumbent on the individual, for a time at least, to take his place exactly opposite every sort of collective" (893). Frau Kapsreiter, née Csmarits, gives Renata a chance for independence and solitude. It is at Frau Kapsreiter's Blue Unicorn that Renata meets Pepi, Kapsreiter's little nephew from Burgenland who dies with his uncle during the socialist demonstration in Schattendorf. Doderer emphasizes that Frau Kapsreiter is a special person who resists reduction to her social class identity:

In every class there are people who fall out of it, whether upstairs or down. Thus, there are high aristocrats who spend almost their full time in libraries and seem no better than humble scholars. There are industrial workers who climb to the heights of culture. There are book binders with touches of genius: consider Hirschkron of the Café Kaunitz. There are petty bourgeois with breadth of soul and magnificent human qualities. One such case was Frau Anna Kapsreiter. (895)

Doderer argued even in the 1940s that "the real, so to say, subcutaneous theme of *The Demons*" is "nothingness as phenomenon."[94] What Frau Kapsreiter did was "nothing. And therein lay the grandeur of her existence" (896). For Doderer, the demonic world of illusion is what appears when we do not apperceive, when we fail to take into account the whole of God's created and historical world.

Doderer defines political ideology as "seeing the world through a slit cut askew, hating what one does not see and does not want to see, from which it is evident that one nevertheless has really seen these things" (565). He provides an account of why revolutionaries have certain kinds of moral/psychological problems—because these ideologies are attempts to escape from their dislike of themselves and from their refusal to see the world as it is. Imre is the epitome of the revolutionary's problematic relation to self (or lack of self), while his countryman, Géza Orkay, eventually sees through the fascists and the kind of thinking they represent.[95] Géza comments on the shooting of the child and the ensuing political furor that led up to the events of July 15 and concludes with a reflection on his right-wing associates in Hungary:

> "So that they too are no more scrupulous than the Reds when it comes to grinding a child's corpse into propagandistic hash. You may wonder at how informed I am—I've spent the last week in the library, looking over the newspapers since the beginning of February. The leftist papers and the rightist ones. If anyone thinks there is the slightest ray of hope in either one of these two movements, he deserves to have a roofing tile fall on his knob."

The exact replication of political events in the dramatic polarization that took place on July 15 is not the real point, even if Doderer sometimes thought it was. Rather, Doderer attempted to portray what was lost during the world wars and the fascist era: the ordinary lives of individual human beings. He wanted to build up his picture of reality from these lives. For Doderer, the fire that dominated the city all day and night symbolized the overwhelming of everyday life by demonic forces—by ideology and the underworld. His point was not that he had achieved historical, ideological, or epistemological objectivity, neutrality, or lack of prejudice, and he was certainly clear that his own views were politically conservative.[96] He was interested in finding ways to overcome the compulsions and fixations that limited his picture of reality, and he was aiming at an ethical attitude, which he believed was exemplified in the erotic situation. He wanted to understand what goes on personally, psychologically, ethically in people who are strongly committed to ideologies, to understand the appeal of totalitarian ideologies, which seemed to function in the individual's emotional economy very much like neurosis. What is sometimes lost in ideological critiques of Doderer is his interest in the pathological moment in ideology—the self-absorption and the attempt to impose abstract change on realities that are not respected or understood. These are qualities that Doderer associates especially with youth, although two young men, René Stangeler and Leonhard Kakabsa become exemplars of freedom from second reality.

Although he was not as intellectual as Musil, Doderer did not intend simply to entertain. He had universal ambitions of portraying life, not in the old abstract way but more concretely and pluralistically. He worked slowly and indirectly, building up his story from the outside by drawing on multiple centers of experience. The beauty of the book is that Doderer portrays totality indirectly through many points of view; even the narrator is relativized in complex ways in this polygraphic novel that is rich in "episodic centers."[97] And yet the theme is consistent: for Doderer, political ideologies are like sexual obsessions, and he believed that the solution in both cases is to see one-self and the world truly. The sexual ideologies of Schlaggenberg and Herzka represent Doderer's own sexual problems, while the political ideologies of the characters are revealed by hatred, which makes clear that they are not ra-tional but rather what Doderer refers to as second reality: the escape from nothingness, courtesy, and the acceptance of the reality of the world. Doderer is not saying that all attempts at improvement are evil, but that the motiva-tion is a problem that leads easily to second reality.[98]

A passage in part 3 of *The Demons* reads very much like a commentary on Doderer's own life as he finished his masterpiece and became Austria's most admired writer: "[E]very so-called success restores equilibrium again. We are rehabilitated, throw off our obligations. What that really comes down to is the opportunity to see the world anew. That way we can more easily get away from ourselves, escape from our own gravitational field, so to speak. That is the spirit in which a success must be pursued, it seems to me; only through this does the success become a success."[99] Doderer continued to be creative after 1956 until his death from cancer at the age of seventy in De-cember 1966, and he attempted to begin anew as a writer. During this decade he designed what he regarded as his most important work, a four-part novel that was to portray the "life that happens in spite of history."[100] He referred to this ambitious project about the years between 1877 and 1961 as *Novel No. 7*—in deference to Beethoven's Symphony no. 7. In his understanding of his own corpus, Doderer discounted *Die Bresche* and *The Secret of the Empire*, and he conceived his projected last four novels as one. His idea of the novel in these years was to have the narrator retreat from view, and in *Novel No. 7* he worked toward the silent novel, at once more objective and more modern than his earlier work—but also less essayistic than Musil or Broch. He was able to complete the first part of the novel, *The Waterfalls of Slunj* (1963), a novel about an English father and his son living in late imperial Vienna, and Doderer was working on the second part, *Der Grenzwald* [The Forest at the Border], when he died. He called *Der Grenzwald* his "first objective work" and his "last eros," his turning away from "deperceptive superstition."[101] He did, however, complete and publish a grotesque novel, *Die Merowinger* (1962), that came to terms with the parts of his personality that could not be assim-ilated to the gracious, elegant Geyrenhoff.[102] Here Doderer portrays the time-less qualities of human experience (in a more or less Schopenhauerian sense), but also a conservative, comic vision and a bewildering response to his own experience of rage and depression as well as his feelings about his family and his father, in particular. But, on the whole, Doderer's work is closer to the re-alities of Vienna and historical developments in the early twentieth century.

Doderer was a problematic person with powerful tendencies toward violence, rage, depression, drinking, and sexual escapades of every kind—and an obsessive inclination toward order and programmatic approaches to life. It is the last of these personal qualities that he believed drew him to National Socialism during the 1930s. But this does not detract from the antidote he prescribed for himself:

> Only the eros of the objective and thereby of the empirical can bring such
> cavemen to step aside and thus at last to take on an inner courtesy: and that
> means not to stand in the way of apperception. This spiritual situation
> brings with it a heightened love for the external world, an externalization in
> a very sublime sense. (443)

By the mid-1950s Doderer had come to views not unlike Musil's in the 1920s: critical of nationalism and the total state, resigned to capitalism, committed to pluralism, and skeptical about the emotional underpinnings of ideologies. Doderer associated these values with Austrian ideology and the Austrian tradition. Musil resisted this narrowing to an Austrian identity, and Doderer's thought certainly bore a more conservative, if not antimodern, stamp. Doderer was above all a storyteller, and his thought lacked the brilliance, flexibility, and complexity of Musil's. Moreover, he always felt a spiritual debt to Weininger, while reminding his friends that, unlike Musil, he was accustomed to finishing his books. Doderer came into his own at the height of the Cold War (and his reception was marked by that), but he was perhaps even more the novelist of the interwar years, who wrote about the disappearance and return of Austria.

$\mathscr{C}$ O N C L U S I O N

∞

$\mathscr{I}$n very different ways, Otto Weininger, Robert Musil, and Heimito von
Doderer all disturbed conventional liberal assumptions about the individual,
in the context of the disintegration of Austrian bourgeois society and culture
in the early twentieth century. For all of them, the irrational was a fundamental power, and they all associated it strongly with sexuality and with
femininity. The theme of sexuality and gender was the form in which these
writers thought through the relationship between self and world. Weininger
appears in my book as the demise of a liberal humanism that had narrowed
too far in the direction of egoism and rationalism, that had become too specifically male and no longer had the capacity to connect with a broader social reality or to endure the realities of modern life. Yet he also began to deconstruct
conventional views of men and women as he rethought eroticism, religion,
and bourgeois sexual conventions. Musil overcame what was rigid in the
grammar of gender defined by Weininger and bourgeois culture, and he developed a more flexible way of thinking about sexuality and gender that was
close to his thinking about ethics and the other condition. Doderer's preoccupation with sexuality was often neurotic and pathological, and his critique
of ideology was more conservative than Musil's, but he also found in sexuality the model for a new understanding of intelligence and an enhanced relationship to the world. These writers explored the balances between thinking
and feeling, conscious and unconscious, masculine and feminine, control and
acceptance, but their meanings were fluid and metaphorical rather than fixed.

My book presents three accounts of nineteenth-century rationalism and individualism. All three authors associated these terms with masculinity, and all of them associated the unconscious and sexuality with femininity; they were critical of bourgeois sexual forms and conventional gender roles, and they were sensitive to the vision of Aristophanes in Plato's *Symposium*. At this point, they begin to diverge. Although enormously influenced by irrationalism and sensitive to the realities of sexuality and the unconscious, Weininger took his stand unambiguously with rationalism, individualism, and consciousness—with an exaggerated version of nineteenth-century liberalism (with powerful religious and idealist overtones). But he also made two other distinctive moves: he associated modern science (and modernity altogether) with the feminine worldview, and he associated Judaism with femininity and modernity rather than with rationalism, individualism, consciousness, and freedom. Musil and Doderer sorted these terms out in very different ways. Doderer's critique of liberalism, rationalism, and the bourgeois ego led him for a time to a form of spirituality that he equated with anti-Semitism, largely along the lines Weininger had argued. Despite his admiration for Weininger, Doderer rejected the one-sided emphasis on the rational and "masculine" in the name of the feminine and henids. More than Musil or Freud, he moved toward the swamps and detours of unconscious thought. Doderer and Musil shared the commitment to the creative person as the model for ethical life, and they both resisted the codification of unconscious life that Ludger Lütkehaus characterizes as the colonization of the unconscious. Doderer's view that the erotic level is the spiritual level is an enormous and fundamental change from Weininger's ideas, although it is anticipated in many regards in Weininger's comments on erotic love and androgyny. Doderer's critique of conscious intention also echoes Musil's efforts to revise the relations between thinking and feeling, masculine and feminine in his culture. Musil's critique of "the liberal scraps of an unfounded faith in reason and progress" was in some respects close to Doderer's view of late nineteenth-century liberalism, but Musil's interests and experience took him into the world of liberalism and secularized Jewish culture, where he seems to have been at home, at least in Berlin.[1] Musil belonged to German liberalism in the broad sense, but he moved away from Liberalism in a narrowly political sense. He gave up on the bourgeois ego and the ethic of achievement and on notions of teleology except of an average, statistical kind that took modern civilization into account in a reasonably optimistic way. Nonetheless, he generally shared in a broad German humanism that identified the interests of individual development with an evolving humanity.

In the early twentieth century, the critique of liberalism was driven to antirationalism and National Socialism, and a conception of spirituality came to be defined in opposition to women and Jews. My explicit theme has been thinking about sexuality and gender, but the question of anti-Semitism has also played a large role in my discussion. The principal reason for this is that gender and anti-Semitism were both central to discourse about liberal rationalism and individualism. But it is also because of the sheer fact of the centrality of National Socialism and anti-Semitism for Central European intellectuals in this period and because a connection is nearly always apparent in writers of this period between their views of women and Jews. What is described as anti-Semitism in discussions of Weininger was an attempt to overcome the conditions of modern life, and what seems to be an attack on women was an attempt to overcome the conditions of human existence. These views may be regarded as reactionary or quixotic, but it is best to see them clearly and to identify what is at stake in them. Musil was, in certain respects, similar to Weininger both in his new ways of talking about gender, androgyny, and human variety and in his awareness of the limitations of modern civilization and the methods of modern science. But, on the whole, Musil embraced modern science and civilization and attempted to create the possibility for a more enriching intellectual and emotional life. In the 1920s Doderer admired both Weininger and Musil, but his experience of war, expressionism, and the collapse of Austria pushed him toward German nationalism and a political break with the bourgeois culture his parents represented. For a time he identified what was wrong in modern civilization with Jews, very much in the spirit of Weininger. He gradually moved away from this association, although he sometimes applied this critique to Germany or to totalitarianism in general. Doderer did not give up his critique of modern life; it remained, but now in a more reconciled and conservative way that emphasized the importance of Austria as the embodiment of a supranational idea of the state.

None of these writers left conventional nineteenth-century notions about the sexual constitution of men and women intact.[2] What is most important about Weininger is that he breaks up automatic, unreflective assumptions about sexuality and gender. This is obscured for most readers because he seems at first glance to be the showcase example of nineteenth-century male prejudice against women. Despite his misogynist impulses, Weininger is far from typical and actually drives the assumptions of this view to the point of absurdity, to what Musil called (in describing Hitler rather than Weininger) "the bankruptcy of the male idea." But Weininger's intent was an attack on sexuality and on the objectification of women in stereotypical roles and a critique of spiritual orthopedics for both men and women, as well as a critique of patriarchal views of religion. Although Weininger advocated a very problematic form of feminism, he posed important issues: the relationship

between the woman as sexual object and the possibilities of women's liberation, as well as the relations among romantic love, sexuality, the body, the
family, and the dignity of the individual. Even if Weininger's answers were
inadequate, he raised important questions. But Weininger's entire approach
to thinking about life is the opposite of Musil's acceptance of the complexity,
irregularity, and imperfection of the world. Doderer eventually moved toward complexity, irony, and objectivity, but not before being powerfully and
fundamentally influenced by Weininger's critique of modern life—and by
his understandings of gender and sexuality, henids and apperception.

The most important theme common to all three authors is the question
of a heightened relation to experience. In Weininger this notion is identified
negatively as female, sexual, and connected to empirical reality. Weininger's
more positive interpretation of eros (which, in his view, is quite distinct from
sexuality) is linked to the male and to rationality, individuality, and logic—
but also to apperception, romantic love, and religion. The possibility of a
heightened relation to experience—and the implications of this for ethics—
were most explicitly worked out in Musil's account of the other condition
and clarified in relation to sexuality and gender, although not reduced to
these. Doderer's view of "first reality" came close to Musil's understanding
of the other condition, and Doderer regarded the erotic (or sexual) situation
as the clearest test of an authentic relation to experience.[3] Indeed, the question of ethics in a post-Nietzschean world is central for all these writers.
Weininger's advocacy of the ethical person is sometimes lost in his critique
of sexuality and femininity, much as the ethical person is what is lost in accounts of Musil's writing about sexuality. And, even in the midst of his sexual obsessions, Doderer is working toward a new ethical relation to his experience and other people. In different ways, Weininger, Musil, and Doderer all
raised the question of whether anything was authentically motivated in
bourgeois society in late nineteenth- and early twentieth-century Europe. In
the midst of the breakup of a society, this could be a terrifying train of thought,
and it led to suicide for Weininger, to a precarious ethical balance for Musil,
and to membership in the National Socialist Party for Doderer.

This book is also intended as a contribution toward seeing the historical
context of psychoanalysis with more complexity and nuance, although my
principal aim is to see these three writers in their own right and not in relation to psychoanalysis. Both Musil and Doderer regarded psychoanalysis as
an important possibility for understanding and organizing emotional life, but
they were both reluctant to set up one of God's possibilities for all eternity.[4]
At the same time, the context for understanding these three writers is also
helpful for understanding Freud's relationship to scientific materialism and

philosophical irrationalism. Freud was not generous in stating his debts to Schopenhauer, Hartmann, and Nietzsche, but no serious scholar of Freud any longer pretends that this debt was trivial, however murky we may be about the details. It is revealing that Freud is disliked both by those who prefer a more sober, experimental, verifiable science and therapy, one more grounded in biochemistry and physiology, one with more dependably universal language and evidence, and by those who prefer something closer to art and a more romantic mode of investigation. The first group faults Freud for not being a scientist, while the second group faults him either for being a scientist at all or for not admitting he was a writer. In fact, Freud was shaped by both scientific materialism and philosophical irrationalism; thus, he was both especially fruitful intellectually for the early twentieth century and especially well suited to address the theme of sexuality. He was also, for these same reasons, one of the most powerful critics of received religious tradition, even though (like Musil) he developed his critique at a distance from religious texts and communities. Freud's commitment to a strong male ego and conscious control was very much a part of the liberal ethos of the late nineteenth century, and genuine respect and tenderness for the unconscious, the "feminine," and the nonego were perhaps not strong in him. But his way of framing these questions was given an Austrian intellectual stamp in the 1870s by the characteristic blend of scientific materialism and philosophical irrationalism. Weininger rejected both scientific materialism and philosophical irrationalism, although he was powerfully shaped by both, while Musil and Doderer sought to balance science and irrationalism in distinctive ways.

Two obvious mistakes offer themselves as conclusions to a book of this kind. One would be an attempt at a comprehensive philosophical position that is faithful neither to the important differences among these three writers nor to the internal inconsistency of each. Weininger valued logic extravagantly, but his whole view is fundamentally contradictory. Musil was a faithful student of Nietzsche who believed in essayism rather than system. And Doderer was all too aware that he was not equipped for philosophical rigor—and in any case did not pursue it. A second (and related) mistake would be to impose our expectations for what a social scientist or a historian of Austrian society might want to say about sexuality and gender today. This might lead at best to a kind of ex post facto labeling that would not correspond to the way these writers thought and experienced the world. It is appropriate for the historian to ask the questions (thinking about sexuality and gender in Vienna during the first half of the twentieth century), but the sources ought to be decisive for the answers.[5]

The process of working on this book has been a kind of intellectual experiment. I began by investigating thinking about sexuality and gender in Vienna in the early twentieth century. My assumption was mainly that Viennese intellectuals were attracted to these themes, but another question began to influence my research: how different was Vienna (or Austria) from Berlin (or Germany)?[6] Perhaps the clearest result of this experiment has been to underscore how closely Austrian intellectual life was connected to Germany in the early twentieth century. This is obvious in the case of Musil, but it is also true of Weininger and Doderer. Weininger was most connected to Germany by his affinity for German thought—whether philosophical idealism or Germanic/Wagnerian ideology—and by his rejection of Ernst Mach and so-called Austrian philosophy. Musil was connected to Germany by his experience in Berlin, by his affinities for the Berlin avant-garde, and by his intention to address German intellectuals, even when he was living in Vienna. Doderer was connected to Germany by two world wars, by his antirationalism, and by his membership in the National Socialist Party during the 1930s. But these strong affinities for Germany in the early twentieth century take on significance precisely in the context of the distinctiveness of Austrian intellectual life in the nineteenth century.

The blend of scientific materialism and philosophical irrationalism that stamped Austrian intellectual life in the late nineteenth century was decisive for all three of these writers. At the same time, Weininger, Musil, and Doderer all moved beyond a narrowly Austrian frame of reference to one that was very broadly European—Russian, German, French, English, Scandinavian. Their philosophical frame of reference was not Austrian in any provincial sense, but it was distinguishable from Germany in its blending of dominant themes, and Austrian writers seem to have been drawn to the theme of sexuality and gender earlier than *Reichsdeutschen*—and in a more nuanced way.[7] Weininger, Musil, and Doderer were intellectual historians of German-speaking Central Europe whose work centered primarily in Vienna during the first half of the twentieth century. But they were also creative minds who shaped their own distinctive visions of human experience.[8] Musil and Doderer were more conscious than Weininger of the importance of "the situation," of the determining power of things and social reality, and they developed richer, wiser perceptions of the world.

I have attempted in this book to begin to recover traditions and perspectives that have been lost to contemporary consciousness, to show how these writers continue to speak to problems of knowledge and experience and how the development of modern science sets limits to our own experience of the world. This is a book about the possibilities for human life and culture after modern science and the series of issues identified by Friedrich Nietzsche. The central intellectual problem of the late nineteenth century was the discrepancy between the developing power and clarity of the scientific worldview and the loss of power of other possible views, whether Christian, liberal, or Marxist. By the turn of the century, the achievements of science were as conspicuous as the need for a new culture that could come to terms with the feelings in a way that liberalism did not. In this regard, Nietzsche was the mentor of German-speaking intellectuals after the turn of the century; in Vienna, in particular, the best minds were shaped by an intellectual context that was both positivist in its antimetaphysical commitment to modern science and empiricism and alert to what was ethically and spiritually problematic in Western culture, especially as it was reflected in the works of writers such as Schopenhauer and Nietzsche.

$\mathcal{N}$OTES

❧

INTRODUCTION

1. *Geschlecht und Charakter: Eine prinzipielle Untersuchung* appeared in Vienna in May 1903. An English translation (*Sex and Character*) appeared in London and New York three years after Weininger's death; this translation is misleading enough on the fundamental issues of the book that I will use my own translations and refer to the German edition (Munich, 1980). For most other texts I will give citations to English works where they are available. Otherwise, I have cited standard German editions; in these cases, the translations are mine.

2. *Der Mann ohne Eigenschaften*, ed. Adolf Frisé (Rowohlt, 1978), *Gesammelte Werke*, vols. 1–4, and *The Man without Qualities*, trans. Sophie Wilkins, ed. and trans. Burton Pike (New York, 1995).

3. *Die Dämonen: Nach der Chronik des Sektionsrates Geyrenhoff* (Munich, 1956) is available in English translation (*The Demons*, trans. Richard and Clara Winston [New York, 1961]).

4. Arthur Schopenhauer, "On Ethics," in *Essays and Aphorisms*, trans. R. J. Hollingdale (New York, 1970), p. 144.

5. Friedrich Nietzsche, "What Is Religious," in *Beyond Good and Evil*, trans. Walter Kaufmann (New York, 1966), p. 59.

6. "Soul" [Seele] refers to a new understanding in this period of the relationships between thinking and feeling and of both to the body and to the unconscious: this was, for example, the word Freud used when he talked about the human mind. See Bruno Bettelheim, *Freud and Man's Soul* (New York, 1983).

7. Jacques Le Rider, *Le Cas Otto Weininger: Racines de l'antiféminisme et de l'antisémitisme* (Paris, 1982). Le Rider emphasizes the importance of Otto Weininger for our understanding of sexuality and gender. See also *Otto Weininger:*

Werk und Wirkung, ed. Jacques Le Rider and Norbert Leser (Vienna, 1984); and Nike Wagner, *Geist und Geschlecht: Karl Kraus und die Erotik der Wiener Moderne* (Frankfurt am Main, 1982).

8. *Wittgenstein's Vienna* (New York, 1973), by Allan Janik and Stephen Toulmin, has done more than any other book in English to identify the importance of Weininger and Kraus and the significance of the theme of gender for Austrian thought after the turn of the century. A recent study by Chandak Sengoopta opens up the discussion of these issues from the perspective of the history of science: *Otto Weininger: Sex, Science, and Self in Imperial Vienna* (Chicago, 2000).

9. See my *Robert Musil and the Crisis of European Culture, 1880–1942* (Berkeley, 1980).

10. The other great Austrian novelist of Musil's generation, Hermann Broch (1886–1951), was less directly interested than Musil or Doderer in portraying Vienna. On Broch's view of eros, art, and mystical ecstasy, see his "Notizen zu einer systematischen Ästhetik," in *Die unbekannte Grösse und Frühe Schriften mit den Briefen an Willa Muir* (Zurich, 1961), pp. 217–236.

11. The classic study is Dietrich Weber, *Heimito von Doderer: Studien zu seinem Romanwerk* (Munich, 1963), and a valuable recent biography is Lutz-W. Wolff, *Heimito von Doderer* (Hamburg, 1996). For an introduction in English to Doderer's fiction, see Michael Bachem, *Heimito von Doderer* (Boston, 1981); and Elizabeth Hesson's study of the origins of *The Demons, Twentieth Century Odyssey: A Study of Heimito von Doderer's Die Dämonen* (Columbia, S.C., 1982). See also Peter Demetz, *Postwar German Literature* (New York, 1970): in the wider context of German literature, Demetz calls Doderer "the legitimate heir to Thomas Mann," a writer who "created in his declining years two or three novels which constitute his indubitable contribution to world literature" (229).

12. Ludger Lütkehaus, *"Dieses wahre innere Afrika": Texte zur Entdeckung des Unbewussten vor Freud* (Frankfurt am Main, 1989), pp. 7–8. We need to see other ways of thinking about sexuality, feelings, and the unconscious rather than locking our understanding within the limits of the psychoanalytic framework.

13. See my "Schopenhauer, Austria, and the Generation of 1905," in *Central European History* 16, no. 1 (March 1983): 53–75.

14. See my "Science and Irrationalism in Freud's Vienna," in *Modern Austrian Literature* 23, no. 2 (1990): 89–97. On the generation of 1905, see *Robert Musil and the Crisis of European Culture,* pp. 13–22; and H. Stuart Hughes, *Consciousness and Society* (New York, 1958), chapter 9. For a comparative view of generations and European intellectuals in the early twentieth century, see Robert Wohl, *The Generation of 1914* (Cambridge, Mass., 1979). On the problem of generations in Austria, see Carl E. Schorske, "Generational Tension and Cultural Change: Reflections on the Case of Vienna," *Daedalus* (fall 1978): 111–122.

15. Carl E. Schorske, *Fin-de-siècle Vienna: Politics and Culture* (New York, 1980). See also William J. McGrath's *Dionysian Art and Populist Politics in Austria* (New Haven, 1974); and *Freud's Discovery of Psychoanalysis: The Politics of Hysteria* (Ithaca, 1986).

16. See Ernst Cassirer, *The Philosophy of the Enlightenment,* trans. Fritz C. A. Koelln and James P. Pettegrove (Princeton, 1951). Cassirer argues that Kant was the culmination of basic themes of the Enlightenment as it emerged in Western Europe; he also demonstrates that German culture belonged to the Enlightenment.

17. See James J. Sheehan, *German Liberalism in the Nineteenth Century* (Chicago, 1978). On Austrian liberalism, see Karl Eder, *Der Liberalismus in Altösterreich: Geisteshaltung, Politik und Kultur* (Munich, 1955); and Georg Franz, *Liberalismus: Die deutschliberale Bewegung in der Habsburgischen Monarchie* (Munich, 1955).

18. On the importance of scientific materialism in Germany after 1848, see Frederick Gregory, *Scientific Materialism in Nineteenth Century Germany* (Dordrecht, 1977).

19. See I. M. Bochenski, *Contemporary European Philosophy* (Berkeley, 1957). Bochenski was thinking of Schopenhauer, Kierkegaard, and Nietzsche not as a school of thought but as a cluster of important thinkers who did not quite fit the categories of the nineteenth century and who turned out to be important in the twentieth century. See also Georg Lukács, *The Destruction of Reason,* trans. Peter Palmer (London, 1980). Lukács, a Hungarian who was sensitized to Austrian intellectual life as a young man, emphasized the importance of irrationalism in nineteenth-century thought, but he was interested almost exclusively in the German context: Dilthey, Simmel, Spengler, Scheler, Heidegger, Jaspers, and Weber; and Lukács argued that this tradition culminated in fascism and racism. As a Marxist and a Hegelian, Lukács was conscious mainly of the reactionary political significance of irrationalism and its links with racism, and he emphasized the tendency of German academic philosophy to minimize the importance of this tradition.

20. "Philosophical irrationalism" is a useful way of referring to this cluster of thinkers, and I distinguish "irrationalism" from "antirationalism," especially "political antirationalism," a term that I use to refer to ideologies that are explicitly opposed to reason.

21. See Maurice Mandelbaum, *History, Man, and Reason* (Baltimore, 1971). Mandelbaum characterizes this cluster of thinkers (Schopenhauer, Kierkegaard, and Nietzsche) as a significant counter-tradition in nineteenth-century European thought, although he describes it as a rebellion against reason, which fits Kierkegaard much better than Schopenhauer.

22. See Joan Wallach Scott, *Gender and the Politics of History* (New York, 1988), p. 2, where Scott defines gender as "the social organization of sexual difference."

23. Weininger's ideas on gender are still largely unfamiliar outside of Austria, but they are important both for understanding Austrian intellectual life in the early twentieth century and for perspective on discussions in the social sciences today. Weininger did not entirely anticipate today's social-science definitions of gender, but his work on *Geschlecht* is more interesting and problematic than most scholars have appreciated. The full significance of Musil's ideas on sexuality and gender becomes apparent precisely in this context, while Doderer simply takes for granted the idioms that Weininger, Musil, Kraus, Freud, and others had established by the 1920s. Weininger argued that "sex" was not a simple biological given but was vari-

able from one individual instance to another and even from one historical period to another—that it was a function of education and culture.

Chapter One

1. For a general history of the Habsburg monarchy, see Robert A. Kann, *A History of the Habsburg Empire, 1526–1918* (Berkeley, 1974). On the political history of Vienna in the late nineteenth century, see John W. Boyer, *Political Radicalism in Late Imperial Vienna: Origins of the Christian Social Movement, 1848–1897* (Chicago, 1981).

2. Karl Eder, *Der Liberalismus in Altösterreich: Geisteshaltung, Politik und Kultur* (Munich, 1955), pp. 246–247 and 12.

3. See W. H. Bruford, *The German Tradition of Self-Cultivation: Bildung from Humboldt to Thomas Mann* (London, 1975); and Raymond Williams's book on the impact of this tradition on nineteenth-century English thought, *Culture and Society: 1780–1950* (New York, 1958).

4. John Stuart Mill's attempt to balance aspects of nineteenth-century liberalism can be characterized in terms of a tension between individuality and individualism. Mill's attempts to reconcile German *Bildung* with his own progressive heritage echoed the tensions within Central European liberalism.

5. Josephinism may refer to the tradition of enlightened, bureaucratic centralism as a whole or, more specifically, to the reform of the Catholic church by the Austrian state in the late eighteenth century. See Fritz Valjavec, *Der Josephinismus: Zur geistigen Entwicklung Österreichs im achtzehnten und neunzehnten Jahrhundert*, 2d ed. (Vienna, 1945); and Ferdinand Maass, *Der Josephinismus: Quellen zu seiner Geschichte in Österreich, 1760–1790*, 5 vols. (Vienna, 1951). See also A. J. Szabo, *Kaunitz and Enlightened Absolutism, 1753–1780* (Cambridge, 1994); and Charles Ingrao, "The Problem of 'Enlightened Absolutism' and the German States," *Journal of Modern History* 58, suppl. (1986): 161–180.

6. See Kant's classic formulation in "What Is Enlightenment?" (1784): "Enlightenment is man's release from his self-incurred tutelage. Tutelage is man's inability to make use of his understanding without direction from another." In Immanuel Kant, *On History*, ed. Lewis White Beck (New York, 1985), p. 3.

7. See Boyer, *Political Radicalism*, p. 23.

8. See Robert Kann, "Die niedergeschlagene Revolution von 1848 und ihr Einfluss auf die österreichische Zukunft," in *Wien und Europa zwischen den Revolutionen (1789–1848)*, ed. Reinhard Urbach (Vienna, 1978), pp. 253–260. Walter Weiss argues that the early nineteenth century was a more distinguished period of literary history than the fin de siècle. See Walter Weiss, "Thematisierung der 'Ordnung' in der österreichischen Literatur," in *Dauer im Wandel*, ed. Walter Strolz and Oscar Schatz (Vienna, 1966). Weiss emphasizes the theme of order from the age of Biedermeier to Musil and Doderer.

9. The social world of the high aristocracy remained distinct even from the high *Bürgertum*, which moved in what was known as second society. The creative intel-

lectual and cultural life of Vienna took place almost entirely within this social context of second society.

10. See *Briefe an, von und um Josephine von Wertheimstein,* ed. Robert A. Kann (Vienna, 1981); Hilde Spiel, *Fanny von Arnstein: A Daughter of the Enlightenment, 1758–1818,* trans. Christine Shuttleworth (New York, 1991); and Spiel, *Vienna's Golden Autumn, 1866–1938* (London, 1987).

11. The separation from German unification was not "complete" until Prussia defeated Austria in 1866. Austria's best minds from Grillparzer to Musil had to come to terms with the realities of Austria's national and cultural complexity in a way that was not typical of countries such as Germany, where national unity and world power were the preoccupations of many thoughtful people between 1848 and 1918.

12. Robert A. Kann, *The Multinational Monarchy: Nationalism and National Reform in the Habsburg Monarchy, 1848–1918,* 2 vols. (New York, 1950). On 1848, see R. John Rath, *The Viennese Revolution of 1848* (Austin, 1957).

13. Universal manhood suffrage was not achieved in Austria until 1907; the restricted franchise of 1873 divided Austrian voters into four curias or classes. See William A. Jenks, *The Austrian Electoral Reform of 1907* (New York, 1950); and Richard Charmatz, *Österreichs innere Geschichte von 1848 bis 1907,* 2 vols. (Leipzig, 1911).

14. The modern liberal press emerged after 1848, especially with *Die Presse,* the "voice of the liberal Viennese *Bürgertum,*" a stratum that wanted to preserve the achievements of 1848 while avoiding the dangers of social upheaval and nationalism. *Die Presse* was reconstituted in 1864 as the *Neue Freie Presse,* in support of an Austria that was "great, German, and free." See Adam Wandruszka, *Geschichte einer Zeitung* (Vienna, 1958), p. 47.

15. On the transformation of Vienna during the *Ringstrassenzeit,* see Carl E. Schorske, "The Ringstrasse, Its Critics, and the Birth of Urban Modernism," in *Fin-de-siècle Vienna,* pp. 24–115; Elisabeth Springer, *Geschichte und Kulturleben der Wiener Ringstrasse* (Wiesbaden, 1979); Hellmut Andics, *Gründerzeit: Das Schwarz-gelbe Wien bis 1867* (Vienna, 1981); and Karlheinz Rossbacher, *Literatur und Liberalismus: Zur Kultur der Ringstrassenzeit in Wien* (Vienna, 1992).

16. On the culture of the German-speaking *Bürgertum* in the middle of the nineteenth century, see James J. Sheehan, *German History, 1770–1866* (Oxford, 1991), chapter 12. On the problems of defining "bourgeois," "middle class," and "bürgerlich," see *Bourgeois Society in Nineteenth-Century Europe,* ed. Jürgen Kocka and Allan Mitchell (Oxford, 1993); and Peter Gay, *The Bourgeois Experience: Victoria to Freud,* vol. 1: *The Education of the Senses* (New York, 1984), chapter 1.

17. According to official estimates, 179 "tolerated" families lived in Vienna before 1848, but the real numbers were larger, probably as many as 10,000 people. See Robert S. Wistrich, *The Jews of Vienna in the Age of Franz Joseph* (Oxford, 1989), pp. 38–42; and Marsha Rozenblit, *The Jews of Vienna: Assimilation and Identity* (Albany, 1983).

18. See, for example, Harry Zohn, *". . . ich bin ein Sohn der deutschen Sprache nur . . .": Jüdisches Erbe in der österreichischen Literatur* (Vienna, 1986), p. 2.

19. See P. G. J. Pulzer, *The Rise of Political Anti-Semitism in Germany and Austria* (New York, 1964); and Steven Beller, *Vienna and the Jews* (Cambridge, 1989).

20. On the conflict between Catholicism and secular education in modern Austrian culture and politics, see Erika Weinzierl-Fischer, *Die österreichischen Konkordate von 1855 und 1933* (Munich, 1960).

21. See Georg Franz, *Liberalismus: Die deutschliberale Bewegung in der Habsburgischen Monarchie* (Munich, 1955); Wilhelm Wadl, *Liberalismus und soziale Frage in Österreich* (Vienna, 1987); and Lothar Höbelt, *Kornblume und Kaiseradler: Die deutsch freiheitlichen Parteien Altösterreichs, 1881–1918* (Vienna, 1993).

22. The Badeni government's attempt in 1897 to resolve the language problem for Germans and Czechs in Bohemia and Moravia—especially with respect to the language of administration—precipitated the end of effective parliamentary government in Habsburg Austria.

23. It was increasingly evident that the ideology of the unbound man had little place for women or for men who were not prepared to compete successfully on the terms of the high *Bürgertum*. The lower *Bürgertum* and the working class produced the two mass parties that eliminated liberalism as a political force, and the liberals themselves largely converted by the 1930s to German nationalism. This political predicament paralleled an intellectual crisis of the broader liberal tradition, but the two were not entirely identical.

24. On the emergence of these political camps in twentieth-century politics, see Pieter Judson, *Exclusive Revolutionaries: Liberal Politics, Social Experience, and National Identity in the Austrian Empire, 1848–1914* (Ann Arbor, 1996); John Boyer, *Culture and Political Crisis in Vienna: Christian Socialism in Power, 1897–1918* (Chicago, 1995); Helmut Gruber, *Red Vienna: Experiment in Working-Class Culture, 1919–1934* (New York, 1991); and Anson Rabinbach, *The Crisis of Austrian Socialism* (Chicago, 1983).

25. Wistrich, *The Jews of Vienna*, p. 261.

26. Schorske, *Fin-de-siècle Vienna*, p. 8.

27. Hermann Broch, *Hugo von Hofmannsthal and His Time: The European Imagination, 1860–1920*, trans. Michael P. Steinberg (Chicago, 1984), pp. 60–81. On the significance of Catholic culture for Austrian Jews, see also Michael P. Steinberg, *The Meaning of the Salzburg Festival: Austria as Theater and Ideology, 1890–1938* (Ithaca, 1990).

28. The literary impressionism of the 1890s has been characterized not only in terms of subjectivity (as an extreme form of individualism and narcissism) but also as a crisis of the coherence of the ego, that is, as a threat to the liberal ideal of individuation. See Judith Ryan, *The Vanishing Subject: Early Psychology and Literary Modernism* (Chicago, 1991).

29. Schorske, *Fin-de-siècle Vienna*, p. 6. It might be fruitful to compare the aestheticization of liberal Vienna with the withdrawal of German idealism from social reality in late nineteenth-century Germany. See Hajo Holborn, "German Idealism in the Light of Social History," in *Germany and Europe* (New York, 1971), pp. 1–31.

30. On the principal spokesman of Viennese modernism in the 1890s, see Donald G. Daviau, *Hermann Bahr* (Boston, 1985). Bahr (1863–1934) brought French ideas of art (symbolism, impressionism, modernism) and decadence to Vienna and became the principal advocate of literary and artistic modernism. Two other important incarnations of Viennese modernism and aestheticism in the 1890s were Richard Beer-Hofmann (1866–1945) and Peter Altenberg (1859–1919).

31. Schorske, *Fin-de-siècle Vienna*, pp. 5–10. Viennese modernism in the 1890s raised challenges to liberal rationalism and individualism in the work of Schnitzler, Hofmannsthal, Klimt, and Freud, but even the narcissism and cult of feeling of Young Vienna were continuous with the individualism of liberal culture.

32. See Jacques Le Rider, *Modernity and Crises of Identity*, trans. Rosemary Morris (New York, 1993). Le Rider also emphasizes the centrality of sexuality for the crisis of Viennese modernism. For Le Rider these years of Viennese modernism represent a crisis of masculine identity and a feminization of culture.

33. Schorske, *Fin-de-siècle Vienna*, p. xxvii.

34. Most liberal intellectuals in Vienna were resistant to nationalism in the late nineteenth century because of their position in a multinational state, but they were receptive to German culture after 1848, despite Austria's exclusion in 1866 from the story of German unification.

35. On the powerful impact of materialism in German culture in the second half of the nineteenth century, primarily through figures such as Ludwig Feuerbach, Karl Vogt, Jacob Moleschott, Ludwig Büchner, and Heinrich Czolbe, see Frederick Gregory, *Scientific Materialism in Nineteenth Century Germany* (Boston, 1977).

36. On the affinities between scientific materialism and historical materialism, see Friedrich Adler, *Ernst Machs Ueberwindung des mechanischen Materialismus* (Vienna, 1918).

37. The most fundamental difference between Austrian culture and the German culture of the north was the virtually total defeat of Protestantism in Bohemia and Austria by the early seventeenth century. Grillparzer characterized the impact of Catholicism at the time of the neoabsolutist Concordat with Rome in 1855: "Catholicism is responsible for everything. Give us a two-hundred-year history as a Protestant state, and we would be the most powerful and talented German people [Volksstamm]. Today all we have left is talent for music and—for the Concordat." Franz Grillparzer, *Sämtliche Werke*, ed. Peter Frank and Karl Pörnbacher (Munich, 1964), 3: 1058.

38. See Friedrich Meinecke, *The Age of German Liberation, 1795–1815*, trans. Peter Paret and Helmut Fischer (Berkeley, 1977).

39. Kant was initially well received in Austria during the 1790s. See Werner Sauer, *Österreichische Philosophie zwischen Aufklärung und Restauration: Beiträge zur Geschichte des Frühkantianismus in der Donaumonarchie* (Würzburg, 1982). Kant's philosophy was regarded in Austria as by no means un-Catholic. See K. Wotke, *Kant in Österreich vor hundert Jahren, Zeitschrift für die österreichischen Gymnasien* 54 (1903): 289 ff.

40. On the distinctive qualities of the Austrian tradition in philosophy, see William M. Johnston, *The Austrian Mind* (Berkeley, 1972); and Roger Bauer, *Ideal-*

ismus und seine Gegner in Österreich (Heidelberg, 1966). Johnston characterizes the Bohemian tradition in philosophy in terms of Leibniz and Bolzano, and Bauer emphasizes the Catholic tradition in Austrian philosophy and literature. See also Bauer, *La realité royaume de Dieu: Études sur l'originalité du théâtre viennois dans la première moitié du XIXe siècle* (Munich, 1965). In *Österreichische Philosophie zwischen Aufklärung und Restauration*, Werner Sauer challenges Bauer's emphasis on the resistance to Kant in Austria but mainly in order to point to the positive Kant reception in the late eighteenth century and to the importance of neo-Kantianism in the late nineteenth century, especially for neopositivism.

41. See also Rudolf Haller, "Wittgenstein and Austrian Philosophy," in *Questions on Wittgenstein* (London, 1988), pp. 1–26; and Kurt R. Fischer, *Philosophie aus Wien*, Geyer edition (Vienna and Salzburg, 1991). Carl von Rokitansky called Bolzano "the only truly great man in the Austrian philosophy faculties." See Rokitansky's *Selbstbiographie und Anrittsrede*, ed. Erna Lesky (Vienna, 1960), p. 46.

42. Grillparzer spoke with considerable reserve about Kant, and he characterized Hegel's philosophy as "the most monstrous prodigy of human self-conceit." See Franz Grillparzer, *Tagebücher*, passage no. 4269 (1860), in *Sämtliche Werke*, 3: 1157.

43. On German universities, see Fritz Ringer, *The Decline of the German Mandarins: The German Academic Community, 1890–1933* (Cambridge, Mass., 1969). On the comparison with French social science, see Ringer, *Fields of Knowledge: French Academic Culture in Comparative Perspective, 1890–1920* (New York, 1992). Rokitansky emphasized the uniformity and mediocrity of Austrian education all the way to the university level before 1848. See *Selbstbiographie*, p. 20. See also Alfred Rhaeticus, "Die Geschichte des Faches Philosophie an der Universität Wien, 1848–1938" (Ph.D. diss., University of Vienna, 1950).

44. On Austrian economics and legal theory, see Johnston, *The Austrian Mind*, pp. 76–98. Johnston cites Karl Pribriam's view that Vienna was "the only outpost of nominalistic reasoning east of the Rhine" (77).

45. Hans Lentze, *Die Universitätsreform des Ministers Graf Leo Thun-Hohenstein* (Vienna, 1962), pp. 22–28.

46. The classic study of materialism was written in this period: Frederick Albert Lange, *The History of Materialism*, 3 vols. (New York, 1974, reprint of the 1879–81 English translation from the German).

47. Auguste Comte, *The Essential Comte: Selected from Cours de Philosophie Positive*, trans. Margaret Clarke (New York, 1974), pp. 19–20. Frank Manuel notes that "Comte was ordinarily classified as the ultimate fulfillment of the eighteenth-century ideal of materialism" (*Prophets of Paris* [New York, 1962], p. 264). To be sure, his emotional life and the later development of his religious ideas displayed the bizarre tendency of nineteenth-century positivists and materialists to have difficulty being faithful to their own rationalist and postreligious values.

48. Social science hardly existed at all in the late nineteenth century in Austria, except in connection with the law school and with the emergence of modern economics. See the approach of Josef Popper-Lynkeus to social science and reform in In-

grid Belke, *Die sozialreformerischen Ideen von Josef Popper-Lynkeus, 1838–1921* (Tübingen, 1978).

49. Ludwig Büchner, *Kraft und Stoff* (Frankfurt am Main, 1858), pp. v–vi. His brother was the German playwright Georg Büchner.

50. Friedrich Jodl (1849–1914), who arrived from Germany to become one of the leading figures in philosophy at Vienna, was the editor of the standard edition of Feuerbach's works, which appeared in thirteen volumes between 1903 and 1911. On Jodl's progressive ideas and his role in the Austrian Ethical Society, see Wilhelm Börner, *Friedrich Jodl* (Stuttgart, 1911); and Margarete Jodl, *Friedrich Jodl: Sein Leben und Wirken* (Stuttgart, 1920).

51. Erna Lesky, *The Vienna Medical School of the 19th Century*, trans. L. Williams and I. S. Levij (Baltimore, 1976), p. 360. See also Julius Braunthal, *Victor und Friedrich Adler: Zwei Generationen Arbeiterbewegung* (Vienna, 1965).

52. Frank J. Sulloway, *Freud, Biologist of the Mind: Beyond the Psychoanalytic Legend* (New York, 1979).

53. See Daniel Gasman, *The Scientific Origins of National Socialism: Social Darwinism in Ernst Haeckel and the German Monist League* (New York, 1971).

54. *The Letters of Sigmund Freud to Eduard Silberstein, 1871–1881*, intro. by Walter Boehlich, trans. Arnold J. Pomerans (Cambridge, Mass., 1990), p. 104. Freud also mentioned Brentano's approval of Auguste Comte. See also William J. McGrath, *Freud's Discovery of Psychoanalysis: The Politics of Hysteria* (Ithaca, 1986): "Brentano taught Freud that the only truly scientific approach to it [the mind-body, or mind-brain, problem] involved both inner and psychological investigation and external physiological and biological research" (126).

55. See Friedrich Stadler, *Vom Positivismus zur "Wissenschaftlichen Weltauffassung": Am Beispiel der Wirkungsgeschichte von Ernst Mach in Österreich von 1895 bis 1934* (Vienna, 1982).

56. See Ernst Mach, *The Analysis of Sensations and the Relation of the Physical to the Psychical*, trans. C. M. Williams (New York, 1959). Regarding Mach's impact on the writers of Vienna in the 1890s and after, see Judith Ryan, "Die andere Psychologie: Ernst Mach und die Folgen," in *Österreichische Gegenwart: Die moderne Literatur und ihr Verhältnis zur Tradition*, ed. Wolfgang Paulsen (Munich, 1980), pp. 11–24.

57. In *The Transformation of Positivism: Alexius Meinong and European Thought, 1880–1920* (Berkeley, 1980), David Lindenfeld challenges the notion that a single Austrian philosophical tradition flows from Leibniz to Bolzano to Brentano to Meinong.

58. Not only did Brentano and Mach have their influence primarily in the twentieth century, but neither was a typical product of liberal Vienna. Brentano was trained in Germany and came to Vienna for his productive years in the 1870s; although Mach studied in Vienna, he did most of his work in Prague and returned to Vienna only in the last years of his career in 1895.

59. On the whole, writing about Austrian philosophy aims at the twentieth century (see especially Rudolf Haller, *Questions on Wittgenstein* [London, 1988])

rather than understanding the mix of influences that formed the late nineteenth-century context. What is most apparent about Brentano in the nineteenth-century context was that he did not contrast philosophical method to scientific method; that is, for Brentano as for Wittgenstein in the *Tractatus*, philosophy used the same methods as the exact natural sciences. On Brentano's significance for Austrian philosophy, see Barry Smith, *Austrian Philosophy: The Legacy of Franz Brentano* (Chicago, 1994).

60. Scientific materialists were increasingly drawn in the direction of the reductions of sex and race and to forms of biologism that threatened the individualistic, emancipatory vision of the liberal tradition.

61. Stefan Jonsson's account of modern subjectivity in *Robert Musil and the History of Modern Identity* (Durham, N.C., 2000) emphasizes German and French rather than Austrian thinkers.

62. Søren Kierkegaard was discovered in Vienna after the turn of the century, particularly through Rudolf Kassner, while Eduard von Hartmann's work on the unconscious often introduced Austrians to Schopenhauer's work. See Georg Lukács, *Die Seele und die Formen: Essays* (Berlin, 1911); and Eduard von Hartmann, *Philosophy of the Unconscious*, trans. William Chatterton Coupland (London, 1950). Even in the wake of existentialism, this tradition is often minimized to an astonishing degree: Stanley Rosen wrote an entire book on nihilism in which he mentioned Schopenhauer only once (*Nihilism* [New Haven, 1968], p. 72), while William Barrett's seminal book on existentialism, *Irrational Man* (New York, 1958), avoids mentioning Schopenhauer altogether.

63. Regarding Austria's indigenous irrationalism, see Franz Grillparzer in *Studien*, 1: 582 of the Schreyvogl edition (Grillparzers Werke in zwei Bänden, ed. Friedrich Schreyvogl): "Drive, inclination, and the instinctual are just as divine as reason."

64. Arthur Schopenhauer, *The World as Will and Representation*, trans. E. F. J. Payne (New York, 1966). On the history of the idea of the unconscious, see *"Dieses wahre innere Afrika": Texte zur Entdeckung des Unbewussten vor Freud*, ed. Ludger Lütkehaus (Frankfurt am Main, 1989); Henri Ellenberger, *The Discovery of the Unconscious: The History and Evolution of Dynamic Psychiatry* (New York, 1970); and Lancelot Law Whyte, *The Unconscious before Freud* (New York, 1960).

65. See my "Schopenhauer, Austria, and the Generation of 1905," in *Central European History* 26 (March 1983): 53–75. Schopenhauer emphasized the stupidity and aggression of the Will, especially as it represents itself in the human body. On the revolutionary significance of Schopenhauer's emphasis on the body before Nietzsche and Freud and his inversion of Descartes's view, see Harald Schöndorf, *Der Leib im Denken Schopenhauers und Fichtes* (Munich, 1982); and Walter Schulz, *Philosophie in der veränderten Welt* (Pfullingen, 1972).

66. See, for example, Emrich du Mont, *Der Fortschritt im Lichte der Lehren Schopenhauer's und Darwin's* (Leipzig, 1876). Du Mont contrasted the progress of civilization (which he associated with the progress of the empirical sciences and the power of human beings over nature) with a "second progress," which is "infinitely slow" and which he characterized as the "increase [Vermehrung] of the power of the

human being in the struggle against his own nature" (187). For du Mont, Schopenhauer and Darwin were the two principal nineteenth-century minds to challenge conventional ideas about progress.

67. Schopenhauer was the key figure in pre-Freudian discussions of the unconscious, and like Freud, he emphasized the mindless drives of sexuality and survival in understanding human behavior.

68. Schopenhauer was not only the intellectual father of the young Nietzsche but also the philosopher of modernism in the arts and the basis for Wagner's thinking about his own music after 1848. For Schopenhauer, genius was "the capacity to remain in a state of pure perception, to lose oneself in perception, to remove from the service of the will the knowledge which originally existed only for this service." See Schopenhauer, *The World as Will and Representation*, 1: 185. The genius was marked by the capacity to "exist only as pure subject" and to forget the individuality, which is in the service of the will (178). Music played a special role in Schopenhauer's understanding of human existence, because music, "like the world, immediately objectifies the will" (265); music ignores the phenomenal world and the illusion of individuation to offer "a copy of the will itself" (257).

69. See William J. McGrath, *Dionysian Art and Populist Politics in Austria* (New Haven, 1974).

70. Houston Stewart Chamberlain, *Foundations of the Nineteenth Century*, trans. John Lees, intro. by George L. Mosse, 2 vols. (New York, 1968).

71. Regarding this German blend of music, spirituality, and anti-Semitic nationalism, see Geoffrey G. Field, *Evangelist of Race: The German Vision of Houston Stewart Chamberlain* (New York, 1981). See also Fritz Stern, *The Politics of Cultural Despair: A Study in the Rise of Germanic Ideology* (Berkeley, 1961); and George L. Mosse, *The Crisis of German Ideology: Intellectual Origins of the Third Reich* (New York, 1964).

72. See Nietzsche's formulations in the early pages of *Schopenhauer as Educator*, trans. James W. Hillesheim and Malcolm Simpson (South Bend, Ind., 1965), p. 5: "[I]t is a painful and dangerous undertaking to dig down into oneself in this way and to descend violently and directly into the shaft of one's being. How easily he could injure himself doing this, so that no doctor could cure him." And on the same page: "[F]or your true being does not lie hidden deep inside you but immeasurably high above you, or at least above what you usually consider to be your ego."

73. Friedrich Nietzsche, *Beyond Good and Evil*, trans. Walter Kaufmann (New York, 1996), p. 100. Nietzsche's awareness of the personal basis of philosophy led him to an impious view of philosophy and academic rationalism: "Gradually it has become clear to me what every great philosophy so far has been: namely, the personal confession of its author and a kind of involuntary and unconscious memoir; also that the moral (or immoral) intentions in every philosophy constituted the real germ of life from which the whole plant had grown." Nietzsche, *Beyond Good and Evil*, p. 13.

74. Friedrich Nietzsche, *The Gay Science*, trans. Walter Kaufmann (New York, 1974), p. 299. This formulation turns the defeat of an individualism based on con-

scious reason into the victory of a new form of individualism. It is also a very different view of the unconscious from Freud's.

75. See George J. Stack, *Lange and Nietzsche* (Berlin, 1983).

76. Nietzsche, *Schopenhauer as Educator*, pp. 11 and 43.

77. See Allan S. Janik, "Schopenhauer and the Early Wittgenstein," in *Philosophical Studies* 15 (1966): 76–95; and Kurt R. Fischer, "Nietzsche und der Wiener Kreis," in his *Philosophie aus Wien* (Vienna, 1991), pp. 170–182.

78. On Klimt's challenge to the Enlightenment tradition of the Josephinist bureaucracy and the liberal elite, see Schorske, "Gustav Klimt: Painting and the Crisis of the Liberal Ego," in *Fin-de-siècle Vienna*, pp. 208–278.

79. See Werner Wolke, *Hugo von Hofmannsthal* (Hamburg, 1967), p. 88.

80. Rudolf Kassner, *Sämtliche Werke*, 1: 477. Kassner invited a less literal reading of Nietzsche's *Übermensch* or of Schopenhauer's denial of the will to live.

81. There are interesting implications here for our understanding of Freud's relationship to Nietzsche. Freud did his best to discount the significance of Nietzsche's influence; yet McGrath has shown the influence of the early Nietzsche on Freud, and Lorin Anderson and others have demonstrated Nietzsche's importance for the late Freud. See Lorin Anderson, "Freud, Nietzsche," in *Salmagundi* 47–48 (1980): 3–29; and Bruce Mazlish, "Freud and Nietzsche," in *Psychoanalytic Review* 55, no. 3 (1968): 360–375. It does seem plausible, however, that during the 1890s, when he was inventing psychoanalysis, Freud was unacquainted with Nietzsche's later works, which seem so close to Freud's ideas.

82. Although her date of birth would seem to locate Rosa Mayreder (1858–1938) firmly in Freud's generation, her intellectual life and cultural production, as well as the peculiar conditions that shaped intellectual work for women, place her in the generation of 1905.

83. Peter Gay, *Weimar Culture* (New York, 1968), p. 7.

84. Edward Timms, *Karl Kraus: Apocalyptic Satirist* (New Haven, 1986), p. 28. Jacques Le Rider argues in *Modernity and Crises of Identity* that Viennese modernism must be understood in terms of the triangle of sexuality, Jewishness, and identity. See also Nike Wagner, *Geist und Geschlecht: Karl Kraus und die Erotik der Wiener Moderne* (Frankfurt am Main, 1982), p. 39: "Im 'Weib' haben die ikonographische und der literarische Symbolismus und Jugendstil ihr Hauptthema gefunden." On the fascination of the themes of sexuality and femininity for the male writers of liberal Vienna, see Rossbacher, *Literatur und Liberalismus*, pp. 319 ff.

85. See Thomas Laqueur, *Making Sex: Body and Gender from the Greeks to Freud* (Cambridge, Mass., 1990). Laqueur is particularly interested in the decision of nineteenth-century scientists and physicians to emphasize the differences between men and women rather than the similarities.

86. See Joan Wallach Scott's discussion of the polarity of gender in "Gender: A Useful Category . . ." in *Gender and the Politics of History* (New York, 1988), p. 7:

> Fixed oppositions conceal the heterogeneity of either category, the extent to which terms presented as oppositional are interdependent—that is, derive their meaning from internally established contrast rather than from some inherent or pure an-

tithesis. Furthermore, the interdependence is usually hierarchical, with one term dominant, prior, and visible, the opposite subordinate, secondary, and often absent or invisible. Yet precisely through this arrangement, the second term is present and central because required for the definition of the first.

Otto Weininger is both an example of the problem of these fixed oppositions and an attempt to make it conscious and address it. Most discussions of Weininger have not sufficiently emphasized the problems raised by translation.

87. On male projection and stereotypes, see Sander L. Gilman, "Male Stereotypes of Female Sexuality in *Fin-de-siècle* Vienna," in *Difference and Pathology: Stereotypes of Sexuality, Race, and Madness* (Ithaca, 1985), pp. 37–58.

88. See Pricilla Smith Robertson, *An Experience of Women: Pattern and Change in Nineteenth-Century Europe* (Philadelphia, 1982); and George L. Mosse, *Nationalism and Sexuality: Middle-Class Morality and Sexual Norms in Modern Europe* (Madison, 1985).

89. Steven Marcus, *The Other Victorians: A Study of Sexuality and Pornography in Mid-Nineteenth-Century England* (New York, 1974). Marcus cites William Acton: "I should say that the majority of women (happily for them) are not very much troubled with sexual feeling of any kind" (31). In *The Education of the Senses,* see Peter Gay's critique of the view that women in the nineteenth century were not very sexual. See also Michel Foucault's critique of "the repressive hypothesis" in *The History of Sexuality, Vol. 1: An Introduction,* trans. Robert Hurley (New York, 1978).

90. Women were first permitted to attend lectures as auditors in 1878. The study of law, the customary path to political power, was not open to women until 1919, a year after women were allowed to vote. See Richard Meister, *Geschichte der Wiener Universität* (Vienna, 1934), pp. 58–62.

91. See Ute Frevert, *Women in German History: From Bourgeois Emancipation to Sexual Liberation,* trans. Stuart McKinnon-Evans (Oxford, 1989); and *Durch Erkenntnis zu Freiheit und Glück. . .,"* ed. Waltraud Heindl and Marina Tichy (Vienna, 1900), p. 9. Austrian scholars still depend heavily on work that deals with Germany in this period, and Eve Nyaradi Dvorak argues that scholarly developments in women's studies over the past two or three decades have hardly touched the study of Austrian women. See *Austrian Women in the Nineteenth and Twentieth Centuries,* ed. David Good, Margarete Grandner, and Mary Jo Maynes (Providence, 1996), p. xi. On German feminism, see Ann Taylor Allen, *Feminism and Motherhood in Germany, 1800–1914* (New Brunswick, N.J., 1991). Liberal, *bürgerlich* culture emphasized notions of the free personality and the professions that were strongly oriented to a certain kind of masculine type and an emphasis on a particular style of rationalism. Only a few (whether men or women) had thought of applying these values to women before 1900. On the masculine coding of liberal individualism, see Brigitte Spreitzer, *TEXTUREN: Die österreichische Moderne der Frauen* (Vienna, 1999).

92. Few recall that Freud's early work on neurosis focused on his attempts to help married couples deal with the neurotic consequences of coitus interruptus. The realities of sexual and family life should be kept in mind before judging values too ahistorically. In the 1890s, the views of intellectuals about sexuality were bounded

by fears of syphilis and prejudices about homosexuality and marriage. On Freud's views in the 1890s, see *The Complete Letters of Sigmund Freud to Wilhelm Fliess, 1887–1904*, trans. and ed. Jeffrey Moussaieff Masson (Cambridge, Mass., 1985).

93. Rossbacher, *Literatur und Liberalismus*, pp. 322–323.

94. Ernest Jones, *The Life and Work of Sigmund Freud* (New York, 1953), 1: 176. The idea of a man concerning himself with running a household was apparently inconceivable to a member of the Austrian liberal *Bürgertum* in the late nineteenth century. "In [Mill's] whole presentation it never emerges that women are different beings—we will not say lesser, rather the opposite from men. He finds the suppression of women an analogy to that of negroes. Any girl, even without a suffrage or legal competence, whose hand a man kisses and for whose love he is prepared to dare all, could have set him right." The main point for Freud, at the age of twenty-seven, seems to have been that women do not belong in the harsh, competitive world of earning a livelihood. See John Stuart Mill, *Ueber Frauenemancipation; Plato; Arbeiterfrage; Socialismus*, trans. Siegmund Freud (Leipzig, 1880).

95. P. J. Möbius, *Über den physiologischen Schwachsinn des Weibes* (Halle, 1905), p. 5. For Möbius, *Schwachsinn* meant less than normal intelligence, and he argued that the woman was in virtually all respects inferior in capacity to the man.

96. See Marianne Hainisch, "Die Geschichte der Frauenbewegung in Österreich," in *Handbuch der Frauenbewegung*, ed. Helene Lange und Gertraud Bäumer, part 1: *Die Geschichte der Frauenbewegung in den Kulturländern* (Berlin, 1901), pp. 167–188. On elementary and secondary education and teachers, see James C. Albisetti, *Schooling German Girls and Women* (Princeton, 1988).

97. See Harriet Anderson, *Utopian Feminism: Women's Movements in Fin-de-siècle Vienna* (New Haven, 1992). The word *Feministin* was not widely used until 1914; before that the word *Feminist* had referred to men who supported the movement (see pp. 9–10).

98. Rossbacher, *Literatur und Liberalismus*, p. 366. On the place of women in scholarship on Viennese modernism, see Lisa Fischer, "Weibliche Kreativität—Oder warum assoziieren Männer Fäden mit Spinnen?" in *Die Wiener Jahrhundertwende*, ed. Jürgen Nautz and Richard Vahrenkamp (Vienna, 1993), pp. 144–158.

99. See Bram Dijkstra, *Idols of Perversity: Fantasies of Feminine Evil in Fin-de-siècle Culture* (New York, 1986).

100. Paul Robinson, *The Modernization of Sex: Havelock Ellis, Alfred Kinsey, William Masters and Virginia Johnson* (New York, 1976). Robinson finds in the years between 1890 and 1910 "a major transformation in sexuality," and he points out that the pioneer modernists—Edward Carpenter, Albert Moll, Auguste Forel, Ivan Bloch, and Magnus Hirschfield—are "now largely forgotten" (2). Although Freud is the best-remembered figure from this period, Robinson argues that it was Havelock Ellis who contributed most to a distinctively modern sexual ethos, which was characterized by new attitudes toward female sexuality and toward "apparently deviant forms of sexuality" (3). For a different, partly Foucauldian, view of these questions, see Lawrence Birken, *Consuming Desire: Sexual Science and the Emergence of a Culture of Abundance, 1871–1914* (Ithaca, 1988). See *The History of Sexuality*, vol. 1, for Foucault's account of the nineteenth century in terms of "the

transformation of sex into discourse" (61) and "the production of sexuality rather than the repression of sex" (114).

101. Schorske, *Fin-de-siècle Vienna*, pp. 15, 212.

102. Michael Worbs, *Nervenkunst: Literatur und Psychoanalyse im Wien der Jahrhundertwende* (Frankfurt am Main, 1983), p. 267.

103. Josef Breuer and Sigmund Freud, *Studies in Hysteria* in *The Standard Edition*, vol. 2. Freud did not work out his view of gender until the First World War. On the asymmetry of Freud's view of gender, see Judith Van Herik, *Freud on Femininity and Faith* (Berkeley, 1982). I make no attempt here to offer an independent history of what sexuality is. See Jeffrey Weeks, *Sexuality* (New York, 1986): a history of sexuality is "a history without a proper subject" (21); and Michel Foucault's discussion of sexuality as "a historical construct" in *A History of Sexuality*, p. 105.

104. Freud was not well known even in Vienna before 1900; the Wednesday night meetings and the psychoanalytic movement came only later.

105. See Sander L. Gilman, *The Jew's Body* (London, 1991), p. 133.

CHAPTER TWO

1. Otto Weininger, *Geschlecht und Charakter: Eine prinzipielle Untersuchung* (Munich, 1980), pp. v–xi.

2. On the connections in this period (especially in the minds of Jewish intellectuals and scientists) between the female and the male Jew, see Sander L. Gilman, *Freud, Race, and Gender* (Princeton, 1993). See also Daniel Boyarin, *Unheroic Conduct: The Rise of Heterosexuality and the Invention of the Jewish Man* (Berkeley, 1997).

3. See Jacques Le Rider, *Modernity and Crises of Identity: Culture and Society in Fin-de-Siècle Vienna*, trans. Rosemary Morris (New York, 1993), p. 166; Le Rider, *Le Cas Otto Weininger: Racines de l'antiféminisme et de l'antisémitisme* (Paris, 1982); and Sander L. Gilman, *The Jew's Body* (New York, 1991), p. 133.

4. See Peter Gay, *Freud, Jews, and Other Germans* (London, 1978), p. 196. See also Hans Mayer, *Aussenseiter* (Frankfurt am Main, 1975), pp. 118–126. Barbara Hyams and Nancy A. Harrowitz describe Weininger's book as "an apotheosis of misogyny that is exacerbated by a penultimate chapter asserting that Jewish male behavior is essentially effeminate." See their "A Critical Introduction to the History of Weininger Reception," in *Jews and Gender: Responses to Otto Weininger* (Philadelphia, 1995), p. 3.

5. Robert Calasso, "Der Philosoph und die 'Kokotte,'" in Weininger, *Geschlecht und Charakter, Anhang*, p. 667. The *Anhang* includes diaries and letters, as well as essays by Annegret Stopczyk, Gisela Dischner, and Robert Calasso.

6. See, for example, Robert S. Wistrich, *The Jews of Vienna in the Age of Franz Joseph* (Oxford, 1990), p. 532; and Hyams and Harrowitz, "A Critical Introduction," in *Jews and Gender*, pp. 5–6.

7. Calasso, "Der Philosoph," in *Geschlecht und Charakter, Anhang*, p. 662.

8. On Weininger's attempt to deconstruct "the concepts 'masculine' and 'feminine,'" see Harriet Anderson, *Utopian Feminism: Women's Movements in Fin-de-siècle Vienna* (New Haven, 1992), p. 5. Weininger was a peculiar but important indicator of how gender was constructed and perceived in Austria around 1900.

9. On the location of Weininger's prejudices within the intellectual world of his time, see Chandak Sengoopta, *Otto Weininger: Sex, Science, and Self in Imperial Vienna* (Chicago, 2000), p. 159: "If, indeed, a historian is expected to condemn past prejudices and apportion blame for them, then I would have to condemn almost the entire *fin-de-siècle* Viennese intelligentsia *including* Otto Weininger, but I would refuse to condemn him alone."

10. Hyams and Harrowitz argue that Weininger's "stance may well have involved homoerotic feelings and rebellion against his family's expectation that he would marry and have a family of his own. Weininger, the apostate Jew and anti-family man, used his constructions of both Jew and gender to exacerbate the crisis of identity felt throughout the culture as a whole." See "A Critical Introduction," in *Jews and Gender*, p. 5. Gilman calls Weininger a "self-hating Jew" and "a repressed homosexual" (*The Jew's Body*, p. 133). Le Rider's defense of Weininger is that his book was not odious but pathetic (*Le Cas*, p. 241). Critics rarely point out that Weininger's views on sexuality and the family were especially appalling to National Socialists.

11. Abrahamsen's book also includes important sources, particularly letters from Freud and from Weininger's sister.

12. See the articles of Karl Kraus and August Strindberg in Kraus's journal, *Die Fackel [The Torch]*, between 1903 and 1907. *Die Fackel* has been reprinted by Kösel Verlag (Munich, 1968–1976) and by Zweitausendeins (Frankfurt, 1977; index by Franz Ögg). See also Hermann Swoboda, *Otto Weiningers Tod*, 2d ed. (Vienna, 1923); Emil Lucka, *Otto Weininger: Sein Werk und seine Persönlichkeit* (Vienna, 1905); Moriz Rappaport, introduction to Otto Weininger, *Über die letzten Dinge* (Vienna, 1907); and Carl Dallago, *Otto Weininger und sein Werk* (Innsbruck, 1912).

13. *Gedanken über Geschlechtsprobleme von Otto Weininger*, ed. Robert Saudek (Berlin, 1907). Saudek (1880–1935) was exactly Weininger's age. It is not clear that these two interpretations exclude each other.

14. Before the First World War, Grete Meisel-Hess, Rosa Mayreder, and Charlotte Perkins Gilman all discussed Weininger's work in relation to the women's movement. See Charlotte Perkins Gilman, "Review of Dr. Weininger's Sex and Character," in *The Critic* 12 (1906): 414–417. In 1912, Bruno Sturm wrote a somewhat sympathetic response to Weininger, although as "a contribution to positivism" and "to a more optimistic worldview." See *Gegen Weininger: Ein Versuch zur Lösung des Moralproblems* (Vienna, 1912). Particularly interesting from the interwar years are two books on Weininger's ethics and his relationship to Kant: Paul Biro, *Die Sittlichkeitsmetaphysik Otto Weiningers: Eine geistesgeschichtliche Studie* (Vienna, 1927); and Leopold Thaler, *Weiningers Weltanschauung im Lichte der kantischen Lehre* (Vienna, 1935). See also Georg Klaren, *Otto Weininger: Der Mensch sein Werk und sein Leben* (Vienna, 1924).

15. Sengoopta, *Otto Weininger*, p. 147. See Charlotte Perkins Gilman, "Review of Dr. Weininger's Sex and Character."

16. See Allan Janik, "Viennese Culture and the Jewish Self-Hatred Hypothesis: A Critique," in *Jews, Antisemitism and Culture in Vienna*, ed. Ivar Oxaal, Michael Pollak, and Gerhard Botz (New York, 1987), pp. 75–88. On Theodor Lessing, see Lawrence Baron, "Theodor Lessing: Between Jewish Self-Hatred and Zionism," *Leo Baeck Institute Yearbook*, 26 (London, 1981), pp. 323–340. In his preface to the German edition of his biography of Weininger, Le Rider points to the openness of discussion of Weininger's misogyny in the scholarship and the tendency to handle his anti-Semitism more awkwardly. See Le Rider, *Der Fall Otto Weininger: Wurzeln des Antifeminismus und Antisemitismus*, trans. Dieter Hornig (Vienna, 1985), p. 9. See also Kurt Lewin, "Self-Hatred among Jews" (1941), in *Resolving Social Conflicts* (New York, 1948), pp. 186–200; André Spire, *Quelques Juifs* (Paris, 1913); and Joshua Sobol, *The Soul of a Jew: The Death of Otto Weininger: Weininger's Last Night*, trans. Betsy Rosenberg and Miriam Schlesinger (Tel Aviv, n.d.).

17. From the scholarship of the postwar period, see Hans Kohn's thoughtful account of Weininger in *Karl Kraus. Arthur Schnitzler. Otto Weininger* (Tübingen, 1962) and the brief discussions of Weininger by Hans Mayer and Peter Gay.

18. Jacques Le Rider and Norbert Leser, *Otto Weininger: Werk und Wirkung* (Vienna, 1984). The reprinting of *Geschlecht und Charakter* in 1980 included essays by Annegret Stopczyk, Gisela Dischner, and Robert Calasso.

19. See Otto Weininger, *Eros und Psyche: Studien und Briefe, 1899–1902*, ed. Hannelore Rodlauer (Vienna, 1990). The early draft of Weininger's dissertation, which is less than forty of the more than two hundred pages in this volume (143–180), was discovered in the Österreichische Akademie der Wissenschaft.

20. See Le Rider, *Le Cas*, pp. 18–19. Le Rider discusses Weininger's comments about homosexuality in his correspondence with Swoboda and speculates about the nature of Weininger's relationship with Artur Gerber. Weininger is often described as a homosexual but usually without much attempt at citation or clarification. See, for example, Ray Monk, *Ludwig Wittgenstein: The Duty of Genius* (New York, 1990), p. 23. Monk also assumes that Weininger constructed his theory to justify his anti-Semitism and his misogyny. In "'The Otto Weininger Case' Revisited" (*Jews and Gender*, pp. 24–25), Le Rider distances himself from the "diagnostic-system" critics have used to interpret Kafka's homosexuality. Instead, Le Rider wants "to examine the deconstruction of the masculine that seems so bound up with the idea of modernity itself." See also John E. Toews, "Refashioning the Masculine Subject in Early Modernism: Narrations of Self-Dissolution and Self-Construction in Psychoanalysis and Literature, 1900–1914," in *MODERNISM/modernity* 4, no. 1 (1997): 31–67.

21. His son Richard later described him as "a Cellini of his times." See Richard Weininger, *Exciting Years* (Hicksville, N.Y., 1978), p. 16.

22. For the early period of Weininger's life, see Rappaport's introduction to *Otto Weininger, Über die letzten Dinge* (Vienna, 1907); and Abrahamsen's *The Mind and Death of a Genius*.

23. Weininger later added Norwegian and Italian on his travels.

24. See Rodlauer, "Fragmente aus Weiningers Bildungsgeschichte," in *Eros und Psyche*, pp. 11–51. Weininger attended a wide range of lectures at the University of

Vienna: on the history of philosophy with Friedrich Jodl, Laurenz Müllner, Alois Höfler, and Adolf Stöhr but also on the physical sciences, mathematics, botany, and zoology, as well as medicine (including Sigmund Exner, Heinrich Obersteiner, Richard von Krafft-Ebing, and Julius von Wagner-Jauregg). Medicine was the Austrian version of the "human sciences": *Naturwissenschaft* not *Geisteswissenschaft*.

25. Rodlauer, *Eros und Psyche*, pp. 17–30.

26. Aside from Weininger's own comments, the most important sources for his intellectual development are two books by his friends, Emil Lucka and Hermann Swoboda.

27. See Richard Avenarius, *Kritik der reinen Erfahrung* (Leipzig, 1888–1890). Avenarius was a Swiss philosopher whose version of empiricism was close to Mach's and was often identified with it.

28. See Hermann Swoboda, *Die gemeinnützige Forschung und der eigennützige Forscher: Antwort auf die von Wilhelm Fliess gegen Otto Weininger und mich erhobenen Beschuldigungen* (Vienna, 1906). It is difficult to avoid the impression that the influence of Fliess on Weininger has been exaggerated because of the significance that Freud later acquired. See Wilhelm Fliess, *Der Ablauf des Lebens* (Leipzig and Vienna, 1906), p. 583: "Dass wirklich über ihn [Freud] meine Ideen zu Weininger und Swoboda gelangt seien, hat er mir auf ein eindringendes Befragen selbst zugestanden." In short, Fliess had to drag it out of Freud [that Fliess's ideas reached Weininger through Freud and Swoboda], whose account is a bit different. Swoboda points out that Fliess had already published on bisexuality at the time. This already murky story is often recast to read that Weininger took Freud's ideas about bisexuality.

29. See Robert D. Richardson, Jr., *Emerson: The Mind on Fire* (Berkeley, 1995), p. 239.

30. Freud later commented on Weininger in his case study of little Hans:

> The castration complex is the deepest unconscious root of anti-semitism; for even in the nursery little boys hear that a Jew has something cut off his penis—a piece of his penis, they think—and this gives them a right to despise Jews. And there is no stronger unconscious root for the sense of superiority over women. Weininger (the young philosopher who, highly gifted but sexually deranged, committed suicide after producing his remarkable book, *Geschlecht und Charakter* [1903]), in a chapter that attracted much attention, treated Jews and women with equal hostility and overwhelmed them with the same insults. Being a neurotic, Weininger was completely under the sway of his infantile complexes; and from that standpoint what is common to Jews and women is their relation to the castration complex.

Sigmund Freud, "Analysis of a Phobia in a Five-Year-Old Boy" (1909), in *Standard Edition*, 10: 36n.

31. Otto Weininger, *Über die letzten Dinge* (Munich, 1980).

32. See Thomas E. Willey, *Back to Kant: The Revival of Kantianism in German Social and Historical Thought, 1860–1914* (Detroit, 1978); and Klaus Christian Köhnke, *The Rise of Neo-Kantianism: German Academic Philosophy between Idealism and Positivism* (Cambridge, 1991). See Weininger in a letter to Swoboda in

Eros und Psyche, p. 121: "Everything that Avenarius and Mach say, Kant already knew. People have no idea of the things that philosophy takes up just beyond their horizon."

33. Weininger discussed the title of his book with Kassner and initially accepted Kassner's suggestion of "Eros und Psyche." See Rodlauer, *Eros und Psyche,* p. 38. Weininger cites Kassner's translation of Aristophanes' speech in Plato's *Symposium* ("Eros und Psyche," in *Eros und Psyche,* p. 171).

34. Weininger's readings of Kant were also shaped by a post-Nietzschean style of intellectual heroism. Robert Reininger, who lectured on philosophical irrationalism when Weininger was a student at the University of Vienna, wrote a book on Nietzsche after the First World War in which he emphasized the similarities between Kant and Nietzsche. Weininger was almost certainly attuned to this connection, despite his and Nietzsche's emphasis on the differences. See Robert Reininger, *Friedrich Nietzsches Kampf um den Sinn des Lebens* (Vienna, 1922).

35. See Sander L. Gilman, *The Case of Sigmund Freud: Medicine and Identity at the Fin de Siècle* (Baltimore, 1993), pp. 79 ff., on conversion as a form of madness, and p. 106: on Weininger as an instance of "the neurotic who was both convert and homosexual."

36. Swoboda argues in *Otto Weiningers Tod* (p. 4) that the book developed in three stages: "a [natural] scientific, a philosophical, and an antifeminist."

37. Weininger, *Über die letzten Dinge,* p. 177.

38. Artur Gerber, "Ecce Homo!" in Otto Weininger, *Taschenbuch und Briefe an einen Freund* (Leipzig, 1919), p. 17.

39. Gerber, "Ecce Homo!" p. 19.

40. Rappaport, in Weininger, *Über die letzten Dinge,* p. xviii.

41. He was found dying from a chest wound in his room on October 4 and pronounced dead at the General Hospital in Vienna at 6:00 A.M. See Le Rider, *Le Cas,* p. 37.

42. Even Gerber emphasized the absence of any sort of recognition for Weininger's book as a reason for his suicide, although Gerber's own evidence argues differently. But Weininger apparently was troubled by the criticisms of Möbius, a more conventional misogynist. See *Le Cas,* p. 36. Möbius rejected everything essential to Weininger's argument but called it plagiarism. Möbius especially disliked Weininger's claim that intermediate sexual forms are normal. P. J. Möbius, *Geschlecht und Unbescheidenheit* (Halle, 1907).

43. Swoboda, *Otto Weiningers Tod,* p. 3.

44. Swoboda, *Otto Weiningers Tod,* pp. 73–74; and Dallago, *Otto Weininger und sein Werk.* Ludwig Wittgenstein, who was then fourteen, assisted at the burial. See Le Rider, *Le Cas,* p. 37.

45. Swoboda, *Otto Weiningers Tod,* p. 80.

46. The posthumous reception of Weininger often transformed him into a quite conventional misogynist, and he was welcomed by fascist intellectuals in Germany and Italy and even perceived at times as an advocate of reproduction. Particularly

striking was Weininger's impact on the generation of 1905 in Italy. See Alberto Cavaglion and Michel David, "Weininger und die italienische Kultur," in Le Rider and Leser, *Otto Weininger*, pp. 37–49. See also Barbara Hyams, "Weininger and Nazi Ideology," in *Jews and Gender*, pp. 155–168.

47. Weininger, *Geschlecht und Charakter*, p. 342. See Karl Kraus, "Weib, Phantasie" (1909), in *Beim Wort Genommen* (Munich, 1955), p. 48: "The division of the human race into two parts has not yet been acknowledged by science."

48. Weininger, *Geschlecht und Charakter*, pp. ix–x.

49. Weininger, *Geschlecht und Charakter*, p. 97.

50. See Gilman, *Freud, Race, and Gender*; Nancy A. Harrowitz, "A Question of Influence," in *Jews and Gender*, pp. 73–90. On Weininger's relationship to the scientific literature of his time, see Sengoopta's *Otto Weininger* and his articles: "Science, Sexuality, and Gender in the Fin de Siècle: Otto Weininger as Baedecker," *History of Science* 30 (1992): 249–279; and "The Unknown Weininger: Science, Philosophy, and Cultural Politics in *Fin-de-siècle* Vienna," *Central European History* 29, no. 4 (1996): 453–493.

51. Weininger, *Geschlecht und Charakter*, p. 6.

52. Weininger, *Geschlecht und Charakter*, p. 8.

53. His word for intermediate forms [Zwischenformen] was "gonochorism." He assumed that the sex of an organism was determined by a combination of masculine and feminine substances (arrhenoplasm and thelyplasm), which is determined at the cellular level. He argued that sex has no localized seat in the body but is distributed throughout. "In a masculine creature, every part is masculine (even the smallest part), however similar it may be to the corresponding part of a feminine creature" (16). On this particularly contradictory moment in Weininger's argument, see Sengoopta, *Otto Weininger*.

54. For a somewhat different account of Weininger's method, see my "Otto Weininger als Figur des Fin de siècle," in *Otto Weininger*, ed. Le Rider and Leser, pp. 71–79. Wittgenstein referred to *Sex and Character* as "that beastly translation" (Sengoopta, *Otto Weininger*, p. 150). Sengoopta also notes Wittgenstein's remark to G. E. Moore that Weininger was "fantastic but *great* and fantastic" (150).

55. See Georg Groddeck, *Das Buch vom Es* (Leipzig, 1923); *The Book of the It*, trans. V. M. E. Collins (London, 1950).

56. The rules that govern relations between the physiological and the psychological (physiognomy) are never entirely clear in Weininger's account, and in the realm of characterology (psychological types) he is free to say almost anything he likes. He defined character not as "something enthroned behind the thinking and feeling of the individual" but rather as "something that reveals itself in *every* thought and *every* feeling" (102).

57. Hyams and Harrowitz argue in their introduction (p. 3) that Weininger's theory of male and female traits "fails because he elides 'W' and 'das Weib' (woman) on more than one occasion in the text." And again: "His essentialist definitions of women and Jews blatantly contradict his claim to be describing poles of behavior." See also *Gedanken über Geschlechtsprobleme*, ed. Saudek, pp. 13–14. In the introduction to his edition of Weininger's work, Saudek emphasized that

"Weib" always means "Nur-Weib" and for Weininger there are no "Nur-Männer" and no "Nur-Weiber" but only hybrids.

58. Weininger argues that "Sappho was only the first of those women who stand on the list of female fame and who at the same time felt homosexual or at least bisexual" (81).

59. *Symposium of Plato,* trans. Tom Griffith (Berkeley, 1986), line 189d-e.

60. Calasso, "Der Philosoph," in *Geschlecht und Charakter, Anhang,* p. 665.

61. See Schopenhauer, *The World as Will and Representation* (New York, 1958), vol. 2, chap. 44.

62. It is not clear how this account fits with the view that any individual is always M or F. It is perhaps a compatible but different view, but Weininger does not bother to sort this out very carefully. See Karl Kraus's mathematical definition of the female soul in Timms, *Karl Kraus,* p. 89.

63. See Judith Van Herik, *Freud on Femininity and Faith* (Berkeley, 1982). See also Simone de Beauvoir, *Second Sex,* trans. H. M. Parshley (New York, 1953; original French ed., 1949).

64. Weininger characterized *The World as Will and Representation* as "the most cheerless of the great books of human literature" and pointed to Schopenhauer's reminder that the will of the species to reproduce is the only immortality (293). The influence of modern science on Schopenhauer is apparent in such contexts.

65. "Matchmaking is the most general quality of the human female. . . ." The "will to be a mother-in-law" is stronger than "the will to motherhood" (350).

66. Weininger was sensitive to the problem of the legitimacy of men discussing women, judging them, and writing about the psychology of F. On page 106, he points out that psychology is ordinarily understood to mean "the psychology of the psychologists, and psychologists are exclusively men"; as a result, the psychology of women had never been developed as a field or attracted the interest of psychologists.

67. Weininger explicitly distinguished his views from people like P. J. Möbius (who thought Weininger had stolen his book from him): "The female is not 'physiologically inferior' [schwachsinnig]." Weininger was also no Max Nordau (who was preoccupied with issues of health and degeneration), and he makes clear that creative women represent not a degeneration but "a progress and an overcoming." Still more strikingly, he returns to an earlier theme, arguing that intermediate forms are not exceptions but the norm in nature. "From a moral point of view one can only happily greet these women, since they are always more masculine than the others . . . ; in biological terms they are just as little or just as much a phenomenon of degeneration as the feminine man (if one does not judge him ethically). The intermediate sexual forms, however, are in the whole range of nature altogether the norm and not a pathological phenomenon, and their appearance is thus still no proof of physical decadence" (343).

68. See p. 457: "[U]ntil two become one, male and female become a third self, neither male nor female." Weininger thought of Schiller as a peer of Kant and Schelling, and at times Weininger seems to come close to Schiller's notion of aesthetic education. On homosexuality in Germany around 1900 and ideas about a

third (or intermediate) sex, see James Steakley's *The Homosexual Emancipation Movement in Germany* (New York, 1975); and Charlotte Wolff, *Magnus Hirschfeld: A Portrait of a Pioneer in Sexology* (London, 1986).

69. In Weininger's view, reproduction was wrong because "it is immoral to make a human being the effect of a cause, to bring it forth as something conditioned, as is given in parenthood" and "because one does not ask a human being for his agreement" before becoming his mother and father (458).

70. Swoboda, *Otto Weiningers Tod*, pp. 23–24. This recalls Sartre's account of human nature in *Being and Nothingness*, trans. Hazel E. Barnes (New York, 1956). The intelligible ego is what Weininger means by "soul."

71. Immanuel Kant, *Foundations of the Metaphysics of Morals*, trans. Lewis White Beck (New York, 1959), p. 39. This was a moral, not a metaphysical or epistemological definition, but Weininger tended to slide from Kant's rational morality to assumptions about ontology and the soul.

72. Kant, *Foundations of the Metaphysics of Morals*, pp. 56–58.

73. This is a moment when the significance of mood in Weininger's argument becomes especially apparent: "Kant's most solitary human being does not laugh or dance, he does not scream and shout: he has no need to make noise, because the cosmos is too deeply silent" (211).

74. At times Weininger takes the view that there is "no practical solipcism" (233), arguing almost as if he were Martin Buber: "I and Thou are reciprocal concepts" and solipsism is nihilism because there is no Thou (233). This seems to contradict the isolation he usually emphasizes. He also argues that "whoever feels his personality in himself feels it in others as well. For him the Tat tvam-asi is no pretty hypothesis but, rather, reality. The highest individualism *is* the highest universalism" (233).

75. "[.] . . ethical individualism as Christianity and German idealism teach it" (228).

76. Gisela Dischner, "Freiheit auf dem Weg der Entsagung?" *Geschlecht und Charakter, Anhang*, p. 657.

77. "What Is Enlightenment?" in Immanuel Kant, *On History*, trans. Lewis White Beck (New York, 1985), p. 3.

78. Anti-*Weib* means anti-irrational, anti-unconscious, antisexuality, antiselfishness. This is Weininger's way of advocating freedom in opposition to selfabsorption.

79. This is very like George Steiner's account of the modern ego from Hegel to Nietzsche to Sartre in Steiner's *In Bluebeard's Castle* (New Haven, 1971).

80. See Le Rider, *Le Cas*, p. 241: "Mais Weininger a voulu confondre culture et nature: c'est là son erreur et sa faute."

81. "The genius has the female, like everything else, entirely in himself; but the female herself is only a part in the universe, and the part cannot contain the whole, and thus femininity cannot contain genius in itself. The lack of genius of the female follows unavoidably from the fact that the female is not a monad and therefore not a

mirror of the universe" (242–243). According to Weininger's original definitions, a woman who is masculine could be a genius.

82. Weininger rejected the aestheticism and hedonism of Young Vienna as well as its positive view of sexuality and of "the coffeehouse concept of the Dionysian" (443). Before Freud was known beyond a small number of people, Weininger characterized his time as an age of the unconscious, and he did not mean this as a compliment. His critique of *das Weib* was an attack on irrationalism in Austrian and German intellectual life.

83. Emil Lucka emphasized the centrality of Weininger's resistance to modern science as the dominant way of looking at the world and Weininger's assertion of the will to value in the face of this (see Lucka, *Otto Weininger*, pp. 13–14).

84. "Apperception" became a central concept for Doderer, although not in Kantian form. On Doderer's reception of Weininger's view of apperception, see Hans Joachim Schröder, *Apperzeption und Vorurteil: Untersuchungen zur Reflexion Heimito von Doderer* (Heidelberg, 1976), pp. 43–57.

85. For Weininger, the proposition A = A is identical with the proposition "I am" (204). Weininger believed that "all purely immanent approaches" to human experience (whether empiricism, positivism, psychologism, or relativism) "instinctively feel that the main problem for them arises from ethics and logic" (206).

86. Weininger believed that "whether a human being has in general a relationship to his own past or not is inwardly extremely closely connected to whether he feels a need for immortality or whether the thought of death leaves him indifferent. The need for immortality is to be sure generally treated very shabbily and condescendingly today" (162). But he was conscious that people were happy to make a psychological rather than an ontological problem out of this.

87. When Weininger discusses Kant and Nietzsche, compassion appears as a virtue. His contrast of Nietzsche to Schopenhauer is very perceptive:

> Schopenhauer's face displays little goodness and a great deal of cruelty (under which he himself must, to be sure, have suffered most terribly: one does not propound an ethic of pity if one is oneself very compassionate. The most compassionate people are those who most find fault with their compassion: Kant and Nietzsche). (316)

88. Bruno Sturm argues in *Gegen Weininger* that if sexuality is a drive that is physiological and aimed at reproduction, eroticism is a "conscious drive" that is abstract and without specific function (36–37). Sturm defends the average person's concern with sexuality against the focus of the genius on eroticism.

89. See Jacques Le Rider, "'The Otto Weininger Case' Revisited," in *Jews and Gender*, p. 26. Le Rider means Weininger's refusal to give up the rational ego. He does credit Weininger with a "sacred eroticism," but this is not quite the Laurencian version of cosmogonic eroticism Le Rider has in mind.

90. Robert Musil believed that love actually changes the object but also that science means looking at the object without love. See Robert Musil, "The German as Symptom," in *Precision and Soul*, ed. and trans. Burton Pike and David S. Luft (Chicago, 1990), p. 185.

91. He sounds almost like Oscar Wilde: "Art creates nature, and not nature, art" (326).

92. "All love is itself only the need for salvation, and all need for salvation is still immoral" (329).

93. On the transcendental homelessness of the modern novel, see Georg Lukács, *The Theory of the Novel*, trans. Anna Bostock (Cambridge, Mass., 1971).

94. "The hygienic punishment for the denial of the real nature of the female is hysteria" (357). Weininger acknowledged Janet, Breuer, and Freud, the importance of their work on hysteria, and their attempt to reconstruct "the psychological process, which led to the illness" (357–358). Weininger regarded the emphasis on sexual repression as the distinctive aspect of this approach.

95. Weininger explains that he does not intend "to idealize men in order to be able to disparage women" and concedes that some might get the impression that he has been too generous to men. He suspects that the Philistines or other scoundrels will be "surprised to learn that they have the whole world in themselves" (403). He admits the inadequacies of empirical men but points to "the better possibilities that are in every man." He argues that the woman simply turns out to lack many things, "which even the most ordinary and plebian man is never entirely without" (403).

96. Weininger's preoccupations with science, modernity, and the crisis of traditional values are obscured by his insistence on labeling issues in terms of what was feminine or Jewish.

97. In *Jews, Antisemitism and Culture in Vienna*, ed. Ivar Oxaal, Michael Pollak, and Gerhard Botz (London, 1987), see especially Sigurd Paul Scheichl, "Contexts and Nuances of Anti-Jewish Language," pp. 89–110; and Robert S. Wistrich, "Social Democracy, Antisemitism, and the Jews," pp. 111–120.

98. "The love for infinite value, that is, for the absolute or for God" (327). This is Weininger's definition of God and of "the transcendental idea of love, if there were such a thing" (327).

99. Allan Janik argues that Weininger's ideal type of the Jew is the Conformist. See Janik, "Viennese Culture and the Jewish Self-Hatred Hypothesis," in *Jews, Antisemitism and Culture in Vienna*, pp. 75–88.

100. See David S. Luft, "Being and German History: Historiographical Notes on the Heidegger Controversy," in *Central European History* 27, no. 4 (1994): 479–501. Although Heidegger would have regarded Weininger's ways of thinking as part of the problematic metaphysics of modernity that derived from the Greeks (and especially from Plato), Weininger's critique of morality in terms of God as a man who created the world resembles Heidegger's critique of Plato and productionist metaphysics.

101. Nietzsche and Mach were the great threats to Weininger, just as they were the great positive influences on Musil.

102. Simone Weil's thought offers a similar understanding of Christianity and classical Greece. See Simone Petrément, *Simone Weil: A Life*, trans. Raymond Rosenthal (New York, 1976), especially pp. 395–396.

103. On Weininger's belief that he might be a religious founder, see Wistrich, *The Jews of Vienna*, pp. 525–526.

104. See two quotations on a somewhat different level from *Über die letzten Dinge:* "The types of the self-loving and the self-hating human beings may thus be extended to the ideas of the father and the son" (36). "The human being can take after the father or the mother even spiritually and intellectually: the father, in that he becomes God; the mother, in that he succumbs psychologically" (68).

105. Weininger believed that this conflict between dualism and monism was the real theme of his book. In 1913 Rosa Mayreder pointed to the centrality of these questions on the first page of her book on femininity: "Psychology has come off very badly in the struggle between the spiritualistic and the materialistic views, between the dualistic and monistic conceptions of the world, so characteristic of the intellectual life of the present day. When we have no certainty as to what is meant by Soul, Spirit, Reason, Intelligence or even Consciousness, when the most divergent views are taken of the relation between the soul and the body." See Rosa Mayreder, *A Survey of the Woman Problem,* trans. Hermann Scheffauer (1913; New York, 1982), p. 1.

106. Heimito von Doderer, "Rede auf Otto Weininger," published by Wendelin Schmidt-Dengler in Le Rider, *Der Fall Otto Weininger,* p. 247. In *The Demons,* Doderer refers to him as the "glorious Weininger." See Heimito von Doderer, *The Demons,* trans. Richard and Clara Winston (New York, 1961), 1: 673.

107. Calasso, "Der Philosoph," in *Geschlecht und Charakter, Anhang,* pp. 662–667.

108. Karl Kraus emphasized the difference between Weininger's critique of Judaism and the Jew-baiting of the bullies in Vienna.

109. See Alexander Centgraf, *Ein Jude treibt Philosophie* (Berlin, 1943). In his preface, Centgraf advocates women against Weininger, Freud, Magnus Hirschfield, and a Jewish strand in Western culture. He opens his discussion by arguing that Jews were mainly in charge of sexual science in 1903, when Weininger wrote. Centraf argues that Weininger's critique of *das Weib* encouraged an unlimited individualism but also Bolshevism, in his recommendation that the education of children be taken out of the hands of the mother (chap. 14, p. 471).

110. Weininger, *Taschenbuch,* p. 66.

111. Weininger, *Taschenbuch,* p. 28.

CHAPTER 3

1. See Robert Musil, *Tagebücher,* ed. Adolf Frisé (Hamburg, 1976), 1: 138 (1905), where Musil refers to "the elimination of the soul from the thinking of the natural sciences."

2. Musil's approach to science was close to William James, as well. James was someone Weininger admired even after turning away from Mach and Avenarius.

3. Musil pointed to the contradictory quality of intellectual life in this period: "Nietzsche and Carlyle intersected with socialism, decadence with the spirit of a nature-cult club, Maeterlinck, Emerson, and Romanticism with veneration of the machine"; these confusing movements introduced a period that was characterized by

"irrationalism along with rationalism. . . . The materialist view of history and the early stages of idealism." But for Musil the "major formula" was "rationalism and irrationalism." See Robert Musil, "The German as Symptom" (unpublished, 1923), in *Precision and Soul* (Chicago, 1990), ed. and trans. Burton Pike and David S. Luft, pp. 150–152. In German literary circles, this conflict was often discussed in terms of naturalism and expressionism.

4. On Musil's informed awareness of early twentieth-century science, see Laurence Dahan-Gaida, *Musil: Savoir et fiction* (Saint-Denis, 1994).

5. *Young Törless* is familiar to English readers, and Volker Schlöndorff directed a film version of *Der junge Törless* in the 1960s.

6. "The Perfecting of a Love" and "The Temptation of Quiet Veronica" have been available in English since 1965, but the two have never appeared together in English in their original form of 1911 (the volume *Vereinigungen*). See *Five Women*, trans. Eithne Wilkins and Ernst Kaiser (New York, 1966); and Lisa Appignanesi, *Femininity and the Creative Imagination* (New York, 1973).

7. The stories were included in *Five Women*. Musil's drama, *Die Schwärmer*, has been translated as *The Enthusiasts*, trans. Andrea Simon (New York, 1983); his farce, *Vinzenz und die Freundin bedeutender Männer*, has not appeared in English.

8. I am concerned here primarily with the ways of thinking that shaped Musil's understanding of sexuality and gender rather than with the fictional portrayals themselves. For a more detailed discussion of Musil's fiction and his intellectual development as a whole, see David S. Luft, *Robert Musil and the Crisis of European Culture* (Berkeley, 1980). On Musil's fiction, see Burton Pike, *Robert Musil: An Introduction to His Work* (Cornell, 1961); and Philip Payne, *Robert Musil's "The Man without Qualities": A Critical Study* (Cambridge, 1988). Christian Rogowski's *Distinguished Outsider: Robert Musil and his Critics* (Columbia, S.C., 1994) is a very helpful introduction to Musil's work and to the history of Musil scholarship.

9. David Landes, *The Unbound Prometheus: Technological Change and Industrial Development in Western Europe from 1750 to the Present* (London, 1969).

10. Musil, "Mind and Experience: Notes for Readers Who Have Eluded the Decline of the West" (1921), in *Precision and Soul*, p. 147.

11. Musil, "Helpless Europe" (1922), trans. Philip H. Beard, in *Precision and Soul*, p. 131. Musil believed that German classicism had been right to emphasize the limitations of science and of the practical requirements resulting from industrialization, but he was also convinced that German humanism had never really come to terms with this new situation. What remained was simply the opposition between scientific and humanistic education, which had never been bridged; and he regarded this split as "the main cause of the disunited, fragmented, and discontented spiritual situation of our time" ("The German as Symptom," p. 180).

12. Although this view also meant a greater tolerance for technological civilization than was common in Musil's generation, the decisive factor was the acceptance of modern science.

13. Musil had a strong background in technology and engineering, but he generally emphasized science rather than technology in his defense of modernity.

14. Carl Stumpf trained the leading figures of Gestalt psychology: Max Wertheimer, Wolfgang Köhler, and Kurt Koffka; and Husserl dedicated his *Logische Untersuchungen* to Stumpf in 1900. Of the two Austrian philosophical traditions in the nineteenth century, Musil was closer to Mach, the more secular tradition, than to Brentano. See Robert Musil, *On Mach's Theories,* intro. by G. H. von Wright, trans. Kevin Mulligan (Washington, D.C., 1982); Robert Musil, *Briefe, 1901–1942,* ed. Adolf Frisé (Hamburg, 1981), pp. 61–64; Silvia Bonacchi, *Die Gestalt der Dichtung* (Bern, 1998); Mitchell G. Ash, *Gestalt Psychology in German Culture, 1890–1967* (Cambridge, 1995); and Luft, *Robert Musil,* pp. 78–88.

15. See Musil, *Tagebücher,* 1: 925.

16. Musil, "Helpless Europe," in *Precision and Soul,* pp. 122–123.

17. Musil, "The German as Symptom," *in Precision and Soul,* p. 151.

18. Musil, *The Man without Qualities,* trans. Sophie Wilkins and Burton Pike, ed. Burton Pike (New York, 1995), 1: 490–491. Musil divided his novel into two books. In the Knopf edition, these correspond to volumes. My references are to these volumes, although other editions (in German and English) are sometimes different.

19. Musil begins his novel with a scene in which he asks that we not take the name of the imperial capital too literally:

> So let us not place any particular value on the city's name. Like all big cities it was made up of irregularity, change, forward spurts, failures to keep step, collisions of objects and interests, punctuated by unfathomable silences; made up of pathways and untrodden ways, of one great rhythmic beat as well as chronic discord and mutual displacement of all its contending rhythms.

Musil, *The Man without Qualities,* p. 4.

20. Musil, "Anschluss with Germany," in *Precision and Soul,* p. 97. If no more than this was meant by "Austrian culture," Musil had no quarrel with it. As Gerald Stourzh has pointed out ("The Multinational Empire Revisited," *Austrian History Yearbook* 23 (1992): 15–16), Musil's significance was surely not his insight into the constitution of the dual monarchy. In fact, when Musil wrote about Kakania in *The Man without Qualities,* he seems often to have been thinking only of Cisleithanian Austria. See, for example, his account of Kakania's constitution in chapter 8 of volume 1 (pp. 29–31). There is, of course, the further question of whether he was even concerned with a realistic historical portrayal of a particular state. It might just as well have been Austria, as it were. See Ulrich's offensive patriotism (1: 13–14) or Musil's playful use of statistics (1: 5) in *The Man without Qualities.*

21. Musil, "Anschluss with Germany," in *Precision and Soul,* p. 95.

22. Robert Musil, "Als Papa Tennis lernte" (April 1931), in *Gesammelte Werke,* 7: 687. The writers of Young Vienna—Schnitzler, Hofmannsthal, Beer-Hofmann, and Bahr—published in Berlin, and during "the first decade of the century, the center of cultural power and modernism seems to have moved from Vienna to Berlin, a shift that was still more apparent in the 1920s." But the influence of Austrian writers was enormous precisely in this context. David S. Luft, "Austria as a Region of German Culture, 1900–1938," *Austrian History Yearbook* 23 (1992): 145.

23. In *"Hölderlin unter den Deutschen" und andere Aufsätze zur deutschen Literatur* (Frankfurt am Main, 1968), Robert Minder calls 1908–1914 "the germcell of the whole of modern art" (p. 25). See also Thomas Harrison's *1910: The Emancipation of Dissonance* (Berkeley, 1996) on Italian intellectuals.

24. See Luft, *Robert Musil*, p. 14.

25. Musil, "The German as Symptom," in *Precision and Soul*, p. 150.

26. Musil, "Sketches and Notes about the Novel, 1920–1929," in *The Man without Qualities*, 2: 1723.

27. Musil, "Politics in Austria" (1912), in *Precision and Soul*, pp. 19–20.

28. Musil, "Political Confessions of a Young Man: A Fragment" (1913), in *Precision and Soul*, pp. 31–37.

29. Musil, "Political Confessions of a Young Man," in *Precision and Soul*, p. 34.

30. On Musil's distinction between a morality based on a rational system and an ethics with affinities to aesthetics, see Werner Ego, *Abschied von der Moral* (Freiburg, 1992). Philip Beard discusses Musil's ambiguities of usage, especially in *The Man without Qualities*, where "morality" is sometimes used in a positive sense to mean ethics. Philip Harper Beard, "Der 'andere Zustand' im *Mann ohne Eigenschaften* und in der Musil-Kritik" (Ph.D. diss., Stanford University, 1971).

31. Musil, "Helpless Europe," in *Precision and Soul*, p. 132. This is the central theme of Musil's work and the source of many of the apparent contradictions in his views.

32. Musil, "Toward a New Aesthetic: Observations on a Dramaturgy of Film" (1925), in *Precision and Soul*, pp. 203–204.

33. In "Analyse und Synthese" (1913), Musil argued that "every metaphor is an unintended analysis." See *Gesammelte Werke*, 8: 1008. Musil distinguished the single-mindedness of scientific, unequivocal language from the figurative language of literature: metaphor "is like the image that fuses several meanings in a dream; it is the gliding logic of the soul, corresponding to the way things relate to each other in the intuitions of art and religion" (*The Man without Qualities*, 1: 647).

34. Musil, "The Religious Spirit, Modernism, and Metaphysics" (1912), in *Precision and Soul*, p. 22.

35. Musil, "The Mathematical Man," in *Precision and Soul*, p. 43.

36. Musil, "Political Confessions," in *Precision and Soul*, p. 34.

37. Musil, "Sketch of What the Writer Knows" (1918), in *Precision and Soul*, p. 63.

38. Musil, "The Religious Spirit," in *Precision and Soul*, p. 24. One of the mistakes in most religions and other ideologies (and in most criticisms of them) is to lapse into the unambiguous and literal, to take metaphors as if they were metaphysical systems or scientific laws.

39. Musil, "The Religious Spirit," in *Precision and Soul*, p. 23. Here "reason" means intellect as it is applied in mathematics and the natural sciences, where the point is the generalizing power.

40. See, for example, Musil's prewar critique of Walther Rathenau: "Commentary on a Metapsychics" (1914), in *Precision and Soul*, pp. 54–58.

41. Musil, "Sketch of What the Writer Knows," in *Precision and Soul,* p. 64.

42. Musil, "Sketch of What the Writer Knows," in *Precision and Soul,* p. 62.

43. Musil, "Political Confessions," in *Precision and Soul,* p. 34.

44. Musil, "The Religious Spirit, Modernism, and Metaphysics" (1912), in *Precision and Soul,* p. 22.

45. "It might easily have been replaced by a new one. But the church was not under any compulsion to do this; it long ago closed the book of essays on its life, and has since successfully steered this book towards mass recognition, with ever-repeated astigmatic reprintings" (25).

46. Musil, "Die Wallfahrt nach innen" (1913), *Gesammelte Werke,* 9: 1447.

47. Musil, *The Man without Qualities,* vol. 1, chap. 62, pp. 267–268.

48. Musil, "Mind and Experience" in *Precision and Soul,* p. 141.

49. Müller was a leading figure of Austrian expressionism and postwar activism. See Robert Müller, *Kritische Schriften III* (Vienna, 1996), pp. 212–216. On the resistance of the field to emphasizing Musil's interest in sexuality, see Andrew Webber, *Sexuality and the Sense of Self in the Works of Georg Trakl and Robert Musil* (London, 1990); and Peter Henninger, *Der Buchstabe und der Geist: Unbewusste Determinierung im Schreiben Robert Musils* (Frankfurt am Main, 1980). Musil scholarship tends to divide between those who minimize the sexual in Musil's work and those who think in specifically psychoanalytic terms.

50. See Roger Shattuck, *Forbidden Knowledge: From Prometheus to Pornography* (New York, 1996). On the dramatic changes in sexual behavior of Europeans even before the war, see Magnus Hirschfeld, *The Sexual History of the World War* (New York, 1941).

51. On the period before 1902, see Sibylle Mulot, *Der junge Musil* (Stuttgart, 1977).

52. See Elias Canetti on Musil in *The Play of the Eyes,* trans. Ralph Manheim (New York, 1986), p. 166: "His attitude toward men was one of combat. He did not feel out of place in war, in war he sought to prove himself. He was an officer, and tried by taking good care of his men to make up for what he regarded as the brutalization of their life. He had a natural or, one might call it, a traditional attitude toward survival and was not ashamed of it. After the war, competition took its place; in that he resembled the Greeks." The novel establishes the tensions between sexuality and violence in Musil's fiction.

53. Musil had apparently not read Freud when he wrote *Törless,* but he did read him seriously thereafter, probably by 1905 or 1906.

54. Robert Musil, *Selected Writing,* ed. Burton Pike (New York, 1986), p. 164.

55. Musil, *Selected Writing,* p. 135.

56. Expressionism is usually associated with Germany, although Austrian expressionism has recently received more attention. See Klaus Amann and Armin A. Wallas, eds., *Expressionismus in Österreich* (Vienna, 1994). The Berlin experience was important for Musil in relation to his understandings of science, literature, art, and politics.

57. Musil, "Profile of a Program" (1912), in *Precision and Soul,* p. 16.

58. Musil, "Profile of a Program," in *Precision and Soul*, p. 13.

59. The great prose writers of the generation of 1905, such as Musil, Kafka, and Thomas Mann, generally kept some distance from expressionism. On the other hand, expressionism was the main literary ideology Doderer was exposed to during and after the war.

60. Musil, "Profile of a Program," in *Precision and Soul*, p. 10.

61. On the importance of Martha's experience for *Vereinigungen*, see Karl Corino, *Robert Musils "Vereinigungen": Studien zu einer historisch-kritischen Ausgabe* (Munich, 1974); and Corino's valuable collection of photographs and passages from Musil's works: *Robert Musil: Leben und Werk in Bildern und Texten* (Hamburg, 1988).

62. Dorrit Cohn, *Transparent Minds: Narrative Modes for Presenting Fiction* (Princeton, 1978), pp. 41–43.

63. Musil, "Profile of a Program," in *Precision and Soul*, p. 15.

64. Robert Musil, cited in Corino, *Robert Musils "Vereinigungen,"* p. 367.

65. See Roy F. Allen, *Literary Life in German Expressionism and the Berlin Circles* (Ann Arbor, 1983), chapter 8; and Peter Paret, *Berlin Seccession: Modernism and Its Enemies in Imperial Germany* (Cambridge, Mass., 1980), pp. 224–225. On modernism in Germany, see Peter Fritzsche, *Reading Berlin 1900* (Cambridge, Mass., 1996); and two books by Peter Jelavich, *Munich and Theatrical Modernism: Politics, Playwriting, and Performance, 1890–1914* (Cambridge, Mass., 1985) and *Berlin Cabaret* (Cambridge, Mass., 1993).

66. Musil, "The Obscene and Pathological," in *Precision and Soul*, pp. 5–6.

67. Musil, "The Obscene and Pathological," in *Precision and Soul*, pp. 8–9.

68. Musil, "Profile of a Program," in *Precision and Soul*, p. 12. Here, as in *The Man without Qualities*, one is reminded of Nietzsche's distance from Wagner. Later Musil distinguished between a decorative art and one that acknowledges the restlessness of life.

69. Musil, "On Robert Musil's Books" (1913), in *Precision and Soul*, p. 28. More than twenty years later Musil emphasized the importance of the ability to appreciate "even the nastiest but wittiest caricature of himself." Musil, "The Serious Writer in Our Time," in *Precision and Soul*, p. 261.

70. Musil, "On the Obscene and Pathological," in *Precision and Soul*, p. 7. This was apparent in *Young Törless*, where a story about adolescent sexuality and cruelty is a way toward thinking about the difficulty of expressing feelings. But it was equally and perhaps more dramatically apparent in *Vereinigungen* [Unions], where Musil demonstrated his inner range (between masculine and feminine) and his interest in something beyond social and sexual convention.

71. Musil, "Moral Fruitfulness," in *Precision and Soul*, pp. 37–39. In the opening scene of "The Perfecting of a Love," Claudine and her husband discuss a sex murderer named "G."

72. Musil, "Moral Fruitfulness," in *Precision and Soul*, p. 38. This draws on the moral atmosphere of *Young Törless* but also touches on "The Perfecting of a Love." This passage is an interesting commentary on Weininger's reliance on dichotomy.

73. Musil, *Tagebücher*, 1: 241.

74. Musil, in a letter to Josef Nadler (December 1, 1924), in *Briefe, 1901–1942*, p. 369.

75. Musil, "Profile of a Program," in *Precision and Soul*, p. 39.

76. Musil, "The German as Symptom," in *Precision and Soul*, p. 166.

77. Musil, "The German as Symptom," in *Precision and Soul*, p. 153.

78. Musil, "Politics in Austria," in *Precision and Soul*, p. 18.

79. See Luft, *Robert Musil*, p. 282. This distance from politics diminished after the war but still separated him somewhat from the literary activists of his generation. See Walter H. Sokel, *The Writer in Extremis: Expressionism in Twentieth-Century German Literature* (Stanford, 1959), on the distinction between an early critical expressionism and a later politically activist stage.

80. See Richard J. Evans, *The Feminist Movement in Germany, 1894–1933* (London, 1976).

81. Musil, "Penthesileiade" (1912), in *Gesammelte Werke*, 8: 986.

82. Musil, "Penthesileiade," in *Gesammelte Werke*, 8: 987.

83. Musil, "Penthesileiade," in *Gesammelte Werke*, 8: 986.

84. Musil, "Penthesileiade," in *Gesammelte Werke*, 8: 986.

85. Musil, "Erinnerung an eine Mode," in *Gesammelte Werke*, 8: 984.

86. Musil, "Penthesileiade," in *Gesammelte Werke*, 8: 986.

87. Musil, "Woman Yesterday and Tomorrow" (1929), in *Precision and Soul*, p. 210.

88. Musil, "Woman Yesterday and Tomorrow," in *Precision and Soul*, p. 209. See Musil, *The Man without Qualities*, vol. 1, chap. 67, p. 301.

89. Musil, "Woman Yesterday and Tomorrow," in *Precision and Soul*, p. 211.

90. See Musil, *Tagebücher*, 2: 1102: "All my apparently immoral people are 'creative.'"

91. Luft, *Robert Musil*, p. 99.

92. This was the point in his adult life when Musil's thinking was most stamped by the specifically Austrian situation and by the political predicaments of its elites.

93. Musil, "The 'Nation' as Ideal and as Reality" (1921), in *Precision and Soul*, 115.

94. Musil, "The 'Nation' as Ideal and as Reality," pp. 115–116.

95. In *Precision and Soul*, see "Mind and Experience" (1921), "The 'Nation' as Ideal and as Reality" (1921), "Helpless Europe" (1922), "The German as Symptom" (unpublished, 1923), and "Toward a New Aesthetics" (1925). On Musil's postwar essays, see Hartmut Böhme, *Anomie und Entfremdung* (Regensburg, 1974); and Luft, *Robert Musil*.

96. See Ernst Hanisch, *Der lange Schatten des Staates* (Vienna, 1994), pp. 265 ff.

97. Musil, "Helpless Europe," in *Precision and Soul*, p. 117.

98. Musil's friends—Franz Blei, Albert Paris Gütersloh, and Robert Müller—were active in the expressionist politics of the postwar period in Austria. Musil resisted "the Gütersloh-Blei" atmosphere of revolution, and he doubted the possibility of a sharp break from the limitations of bourgeois society. See Ernst Fischer, "Expressionismus—Aktivismus—Revolution: Die österreichische Schriftsteller zwischen Geistpolitik und Roter Garde," in *Expressionismus in Österreich*, pp. 19–48.

99. Musil, "Mind and Experience," in *Precision and Soul*, p. 149.

100. Musil, "The 'Nation' as Ideal and as Reality," in *Precision and Soul*, p. 113.

101. Musil, "The 'Nation' as Ideal and as Reality," in *Precision and Soul*, p. 154.

102. Musil, "The 'Nation' as Ideal and as Reality," in *Precision and Soul*, p. 113. Musil was not thinking here of German idealism in the philosophical sense; Austrian commentators sometimes blur this distinction.

103. Musil, "The 'Nation' as Ideal and as Reality," in *Precision and Soul*, p. 105.

104. Musil, "Ruminations of a Slow-witted Mind" (unpublished, 1933), in *Precision and Soul*, p. 233.

105. Musil, "The German as Symptom," in *Precision and Soul*, p. 161.

106. Musil, "The German as Symptom," in *Precision and Soul*, p. 157.

107. Musil, "The German as Symptom," in *Precision and Soul*, pp. 154–155. In his *Erkenntnis und Freiheit: Der Mann ohne Eigenschaften als "Übergangswesen"* (Munich, 1994), Cay Hehner is unsympathetic to Musil's resigned acceptance of capitalism—not as the cause of greed but as the most dependable organizing form for violence in our time.

108. In "The 'Nation' as Ideal and as Reality," p. 110, and "The German as Symptom," in *Precision and Soul*, p. 152.

109. See Elias Canetti on Musil in *The Play of the Eyes*, p. 168: "He was right not to recognize anyone's superiority; among those who passed as writers in Vienna, or perhaps in the whole German-speaking world, there was none of his rank."

110. Musil, "Mind and Experience," in *Precision and Soul*, p. 148. Some commentators see only that Musil criticized the excessive emphasis on feelings in expressionism, while others notice that Musil belonged to the revolt against the rigidities of bourgeois society and culture. This discussion is often formulated as a choice between reason and feeling, or between civilization and revolt, or as a reaction versus revolution. Musil argued that "the humanly essential questions are only confused by all the scribbling about rationalism and antirationalism. The only possible longing in which one does not lose as much as one gains is the longing for suprarationalism" ("Mind and Experience," p. 142). The younger Doderer was more strongly drawn toward expressionism and revolt.

111. Musil, "Mind and Experience," in *Precision and Soul*, pp. 145–146.

112. Musil, "The German as Symptom," in *Precision and Soul*, p. 153.

113. Musil, "The German as Symptom," in *Precision and Soul*, p. 174.

114. Musil, "The German as Symptom," in *Precision and Soul*, p. 175.

115. Musil, "Helpless Europe," in *Precision and Soul*, p. 131.

116. Musil, "Helpless Europe," in *Precision and Soul*, pp. 131–132.

117. Musil, "Toward a New Aesthetic," in *Precision and Soul*, p. 199.

118. Musil, "Toward a New Aesthetic," in *Precision and Soul*, p. 199.

119. Musil, "The German as Symptom," in *Precision and Soul*, p. 156.

120. Musil noted that bishops in the early Church had trouble deciding whether to sign their pastoral letters with agape or eros. See Musil, *Tagebücher*, 1: 506 and 2: 325–327.

121. Musil, "The German as Symptom," in *Precision and Soul*, p. 157.

122. Musil, "Mind and Experience," in *Precision and Soul*, p. 145.

123. Musil, "The German as Symptom," in *Precision and Soul*, p. 186. "It is possible that this masculine-feminine principle lay at the basis of the ancient mystery cults."

124. Musil, "Alfred Döblins Epos" (1927), in *Gesammelte Werke*, 9: 1677.

125. Musil, "The German as Symptom," in *Precision and Soul*, p. 185.

126. Egoism and altruism, good and evil give way to the pair enhancement and diminution.

127. Musil, *The Man without Qualities*, p. 391.

128. See J. M. Coetzee, "The Man with Many Qualities," *New York Review of Books*, March 18, 1999, pp. 52–55.

129. Musil, *The Man without Qualities*, 2: 944.

130. Musil, *The Man without Qualities*, 2: 804. Ulrich offers a provocative account of masculine values: "'The moral argumentation is just one more means to an end, a weapon used in much the same way as lies. This is the world that men have made, and it would make me want to be a woman—if only women did not love men!'" (803). Ulrich thinks of the morality of achievement as "the morality of the careerists."

131. Musil, *The Man without Qualities*, 1: 62–63.

132. Musil, *The Man without Qualities*, 1: 307.

133. Musil, *The Man without Qualities*, 2: 957–958.

134. Musil, *The Man without Qualities*, 2: 1020.

135. Musil, *The Man without Qualities*, 1: 306–307. Musil wants to draw on this "pure pleasure two people have in each other, this simplest and deepest of all feelings in love" (307).

136. Musil, *The Man without Qualities*, 2: 982.

137. Musil, *The Man without Qualities*, 2: 980.

138. Musil, *The Man without Qualities*, 2: 981.

139. Musil, *The Man without Qualities*, 2: 898.

140. Musil, *The Man without Qualities*, 1: 119.

141. Musil, *The Man without Qualities*, 1: 127–128. See also "Helpless Europe," in *Precision and Soul*, p. 132.

142. Musil, *The Man without Qualities*, 1: 646–647.

143. Musil, *The Man without Qualities*, 2: 1021.

144. See Musil, *The Man without Qualities*, 1: 25.

145. Musil, *The Man without Qualities*, 1: 645.

146. Musil, *The Man without Qualities*, 2: 1019–1020.

147. Musil, *The Man without Qualities*, 2: 745.

148. Musil was inclined to speak of "the hermaphroditism of the primal imagination" (2: 819) rather than the mind's primal androgyny.

149. Musil was exploring the culture's division between male and female—as well as the possibilities within these roles—and he consistently criticized male courtship patterns.

150. Musil was finishing the first volume of *The Man without Qualities* just as Virginia Woolf was writing *A Room of One's Own* between 1928 and 1929. There Woolf reflects on the idea of androgyny, the balance of masculine and feminine qualities in the mind—as well as on why men write about women.

151. Musil, *Tagebücher* (entry from 1941), 1: 811. On "Le conseiller Ulrichs" and the soul of a woman in a man's body, see Scipio Sighele, *Le Crime à deux: Essai de psycho-pathologie sociale* (Paris, 1910), p. 153.

152. Luft, *Robert Musil*, p. 270 ff. Shortly after the Anschluss, Musil received a visit from publishers in Hamburg; he left for Switzerland the next day. Once, when Ignazio Silone asked him why he left, Musil replied that all his readers had left. He died in 1942, mainly forgotten and unread but confident that the Nazis would lose the war as a result of the intellectual deficiencies that would follow from the moral ones.

153. Musil, "Aus einem Rapial" [*Nachlass*], in *Gesammelte Werke*, 7: 840.

154. Musil provided a particularly acute rendering of his resistance to reductionism in a passage from the *Nachlass:* "What is so attractive, so specially tempting to the mind, that it finds it necessary to reduce the world of emotions to pleasure and its lack, or to the simplest psychological processes? Why does it grant a higher explanatory value to something psychological, the simpler it is? Why a greater value to something physiological-chemical than to something psychological, and finally, why does it assign the highest value of all to reducing things to the movement of physical atoms?. . . . Upon what, in other words, rests this faith that nature's mystery has to be simple?" From posthumous papers in Musil, *The Man without Qualities*, 2: 1247.

Chapter 4

1. The first of Doderer's Vienna novels appeared recently in English as *The Lighted Windows, or The Humanization of the Bureaucrat Julius Zihal*, trans. John S. Barrett (Riverside, 2000). The more important (and much longer) *The Strudlhof Steps, or Melzer and the Depth of the Years* has not appeared in English, although Vincent Kling published the beginning of an English translation in *Chicago Review* 26, no. 2 (1974): 107–138.

2. See Hans Joachim Schröder, *Apperzeption und Vorurteil: Untersuchungen zur Reflexion Heimito von Doderers* (Heidelberg, 1976); and Anton Reininger, *Die Erlösung des Bürgers: Eine ideologiekritische Studie zum Werk Heimito von Doderers* (Bonn, 1975).

3. Robert Wohl argues that "the generation of 1914" was mainly myth rather than reality, a myth that blurred two fairly distinct generations— roughly those who were thirty-five and those who were twenty in 1914—because they participated in the Great War. Musil belonged to the former group, and Doderer to the latter. See Robert Wohl, *The Generation of 1914* (Cambridge, Mass., 1979). Ernst Schönwiese divides Austrian writers who were born between 1880 and 1912 into three groups: what I call the generation of 1905, Doderer's generation, and those born just before the war. See Schönwiese, *Literatur in Wien zwischen 1930 und 1980* (Vienna, 1980), p. 7.

4. For Doderer, the events of 1927 had much the same significance that the Russian Revolution of 1905 and the ensuing diplomatic revolution had for Musil's generation—in the form of an enforced awareness of politics. On the significance of these events for Doderer and what I call the generation of 1927, see Luft, "Austrian Intellectuals and the Palace of Justice Fire," in *The Austrian Socialist Experiment: Social Democracy and Austromarxism, 1918–1934,* ed. Anson Rabinbach (Boulder, Colo., 1985), pp. 151–156.

5. Doderer's background is a recipe for someone who would be *grossdeutsch* after 1918: a recently arrived German family that was professional, Protestant, and disinherited politically, socially, and economically by the war.

6. There are echoes here of Max Weber's childhood—and Doderer's parents were Protestants, only a generation removed from Germany. But Doderer was the youngest child in a large family, and his mother was far more nurturing than Weber's, to say nothing of the older sisters who took a great interest in their younger brother.

7. On Doderer's personal life, see his *Tagebücher: 1920–1939,* 2 vols., ed. Wendelin Schmidt-Dengler, Martin Loew-Cadonna, and Gerald Sommer (Munich, 1996); Wolfgang Fleischer, *Das verleugnete Leben: Die Biographie des Heimito von Doderer* (Vienna, 1996); Lutz-W. Wolff, *Heimito von Doderer* (Hamburg, 1996); *Heimito von Doderer, 1896–1966: Selbstzeugnisse,* intro. by Wendelin Schmidt-Dengler (Munich, 1995); and Engelbert Pfeiffer, *Heimito Doderers Alsergrund-Erlebnis* (Vienna, 1983) and *The Writer's Place: Heimito von Doderer and the Alsergrund District of Vienna,* trans. Vincent Kling (Riverside, Calif., 2001).

8. Heimito von Doderer, *Tangenten: Tagebuch eines Schriftstellers, 1940–1950* (Munich, 1964), p. 331.

9. Heimito von Doderer, "Der Abschied," in *Die sibirische Klarheit,* ed. Wendelin Schmidt-Dengler and Martin Loew-Cadonna (Munich, 1991). See also Doderer, *Frühe Prosa,* ed. Hans Flesch-Brunningen, Wendelin Schmidt-Dengler, and Martin Loew Cadonna (Munich, 1996), pp. 5–117.

10. On the transition from the empire to the First Republic and the mounting conflicts of the 1920s, see Klemens von Klemperer, *Ignaz Seipel: Christian Statesman in a Time of Crisis* (Princeton, 1972).

11. He preferred Oscar Wilde to all Heinrich Ritter von Srbik's learning: "[W]hat is all this learnedness next to half a page from a dialog by Oscar Wilde!" Doderer, *Tagebücher*, 1: 101. The originals are in Doderer's papers in the Österreichischen Nationalbibliothek in Vienna. Page numbers in parentheses in this section are to the *Tagebücher*.

12. Doderer, *Tagebücher*, 2: 839.

13. Doderer, *Tagebücher*, 1: 39.

14. "Zur bürgerlichen Geschichtsschreibung in Wien während des 15. Jahrhunderts" (Ph.D. diss, University of Vienna, 1925). In the 1920s, Doderer wrote a sketch for Haybach of a biography of Vienna in which he characterized "the city as a lifeform of a higher order." See Heimito von Doderer, *Gedanken über eine zu schreibende Geschichte der Stadt Wien*, ed. Erich Fitzbauer (Vienna, 1996).

15. As a student of psychology and of Swoboda in particular, Doderer was already aware of the importance of Freud at this time. In a diary entry from 1926, Doderer argued that the significance of Freud lay "not in the details of his system" and not even "in the clinical side, in the therapy. No, more important than the whole of 'psychoanalysis' is the appearance—and, to be sure, the appearance *for the first time*—of modern psychological thinking altogether. It is a matter of *Freud's way of thinking*, not his individual teachings, partly exaggerated by his students, in part 'refuted' by them. The way of thinking: the recognition of *the meaning of symptoms* (N.B. meaning!) was something *completely* new for the psychiatry of that time." Doderer, *Tagebücher*, 1: 239.

16. Doderer, *Tagebücher*, 1: 12.

17. Doderer, *Tagebücher*, 1: 208.

18. See Klaus Amann and Armin A. Wallas, ed., *Expressionismus in Österreich* (Vienna, 1994), p. 9 and passim. Austrian expressionism has generally not been very clearly defined, and its themes often blur with modernism in general. The expressionists were usually a bit younger than Musil and inclined to emphasize themes of revolt, father-son conflict, and opposition to civilization (whether modern or bourgeois).

19. Doderer, *Tagebücher*, 1: 80.

20. Doderer, *Tagebücher*, 1: 127.

21. Regarding his detailed records of masturbation and visits to prostitutes, see his *Tagebücher*, particularly volume 1, and Fleischer's comprehensive biography, *Das verleugnete Leben*. In 1982 Doderer's friend Dorothea Zeemann published an account of their relationship that drew attention to the tremendous role that sexuality continued to play in Doderer's personal life. Dorothea Zeemann, *Jungfrau und Reptil: Leben zwischen 1945 und 1972* (Frankfurt am Main, 1982).

22. In 1923 Doderer published a volume of poetry, *Gassen und Landschaft*, with his friend, Haybach; Lang, another friend from Siberia, did the illustrations for *Die Bresche*. Doderer wrote six divertimentos between 1921 and 1926, although they did not appear in print together until 1972. See Doderer's "Divertimenti und Variationen," in *Die Erzählungen*, ed. Wendelin Schmidt-Dengler (Munich, 1972), pp. 7–207.

23. "Jutta Bamberger: Ein Fragment aus dem Nachlass," *Frühe Prosa*, pp. 207–293. See also the closely related "Episode f," pp. 294–329.

24. See Engelbert Pfeiffer, "Heimito von Doderer in Döbling," *Literatur und Kritik* 123 (April 1978): 158–170.

25. Doderer, *Tagbücher*, 1: 292–293.

26. See *The Secret of the Empire*, trans. John S. Barrett (Riverside, 1998), pp. 40–41, translation of *Das Geheimnis des Reichs: Roman aus dem russischen Bürgerkrieg* (Vienna, 1930), in *Frühe Prosa*, pp. 217–357. Doderer wrote a second novel about the Russian Civil War near the end of his life: *Der Grenzwald, Roman No. 7, Zweiter Teil* (Munich, 1967).

27. Alwersik is completely evenhanded in his object choice (Dorian and Katia), and Doderer portrays Alwersik's conflicts much as Sartre would have a few years later: "It was unthinkable to lose Katia. And it was equally unthinkable to lose Dorian. Caught between these two impossibilities, he hurled his schnaps glass against the dirty table top" (95).

28. Doderer, *Der Fall Gütersloh: Ein Schicksal und seine Deutung* (Vienna, 1930), pp. 52–53.

29. See also Gütersloh's *Bekenntnisse eines modernen Malers* (1926) and *Heimito von Doderer/Albert Paris Gütersloh: Briefwechsel, 1928–1962*, ed. Reinhold Treml (Munich, 1986).

30. In *Sonne und Mond: Ein historischer Roman aus der Gegenwart* (Munich, 1962), Gütersloh satirized his still loyal disciple as Ariovist von Wissendrum. He mocked Doderer's pose as a great writer rather than just an ordinary, everyday person, and satirized him as a Nazi, although Doderer had been influenced in this direction very largely by Gütersloh.

31. Doderer, *Tagebücher*, 1: 372–374.

32. Doderer, *Tagebücher*, 1: 372.

33. See Ernst Hanisch, *Der lange Schatten des Staates: Österreichische Gesellschaftsgeschichte im 20. Jahrhundert* (Vienna, 1994).

34. In the 1930s Doderer established a close and lifelong friendship with a young medical student named Gabriele (Licea) Murad, who became the model for Renata in *The Demons*. On his deep affinity for Licea, see a note from April 1935: "This whole time is tinged moreover with the experience of living with Licea. . . . Whether we were gliding through the forests on skis, dreaming afterward with tea by the open fire, whether Licea helped me with my work or sat with me in a little bar," he was conscious of having "the best of his life across from him and of being surrounded in . . . unlimited trust." Doderer, *Tagebücher*, 2: 702.

35. Doderer, *Tagebücher*, 2: 819.

36. Doderer, *Tagebücher*, 2: 819.

37. Doderer, *Tagebücher*, 2: 813–821. See also Doderer's responses to a questionnaire from the Reich Ministry, cited in Gerald Stieg, *Frucht des Feuers: Canetti, Doderer, Kraus und der Justizpalastbrand* (Vienna, 1990), pp. 220–227. The passage is a combination of sincerity and expedience in which Doderer fit his own work into the signs of the times; his account of his novel expresses his own views, but it is also an author's pretension and an attempt to accommodate politically.

38. On the almost matter-of-fact anti-Semitism in all Austrian political camps in the interwar years, see Herbert Rütger, "Antisemitismus in allen Lagern" (Ph.D. diss., University of Graz, 1989).

39. For a nuanced and highly informative account of the political camps of the interwar years in Austria, see Adam Wandruszka, "Österreichs politische Struktur: Die Entwicklung der Parteien und politischen Bewegungen," in *Geschichte der Republik Österreich*, ed. Heinrich Benedikt and Walter Goldinger et al. (Vienna, 1954), pp. 289–486.

40. Doderer, *Tagebücher*, 2: 819.

41. His short fiction from this period includes *Ein Umweg*, which appeared in 1940, and *Das Letzte Abenteuer*, which appeared in 1953. A fascinating short story from these years has been translated by Vincent Kling as "A Person Made of Porcelain," *Chicago Review* 26, no. 2 (1974): 70–73. This story from Doderer's diary (entry from May 27, 1935, in *Tagebücher*, 2: 706–710) shows how aware Doderer was of the aspects of human nature that are not rational or socially presentable.

42. See *Die Daemonen*, Roman Studien I, II, III; ser. n. 14.238–14.240. Part of Doderer's papers in the Handschriftensammlung der Österreichischen Nationalbibliothek. I will refer to this as "The Demons of Ostmark" to distinguish it from the later version.

43. Hilde Spiel characterizes Doderer's account of these three autobiographical figures in the final version of *The Demons* as so pitiless that "Freud's self-analysis seems like child's play by comparison." Hilde Spiel, *Welt im Widerschein: Essays* (Munich, 1960), p. 293.

44. Doderer's fiction in the 1930s had already begun to display his fascination with portraying primitive stages of development in the natural world. See Ivar Ivask, "Psychologie and Geschichte in Doderers Romanwerk," in *Literatur und Kritik* 24 (April 1968): 213–233.

45. Doderer, "Die Daemonen," typescript, pp. 20–21. I am citing here from the English translation of the completed novel: *The Demons*, trans. Richard and Clara Winston (New York, 1961), p. 17.

46. Doderer, *Tagebücher*, 2: 831.

47. Doderer, *Tagebücher*, 2: 818.

48. See Dietrich Weber, *Heimito von Doderer: Studien zu seinem Romanwerk* (Munich, 1963), chapter 3, pp. 31 ff. See also Martin Loew-Cadonna, *Zug um Zug: Studien zu Heimito von Doderers Roman "Ein Mord den jeder begeht,"* (Vienna, 1991).

49. This is my translation, but it is close to the rendering in *Every Man a Murderer*, trans. Richard and Clara Winston (New York, 1964), p. 3.

50. See Wolff, *Heimito von Doderer*, p. 64.

51. And a few lines later: "If I were to exaggerate a trifle, for the sake of clarity, I would say that most people noticed the Inquisition no more than the contemporaries of the great age of art in Italy noticed the 'Renaissance'" (204). This novel, whose title might be translated more literally as *A Murder That Everyone Commits*, seems to suggest that everyone is implicated in evil. Even more than Weininger, Do-

derer apparently became a critic of the ideology he is accused of, in this case, conformity.

52. Dietrich Weber's comprehensive study begins with 1938, and Doderer did not "count" *Die Bresche* and *The Secret of the Empire* when he looked back over his novels.

53. Unless otherwise indicated, page numbers in parentheses in this section are to Doderer's *Tangenten*. On his diaries during the 1940s, see my "Eros and Apperception in Heimito von Doderer's *Tangenten*" in *Philosophie, Psychoanalyse, Emigration* (Vienna, 1992), pp. 194–209; and Simone Leinkauf's excellent study of the centrality of diaries in Doderer's work: *Diarium in principio: Das Tagebuch als Ort der Sinngebung* (Frankfurt am Main, 1992).

54. Leibniz, "Principles of Nature and Grace," in *The Monadology and Other Philosophical Writings*, trans. Robert Latta (1898; London, 1965), p. 411.

55. G. W. Leibniz, *New Essays on Human Understanding*, trans. Peter Remnant and Jonathan Bennett (Cambridge, 1982), p. 134.

56. Karl Lange, *Apperception: A Monograph on Psychology and Pedagogy*, trans. the Herbart Club (Boston, 1896), p. 248.

57. Lange, *Apperception*, pp. 274–275. See also Herbart's *Science of Education*, trans. Henry M. and Emmie Felkin (Boston, 1896).

58. Heimito von Doderer, *The Lighted Windows, or The Humanization of the Bureaucrat Julius Zihal*, trans. John S. Barrett (Riverside, 2000). See Fleischer, *Das verleugnete Leben*, p. 288.

59. Doderer's comments in *The Lighted Windows* about modern experience and modern civilization help to clarify some of his arguments in *The Demons* and to suggest the way in which philosophical irrationalism could come to the defense of civilizational values: "As long as people, in the beginning of this newest of all civilizations, were still inured and tolerant toward their own, already present emptiness, and endured it patiently like a roommate, considered it legitimate, just that long was it impossible to draw the basic, inherent consequences from that civilization, achieve its real power, and put the null point decisively behind." *The Lighted Windows*, p. 85.

60. Doderer, *Tangenten*, p. 762.

61. Doderer, *Tangenten*, p. 471. He goes on to counter this quotation with one from Gütersloh: Gütersloh wondered why "any particular category of human activity should be more impure in itself than any other. Surely the categories as such are innocent."

62. See *Erinnerungen an Heimito von Doderer*, ed. Xaver Schaffgotsch (Munich, 1972). Doderer told his friend and fellow officer Qualtinger (111) in 1943 that they were watching "the burial of a high culture" and both were convinced that the war would be lost (112). See also Vincent Kling's translation of "Unter schwarzen Sternen" [Under Black Stars] in *Chicago Review* 26, no. 2 (1974): 36–45.

63. See Heimito von Doderer, "Sexualität und totaler Staat," *Die Wiederkehr der Drachen: Aufsätze/Traktate/Reden*, ed. Wendelin Schmidt-Dengler (Munich, 1970), pp. 275–298.

64. In the 1940s Doderer was usually thinking of "existential apperception" (265), and the distinction itself emphasizes Doderer's move beyond an understanding of apperception simply in terms of consciousness.

65. Doderer's emphasis on the relationship between inner and outer preceded his Thomism, but his conversion to Catholicism in 1939–1940 and his discovery of Thomism in 1942 intensified the appeal of this way of thinking. On Thomism, see Siegmund Kastner, "Thomismus und Roman" (Ph.D. diss., University of Vienna, 1977); and Wendelin Schmidt-Dengler, "'Analogia entis' oder das 'Schweigen unendlicher Räume': Theologische Themen bei Heimito von Doderer und Thomas Bernhard," in Gott in der Literatur, ed. Gottfried Bachl and Helmut Schink (Linz, 1976).

66. The distinction between sexuality and eros had no significance for Doderer, and he simply used these words interchangeably.

67. Doderer's conception of the mind recalls Musil: "There is nothing else left: one must simply become highly intelligent—by which I always want to have a double meaning understood, the forming thinking and the analytic mode" (743).

68. See Engelbert Pfeiffer, The Writer's Place: Heimito von Doderer and the Alsergrund District of Vienna, trans. Vincent Kling (Riverside, 2001), pp. 37–38. Dr. Rudolf Allers was an important source of Doderer's knowledge of both psychoanalysis and Thomism. In 1944 Doderer remembered hearing about Weininger as a little boy and argued that it was time to build Weininger a monument for the discovery of the concept of the "henid" alone. Doderer, Tangenten, pp. 230–231.

69. Some commentators have found it difficult to appreciate the "Braudelian" element in Doderer, his portrayal of structures and his sense of longue durée. Particularly in Die Strudlhofstiege, he represents the years before and after the First World War as if they belonged to the same period, despite the conspicuous political changes.

70. The German word Befangenheit may mean either shyness or bias in a way that is difficult to capture in a single English word. Doderer used the word in the sense of constraint to mean an entrapment in subjectivity of the sort he suffered from himself in the 1920s and 1930s. Thus, he thought of Befangenheit as the inhibition of open perception, as entanglement in subjectivity. This pseudological egocentricity breaks off "the bridge of reality that binds and coordinates inner and outer" (628). As in The Lighted Windows, the voyeur is trapped behind the window with his records.

71. For a recent attempt to transcend the assumptions of the two main traditions of Doderer-interpretation, see Rudolf Helmstetter, Das Ornament der Grammatik in der Eskalation der Zitate: "Die Strudlhofstiege," Doderers moderne Poetik des Romans, und die Rezeptionsgeschichte (Munich, 1995). Helmstetter points to Doderer's similarities to Mikhail Bakhtin and Julia Kristeva.

72. See Reininger, Die Erlösung des Bürgers, especially chapter 10.

73. Heimito von Doderer, Die Strudlhofstiege oder Melzer und die Tiefe der Jahre (Munich, 1980), p. 678.

74. Joachim Schröder, for example, has questioned the possibility of an unprejudiced apperception and emphasized the role of Doderer's conservative views in lim-

iting the openness of his apperception and defining his critique of political ideologies. See Schröder, *Apperzeption*, pp. 71–80. See also the comparison of Doderer to Heidegger in Reininger, *Die Erlösung des Bürgers*, pp. 88–89.

75. See Eilizabeth C. Hesson, *Twentieth Century Odyssey: Study of Heimito von Doderer's Die Dämonen* (Columbia, S.C., 1982).

76. See Helmut Luger, "Eine ideologiekritische Analyse der theoretische Schriften Heimito von Doderers" (Ph.D. diss., University of Innsbruck, 1990), p. 245.

77. In *Democracy in Plural Societies* (New Haven, 1977), Arend Lijphart characterizes Austria from 1945 to 1966 as the pure case of consociational democracy (105) in response to the sharp conflicts between Catholic and socialist elites from 1918 to 1945.

78. See Ulrike Schupp, *Ordnung und Bruch: Antinomien in Heimito von Doderers Roman Die Dämonen* (Frankfurt am Main, 1994).

79. Indeed, Geyrenhoff states this in the Overture as a characteristic principle of the novel: "[I]n fact you need only draw a single thread at any point you choose out of the fabric of life and the run will make a pathway across the whole, and down that wider pathway each of the other threads will become successively visible, one by one. For the whole is contained in the smallest segment of anyone's life-story" (7).

80. See Stieg, *Frucht des Feuers*.

81. In *The Demons*, 1: 452, René Stangeler describes history as "the science of the future" in a discussion of the Middle Ages.

82. Doderer, *The Demons*, p. 1020. On Doderer's portrayal of 1927, see Schupp, *Ordnung und Bruch*. Other critics have emphasized the limits of Doderer's perspective from a Social Democratic point of view, but much more striking is his attempt to take his own period and the people he knew this seriously.

83. See Anton Reininger, "'Die Dämonen': Totaler Roman und antirevolutionärer Traktat," in *Literatur und Kritik* 80 (1973): 599–608; and Reininger, *Die Erlösung des Bürgers*. Reininger argues that Doderer had simply mistakenly associated some of his themes with National Socialism but emphasizes the continuity of Doderer's conservatism throughout his work. Hesson contends in *Twentieth Century Odyssey* (86) that Reininger exaggerates the degree to which Doderer tried to expurgate his earlier fascism and anti-Semitism. See also Hubert Kerscher, *Zweite Wirklichkeit* (Frankfurt am Main, 1998), p. 161. Kerscher emphasizes that the mainly conservative reception of Doderer's work in the 1950s tended to overlook what was disguised and never explicitly thematized: Doderer's own critique of National Socialism.

84. See Hesson, *Twentieth Century Odyssey* (39–53) on Doderer's revisions between 1951 and 1956 and his introduction of the "'ideologically disinfected'" group.

85. See Karl Heinrich Schneider, *Die technisch-moderne Welt im Werk Heimito von Doderers* (Frankfurt am Main, 1985).

86. See Doderer's comments on positivism and the bourgeois ideology of progress in *Tangenten*: "[F]or all acts of the spirit the *hic et nunc* is absolutely constitu-

tive; by this we distinguish ourselves from the revolutionaries who always need a program and projects and a future as a garbage dump for what is unrealized" (223).

87. Doderer makes the modern city palpable (telephones, electric lights, automobiles) as it emerged just before and after the First World War, but he also concurs with the view "that low-grade minds are always most susceptible to progress and its technical toys" (553).

88. An aspect of Doderer's work that has not been emphasized enough is his attempt (particularly in *The Demons*) to extend the values of liberalism to women. Women play prominent roles in the novel, and Doderer was gifted at portraying the social predicament of women and the ways they are forced to negotiate female roles and identities. Notable in addition to the characters based on Gusti are Frau Ruthmayr, the captain's wealthy widow, who after years of being escorted by Levielle finds her way to Geyrenhoff; Anny Gräven, who is Weininger's ideal prostitute; Quapp, who turns out not to be Schlaggenberg's sister but the daughter of Captain Ruthmayr and Countess Chargiel; and Mary K., who is based on a woman Doderer met through Gusti.

89. Doderer, *The Demons*, p. 691 ff.

90. This is chapter 7 of part 2; Doderer wrote the document in late medieval German.

91. Doderer, *The Demons*, p. 1018. René Stangeler emphasizes that he does not think of political ideologies as sublimations of sexuality. Rather, Achaz's "artificial, arranged sexual experiences" and political ideology are both forms of second reality.

92. See George Steiner, *In Bluebeard's Castle* (New Haven, 1971).

93. See also "Jutta Bamberger" and Doderer's own dislike for his childhood and the world in which he grew up. The liberal era was his childhood—and what he disliked.

94. Doderer, *Tangenten*, p. 586.

95. Doderer emphasizes Imre von Gyurkicz's lack of memory and his ability to lie to himself. Renata and her friend Sylvia actually meet Imre in the scene in which he defends himself against Meisgeier's knife attack; Imre dies in the fighting on July 15, perhaps because of the troubles Meisgeier starts for (entirely nonideological) reasons of his own.

96. Even when Schröder makes Doderer's ethical and aesthetic intentions explicit, he is reluctant to accept them at face value. Schröder wants to protect the epistemological validity of claims to objectivity that Doderer sometimes criticizes as ideological. But what was central for Doderer was overcoming his own psychological and ideological entrapment in order to be able to write. He concluded that the key to writing (for him at least) was apperception (and the ethical attitude that came with it) and that the model of apperception was the erotic situation.

97. See Dietrich Weber, *Heimito von Doderer: Studien zu seinem Romanwerk* (Munich, 1963), pp. 6–7; and Doderer, "Grundlagen und Funktion des Romans," *Die Wiederkehr der Drachen: Aufsätze/Traktate/Reden*, ed. Wendelin Schmidt-Dengler (Munich, 1970), pp. 149–175. *The Demons* is not meant to be a rationally coherent whole but an image of the complexity and unevenness of life.

98. See Stangeler on the philosophical content of the ideologies of his time: "'Today such a thing is falsely called a philosophy. As if it were of rational origin!

But the mutual hatred that constantly breaks out between these rival philosophies should tell us something. That alone should indicate that their real source has nothing to do with divergent opinions on how "humanity" can be helped, or on this class or that race, six of one and half a dozen of the other, and such like idiocies'" (1019).

99. Doderer, *The Demons*, p. 985. See also p. 831: "Every triumph is a cancellation," Williams said. "Every success in general. By the laws of compensation, the tension is relieved. And that produces an insipid aftertaste. At bottom there is something repellent about everyone who, after a long effort, is what you might call exonerated by success. It's a dubious stage in a person's life."

100. Doderer, *Tangenten*, p. 230.

101. See Doderer, *Der Grenzwald: Roman Nr. 7, Zweiter Teil* (Munich, 1967), pp. 246–247.

102. *Die Merowinger* is scurrilous like Doderer himself—he was very different from Geyrenhoff, as Dietrich Weber was surprised to discover, but *Merowinger* is also very different from *The Demons. The Merowingians, or The Total Family*, trans. Vinal Overing Binner (Los Angeles, 1996).

Conclusion

1. Robert Musil, "Helpless Europe," in *Precision and Soul: Essays and Addresses* (Chicago, 1990), p. 127.

2. Musil and Doderer both developed Weininger's understanding of female sexuality in more positive directions.

3. On the similarities between the other condition and Doderer's notion of "first reality," see Wolfgang Rath, "Leben als maximale Forderung. Der ,aZ' bei Robert Musil und Heimito von Doderers Erste Wirklichkeit," in *Excentrische Einsätze: Studien und Essays zum Werk Heimito von Doderers*, ed. Kai Luehrs (Berlin, 1998), pp. 302–318.

4. Musil thought of Freud as more a writer than a scientist, and Doderer emphasized that Freud's significance lay in his whole way of thinking rather than in any particular theory. Musil believed that psychoanalysis had made it possible to talk about sexuality: "That is its enormous achievement for civilization. Next to that, it may even seem unimportant [to ask?] what value it has as psychology." Robert Musil, "Aus einem Rapial," *Gesammelte Werke*, vol. 7, p. 832. Although Doderer's critique of ideology in *The Demons* extends to the uses of psychoanalysis, it aims not at Freud's ideas but at the way psychoanalysis can be used to satisfy the individual's need for order and control. See Heimito von Doderer, *The Demons*, trans. Richard and Clara Winston (New York, 1961), p. 439.

5. Perhaps the strangest yield of this research has been a variation on Wittgenstein's view in the *Tractatus* that philosophy properly understood is something that has nothing to do with philosophy at all; as I explored thinking about sexuality and gender in Vienna, this thinking seemed at times to have nothing to do with sexuality and gender at all.

6. See my "Austria as a Region of German Culture: 1900–1938," *Austrian History Yearbook* 28 (1992): 135–148.

7. This study also draws attention to what these three Austrian thinkers did not share—and to some of the limits of generalizing about Austrian culture. What was most important about Weininger, Musil, and Doderer as individual, creative people is only obliquely connected to Vienna, except as a location for receiving international impulses in science and literature. Nonetheless, all three writers were shaped by an intellectual structure that differed from England or France or even Germany.

8. In "The Serious Writer" (*Precision and Soul*, p. 261), Musil offers a nice formulation (drawn from Wilhelm von Humboldt) about the causes of intellectual creativity. Musil characterizes "significant individuality as a power of the spirit that springs up without reference to the course of events and begins a new series."

$\mathscr{S}$ELECT $\mathscr{B}$IBLIOGRAPHY

◈

GENERAL

Adler, Friedrich. *Ernst Machs Ueberwindung des mechanischen Materialismus.* Vienna, 1918.

Albisetti, James C. *Schooling German Girls and Women: Secondary and Higher Education in the Nineteenth Century.* Princeton, 1988.

Anderson, Harriet. *Utopian Feminism: Women's Movements in fin-de-siècle Vienna.* New Haven, 1992.

Anderson, Lorin. "Freud, Nietzsche." *Salmagundi* 47–48 (1980): 3–29.

Andics, Hellmut. *Gründerzeit: Das Schwarzgelbe Wien bis 1867.* Vienna, 1981.

Austrian Women in the Nineteenth and Twentieth Centuries. Ed. David Good, Margarete Grandner, and Mary Jo Maynes. Providence, 1996.

Bader, William B. *Austria between East and West, 1945–1955.* Stanford, 1966.

Barrett, William. *Irrational Man: A Study in Existential Philosophy.* New York, 1958.

Bauer, Roger. *Idealismus und seine Gegner in Österreich.* Heidelberg, 1966.

———. *La realité royaume de Dieu: Études sur l'originalité du théâtre viennois dans la première moitié du XIXe siècle.* Munich, 1965.

Belke, Ingrid. *Die sozialreformerischen Ideen von Josef Popper-Lynkeus (1838–1921).* Tübingen, 1978.

Beller, Steven. *Vienna and the Jews, 1867–1938: A Cultural History.* Cambridge, 1989.

Bettelheim, Bruno. *Freud and Man's Soul.* New York, 1983.

Birken, Lawrence. *Consuming Desire: Sexual Science and the Emergence of a Culture of Abundance, 1871–1914.* Ithaca, 1988.

Bochenski, I. M. *Contemporary European Philosophy.* Berkeley, 1957.

Börner, Wilhelm. *Friedrich Jodl.* Stuttgart, 1911.

Bourgeois Society in Nineteenth-Century Europe. Ed. Jürgen Kocka and Allan Mitchell. Oxford, 1993.

Boyer, John W. *Culture and Political Crisis in Vienna: Christian Socialism in Power, 1897–1918.* Chicago, 1995.

———. *Political Radicalism in Late Imperial Vienna: Origins of the Christian Social Movement, 1848–1897.* Chicago, 1981.

Braunthal, Julius. *Victor und Friedrich Adler: Zwei Generationen Arbeiterbewegung.* Vienna, 1965.

Briefe an, von und um Josephine von Wertheimstein. Ed. Robert A. Kann. Vienna, 1981.

Broch, Hermann. *Hugo von Hofmannsthal and His Time: The European Imagination, 1860–1920.* Trans. Michael P. Steinberg. Chicago, 1984.

———. "Notizen zu einer systematischen Ästhetik." In *Die unbekannte Grösse und Frühe Schriften mit den Briefen an Willa Muir.* Ed. Ernst Schönwiese, pp. 217–236. Zurich, 1961.

Bruford, W. H. *The German Tradition of Self-Cultivation: Bildung from Humboldt to Thomas Mann.* London, 1975.

Büchner, Ludwig. *Kraft und Stoff.* Frankfurt am Main, 1858.

Bukey, Evan Burr. *Hitler's Austria: Popular Sentiment in the Nazi Era, 1938–1945.* Chapel Hill, N.C., 2000.

Canetti, Elias. *The Play of the Eyes.* Trans. Ralph Manheim. New York, 1986.

Cassirer, Ernst. *The Philosophy of the Enlightenment.* Trans. Fritz C. A. Koelln and James P. Pettegrove. Princeton, 1951.

Chamberlain, Houston Stewart. *Foundations of the Nineteenth Century.* Trans. John Lees. Intro. by George L. Mosse. 2 vols. New York, 1968.

Charmatz, Richard. *Österreichs innere Geschichte von 1848 bis 1907.* 2 vols. Leipzig, 1911.

Comte, Auguste. *The Essential Comte: Selected from Cours de philosophie positive.* Trans. Margaret Clarke. New York, 1974.

Daviau, Donald G. *Hermann Bahr.* Boston, 1985.

Demetz, Peter. *Postwar German Literature: A Critical Introduction.* New York, 1970.

Die Wiener Jahrhundertwende. Ed. Jürgen Nautz and Richard Vahrenkamp. Vienna, 1993.

Dijkstra, Bram. *Idols of Perversity: Fantasies of Feminine Evil in Fin-de-siècle Culture.* New York, 1986.

Du Mont, Emrich. *Der Fortschritt im Lichte der Lehren Schopenhauer's und Darwin's.* Leipzig, 1876.

"Durch Erkenntnis zu Freiheit und Gluck . . .": Frauen an der Universität Wien (ab 1897). Ed. Waltraud Heindl and Marina Tichy. Vienna, 1990.

Eder, Karl. *Der Liberalismus in Altösterreich: Geisteshaltung, Politik und Kultur*. Munich, 1955.

Ellenberger, Henri. *The Discovery of the Unconscious: The History and Evolution of Dynamic Psychiatry*. New York, 1970.

Evans, Richard J. *The Feminist Movement in Germany, 1894–1933*. London, 1976.

Expressionismus in Österreich. Ed. Klaus Amann and Armin A. Wallas. Vienna, 1994.

Field, Geoffrey G. *Evangelist of Race: The German Vision of Houston Stewart Chamberlain*. New York, 1981.

Fischer, Kurt R. *Philosophie aus Wien*. Vienna, 1991.

Fliess, Wilhelm. *Der Ablauf des Lebens*. Leipzig and Vienna, 1906.

Foucault, Michel. *The History of Sexuality, Vol. I: An Introduction*. Trans. Robert Hurley. New York, 1978.

Franz, Georg. *Liberalismus: Die deutschliberale Bewegung in der Habsburgischen Monarchie*. Munich, 1955.

Freud, Sigmund. *The Complete Letters of Sigmund Freud to Wilhelm Fliess, 1887–1904*. Trans. and ed. Jeffrey Moussaieff Masson. Cambridge, Mass., 1985.

———. *The Letters of Sigmund Freud to Eduard Silberstein, 1871–1881*. Intro. by Walter Boehlich. Trans. Arnold J. Pomerans. Cambridge, Mass., 1990.

———. *The Standard Edition of the Complete Psychological Works of Sigmund Freud*. 24 vols. London, 1963.

Frevert, Ute. *Women in German History: From Bourgeois Emancipation to Sexual Liberation*. Trans. Stuart McKinnon-Evans. Oxford, 1989.

Fritzsche, Peter. *Reading Berlin 1900*. Cambridge, Mass., 1996.

Fuchs, Albert. *Geistige Strömungen in Österreich, 1867–1918*. 1949. Reprint, Vienna, 1984.

Gasman, Daniel. *The Scientific Origins of National Socialism: Social Darwinism in Ernst Haeckel and the German Monist League*. New York, 1971.

Gay, Peter. *The Bourgeois Experience: Victoria to Freud, Vol. I: The Education of the Senses*. New York, 1984.

———. *Freud, Jews, and Other Germans*. New York, 1978.

———. *Freud: A Life for Our Time*. New York, 1988.

———. *Weimar Culture*. New York, 1968.

Gilman, Sander L. *Difference and Pathology: Stereotypes of Sexuality, Race, and Madness*. Ithaca, 1985.

———. *The Jew's Body*. London, 1991.

Greiner, Ulrich. *Der Tod des Nachsommers*. Vienna, 1979.

Gregory, Frederick. *Scientific Materialism in Nineteenth Century Germany*. Dordrecht, 1977.

Grillparzer, Franz. *Sämtliche Werke.* 4 vols. Ed. Peter Frank and Karl Pörnbacher. Munich, 1964.

Gruber, Helmut. *Red Vienna: Experiment in Working-Class Culture, 1919–1934.* New York, 1991.

Gütersloh, Albert Paris. *Sonne und Mond: Ein historischer Roman aus der Gegenwart.* Munich, 1962.

Hacohen, Malachi Haim. *Karl Popper: The Formative Years, 1902–1945. Politics and Philosophy in Interwar Vienna* (Cambridge, 2000).

Haeckel, Ernst. *The Riddle of the Universe: At the Close of the Nineteenth Century.* Trans. Joseph McCabe. Buffalo, 1992.

Hainisch, Marianne. "Die Geschichte der Frauenbewegung in Österreich." In *Die Geschichte der Frauenbewegung in den Kulturländern.* Part 1 of *Handbuch der Frauenbewegung.* Ed. Helene Lange und Gertraud Bäumer, 167–188. Berlin, 1901.

Haller, Rudolf. *Questions on Wittgenstein.* London, 1988.

Hanisch, Ernst. *Der lange Schatten des Staates: Österreichische Gesellschaftsgeschichte im 20. Jahrhundert.* Vienna, 1994.

Harrison, Thomas. *1910: The Emancipation of Dissonance.* Berkeley, 1996.

Hartmann, Eduard von. *Philosophy of the Unconscious.* Trans. William Chatterton Coupland. London, 1950.

Heer, Friedrich. *Land im Strom der Zeit: Österreich gestern, heute, morgen.* Vienna, 1958.

Herbart, J. F. *Science of Education.* Trans. Henry M. and Emmie Felkin. Boston, 1896.

Hirschfeld, Magnus. *The Sexual History of the World War.* New York, 1941.

Höbelt, Lothar. *Kornblume und Kaiseradler: Die deutsch freiheitlichen Parteien Altösterreichs, 1881–1918.* Vienna, 1993.

Holborn, Hajo. "German Idealism in the Light of Social History." In *Germany and Europe: Historical Essays,* 1–32. New York, 1971.

Hughes, H. Stuart. *Consciousness and Society.* New York, 1958.

Ingrao, Charles. "The Problem of 'Enlightened Absolutism' and the German States." *Journal of Modern History* 58 suppl. (1986): 161–180.

Janik, Allan S. "Schopenhauer and the Early Wittgenstein." *Philosophical Studies* 15 (1966): 76–95.

Janik, Allan S., and Stephen Toulmin. *Wittgenstein's Vienna.* New York, 1973.

Jelavich, Peter. *Berlin Cabaret.* Cambridge, Mass., 1993.

———. *Munich and Theatrical Modernism: Politics, Playwriting, and Performance, 1890–1914.* Cambridge, Mass., 1985.

Jenks, William A. *The Austrian Electoral Reform of 1907.* New York, 1950.

Jodl, Margarete. *Friedrich Jodl: Sein Leben und Wirken.* Stuttgart, 1920.

Johnston, William M. *The Austrian Mind: An Intellectual and Social History, 1848–1938.* Berkeley, 1972.

Jones, Ernst. *The Life and Work of Sigmund Freud.* 3 vols. New York, 1953.

Judson, Pieter. *Exclusive Revolutionaries: Liberal Politics, Social Experience, and National Identity in the Austrian Empire, 1848–1914.* Ann Arbor, 1996.

Kann, Robert A. "Die niedergeschlagene Revolution von 1848 und ihr Einfluss auf die österreichische Zukunft." In *Wien und Europa zwischen den Revolutionen (1789–1848)*. Ed. Reinhard Urbach, 253–260. Vienna, 1978.

———. *A History of the Habsburg Empire, 1526–1918*. Berkeley, 1974.

———. *The Multinational Monarchy: Nationalism and National Reform in the Habsburg Monarchy, 1848–1918*. 2 vols. New York, 1950.

Kant, Immanuel. *Foundations of the Metaphysics of Morals*. Trans. Lewis White Beck. New York, 1959.

———. *On History*. Ed. Lewis White Beck. New York, 1985.

Kassner, Rudolf. *Sämtliche Werke*. 10 vols. Pfullingen, 1969–1991.

Klemperer, Klemens von. *Ignaz Seipel: Christian Statesman in a Time of Crisis*. Princeton, 1972.

Krafft-Ebing, Richard von. *Psychopathia Sexualis*. Trans. Harry E. Wedeck. New York, 1965.

Kruntorad, Paul. "Prosa in Österreich seit 1945." In *Kindlers Literaturgeschichte der Gegenwart: Die Zeitgenössische Literatur Österreichs, I*. Ed. Hilde Spiel. Frankfurt am Main, 1976–1980.

Lange, Frederick Albert. *The History of Materialism*. 3 vols. 1879–1881. Reprint, New York, 1974.

Landes, David. *Unbound Prometheus: Technological Change and Industrial Development in Western Europe from 1750 to the Present*. London, 1969.

Lange, Karl. *Apperception: A Monograph on Psychology and Pedagogy*. Ed. Charles De Garno. Trans. by members of the Herbart Club. Boston, 1896.

Laqueur, Thomas. *Making Sex: Body and Gender from the Greeks to Freud*. Cambridge, Mass., 1990.

Leibniz, G. W. *The Monadology and Other Philosophical Writings*. Trans. Robert Latta. London, 1965.

———. *New Essays on Human Understanding*. Trans. Peter Remnant and Jonathan Bennett. Cambridge, 1982.

Lentze, Hans. *Die Universitätsreform des Ministers Graf Leo Thun-Hohenstein*. Vienna, 1962.

Le Rider, Jacques. *Modernity and Crises of Identity: Culture and Society in Fin-de-siècle Vienna*. Trans. Rosemary Morris. New York, 1993.

Lesky, Erna. *The Vienna Medical School of the 19th Century*. Trans. L. Williams and I. S. Levij. Baltimore, 1976.

Lijphart, Arend. *Democracy in Plural Societies: A Comparative Exploration*. New Haven, 1977.

Lindenfeld, David. *The Transformation of Positivism: Alexius Meinong and European Thought, 1880–1920*. Berkeley, 1980.

Luft, David. S. "Austria as a Region of German Culture: 1900–1938." *Austrian History Yearbook* 23 (1992): 135–148.

———. "Schopenhauer, Austria, and the Generation of 1905." *Central European History* 16, no. 1 (March 1983): 53–75.

———. "Science and Irrationalism in Freud's Vienna." *Modern Austrian Literature* 23, no. 2 (1990): 89–97.

Lukács, Georg. *Die Seele und die Formen: Essays.* Berlin, 1911.

———. *The Destruction of Reason.* Trans. Peter Palmer. London, 1980.

———. *The Theory of the Novel: A Historico-philosophical Essay on the Forms of the Great Epic Literature.* Trans. Anna Bostock. Cambridge, Mass., 1971.

Lütkehaus, Ludger. *"Dieses wahre innere Afrika": Texte zur Entdeckung des Unbewussten vor Freud.* Frankfurt am Main, 1989.

Maas, Ferdinand. *Der Josephinismus: Quellen zu seiner Geschichte in Österreich, 1760–1790.* 5 vols. Vienna, 1951.

Mach, Ernst. *The Analysis of Sensations and the Relation of the Physical to the Psychical.* Trans. C. M. Williams. New York, 1959.

Mandelbaum, Maurice. *History, Man and Reason: A Study in Nineteenth-Century Thought.* Baltimore, 1971.

Manuel, Frank. *The Prophets of Paris.* New York, 1962.

Marcus, Steven. *The Other Victorians: A Study of Sexuality and Pornography in Mid-Nineteenth Century England.* New York, 1974.

Mazlish, Bruce. "Freud and Nietzsche." *Psychoanalytic Review* 55, no. 3 (1968): 360–375.

Mayreder, Rosa. *A Survey of the Woman Problem.* Trans. Hermann Scheffauer. 1913. Reprint, Westport, Conn., 1982.

McGrath, William J. *Dionysian Art and Populist Politics in Austria.* New Haven, 1974.

———. *Freud's Discovery of Psychoanalysis: The Politics of Hysteria.* Ithaca, 1986.

Meinecke, Friedrich. *The Age of German Liberation: 1795–1815.* Trans. Peter Paret and Helmut Fischer. Berkeley, 1977.

Meister, Richard. *Geschichte der Wiener Universität.* Vienna, 1934.

Minder, Robert. *"Hölderlin unter den Deutschen" und andere Aufsätze zur deutschen Literatur.* Frankfurt am Main, 1968.

Möbius, P. J. *Geschlecht und Unbescheidenheit.* Halle, 1907.

———. *Über den physiologischen Schwachsinn des Weibes.* Halle, 1905.

Mosse, George L. *The Crisis of German Ideology: Intellectual Origins of the Third Reich.* New York, 1964.

———. *Nationalism and Sexuality: Middle-Class Morality and Sexual Norms in Modern Europe.* Madison, 1985.

Müller, Robert. *Kritische Schriften III (Schriften 1921–1924).* Vienna, 1996.

Nietzsche, Friedrich. *Beyond Good and Evil.* Trans. Walter Kaufmann. New York, 1996.

———. *The Gay Science.* Trans. Walter Kaufmann. New York, 1974.

———. *Schopenhauer as Educator.* Trans. James W. Hillesheim and Malcolm R. Simpson. South Bend, 1965.

Paret, Peter. *Berlin Secession: Modernism and Its Enemies in Imperial Germany.* Cambridge, Mass., 1980.

Pulzer, P. G. J. *The Rise of Political Anti-Semitism in Germany and Austria.* New York, 1964.

Rabinbach, Anson. *The Crisis of Austrian Socialism: From Red Vienna to Civil War, 1927–1934.* Chicago, 1983.

Rath, R. John. *The Viennese Revolution of 1848.* Austin, 1957.

Reininger, Robert. *Friedrich Nietzsches Kampf um den Sinn des Lebens.* Vienna, 1922.

Rhaeticus, Alfred. "Die Geschichte des Faches Philosophie an der Universität Wien, 1848–1938." Ph.D. diss., University of Vienna, 1950.

Richardson, Robert D., Jr. *Emerson: The Mind on Fire. A Biography.* Berkeley, 1995.

Ringer, Fritz. *The Decline of the German Mandarins: The German Academic Community, 1890–1933.* Cambridge, Mass., 1969.

———. *French Academic Culture in Comparative Perspective, 1890–1920.* New York, 1992.

Robertson, Priscilla Smith. *An Experience of Women: Pattern and Change in Nineteenth-Century Europe.* Philadelphia, 1982.

Robinson, Paul. *The Modernization of Sex: Havelock Ellis, Alfred Kinsey, William Masters and Virginia Johnson.* New York, 1976.

Rokitansky, Carl von. *Selbstbiographie und Anrittsrede.* Ed. Erna Lesky. Vienna, 1960.

Rosen, Stanley. *Nihilism: A Philosophical Essay.* New Haven, 1969.

Rossbacher, Karlheinz. *Literatur und Liberalismus: Zur Kultur der Ringstrassenzeit in Wien.* Vienna, 1992.

Rozenblit, Marsha. *The Jews of Vienna, 1867–1914: Assimilation and Identity.* Albany, 1983.

Ryan, Judith. "Die andere Psychologie: Ernst Mach und die Folgen." In *Österreichische Gegenwart: Die moderne Literatur und ihr Verhaltnis zur Tradition.* Ed. Wolfgang Paulsen. Munich, 1980.

———. *The Vanishing Subject: Early Psychology and Literary Modernism.* Chicago, 1991.

Sartre, Jean Paul. *Being and Nothingness.* Trans. Hazel E. Barnes. New York, 1956.

Sauer, Werner. *Österreichische Philosophie zwischen Aufklärung und Restauration: Beiträge zur Geschichte des frühkantianismus in der Donaumonarchie.* Würzburg, 1982.

Schöndorf, Harald. *Der Leib im Denken Schopenhauers und Fichtes.* Munich, 1982.

Schönwiese, Ernst. *Literatur in Wien zwischen 1930 und 1980.* Vienna, 1980.

Schopenhauer, Arthur. *Essays and Aphorisms.* Trans. R. J. Hollingdale. New York, 1970.

———. *The World as Will and Representation.* 2 vols. Trans. E. F. J. Payne. New York, 1966.

Schorske, Carl E. *Fin-de-siècle Vienna: Politics and Culture.* New York, 1980.

———. "Generational Tension and Cultural Change: Reflections on the Case of Vienna." *Daedelus* 107, no. 4 (fall 1978): 111–122.

Schulz, Walter. *Philosophie in der veränderten Welt.* Pfulligen, 1972.

Scott, Joan Wallach. *Gender and the Politics of History.* New York, 1988.

Shattuck, Roger. *Forbidden Knowledge: From Prometheus to Pornography.* New York, 1996.

Sheehan, James J. *German History, 1770–1866.* Oxford, 1991.

———. *German Liberalism in the Nineteenth Century.* Chicago, 1978.

Sighele, Scipio. *Le Crime à deux: Essai de psycho-pathologie sociale.* Paris, 1910.

Smith, Barry. *Austrian Philosophy: The Legacy of Franz Brentano.* Chicago, 1994.

Sokel, Walter H. *The Writer in Extremis: Expressionism in Twentieth-Century German Literature.* Stanford, 1959.

Spiel, Hilde. *Fanny von Arnstein: A Daughter of the Enlightenment, 1758–1818.* Trans. Christine Shuttleworth. New York, 1991.

———. *Vienna's Golden Autumn, 1866–1938.* London, 1987.

Spreitzer, Brigitte. *TEXTUREN: Die österreichische Moderne der Frauen.* Vienna, 1999.

Springer, Elizabeth. *Geschichte und Kulturleben der Wiener Ringstrasse.* Wiesbaden, 1979.

Stack, George J. *Lange and Nietzsche.* Berlin, 1983.

Stadler, Friedrich. *Vom Positivismus zur "Wissenschaftlichen Weltauffassung": Am Beispiel der Wirkungsgeschichte von Ernst Mach in Österreich von 1895 bis 1934.* Vienna, 1982.

Steinberg, Michael P. *The Meaning of the Salzburg Festival: Austria as Theater and Ideology, 1890–1938.* Ithaca, 1990.

Steiner, George. *In Bluebeard's Castle: Some Notes Towards the Redefinition of Culture.* New Haven, 1971.

Stern, Fritz. *The Politics of Cultural Despair: A Study in the Rise of Germanic Ideology.* Berkeley, 1961.

Stourzh, Gerald. "The Multinational Empire Revisited." *Austrian History Yearbook* 23 (1992): 1–22.

Strelka, Joseph. *Brücke zu vielen Ufern: Von Wesen und Eigenart der österreichischen Literatur.* Vienna, 1966.

Szabo, Franz A. J. *Kaunitz and Enlightened Absolutism, 1753–1780.* New York, 1994.

Timms, Edward. *Karl Kraus, Apocalyptic Satirist: Culture and Catastrophe in Habsburg Vienna.* New Haven, 1986.

Trommler, Frank. "Österreich im Roman und Wirklichkeit. Eine Untersuchung zur dargestellten Wirklichkeit bei Joseph Roth, Robert Musil, und Heimito von Doderer." Ph.D. diss., University of Munich, 1965.

Valjavec, Fritz. *Der Josephinismus: Zur geistigen Entwicklung Österreichs im achtzehnten und neunzehnten Jahrhundert.* 2d ed. Vienna, 1945.

Van Herik, Judith. *Freud on Femininity and Faith.* Berkeley, 1982.

Wadl, Wilhelm. *Liberalismus und soziale Frage in Österreich.* Vienna, 1987.

Wagner, Nike. *Geist und Geschlecht: Karl Kraus und die Erotik der Wiener Moderne.* Frankfurt am Main, 1982.

Wandruszka, Adam. *Geschichte einer Zeitung: Das Schicksal "der Presse" und der "Neuen freien Presse" von 1848 zur Zweiten Republik,* Vienna, 1958.

———. "Österreichs politische Struktur: Die Entwicklung der Parteien und politischen Bewegungen." In *Geschichte der Republik Österreich.* Ed. Heinrich Benedikt, Walter Goldinger, et. al., 289–486 Vienna, 1954.

Weeks, Jeffrey. *Sexuality.* New York, 1986.

Weinzierl-Fischer, Erika. *Die österreichischen Konkordate von 1855 und 1933.* Munich, 1960.

Weiss, Walter. "Thematisierung der 'Ordnung' in der österreichischen Literatur." In *Dauern im Wandel.* Ed. Walter Strolz and Oscar Schatz. Vienna, 1966.

Whyte, Lancelot Law. *The Unconscious before Freud.* New York, 1960.

Williams, Raymond. *Culture and Society: 1780–1950.* New York, 1958.

Wistrich, Robert S. *The Jews of Vienna in the Age of Franz Joseph.* Oxford, 1990.

Wohl, Robert. *The Generation of 1914.* Cambridge, Mass., 1979.

Wolke, Werner. *Hugo von Hofmannsthal.* Hamburg, 1967.

Woolf, Virginia. *A Room of One's Own.* New York, 1981.

Worbs, Michael. *Nervenkunst: Literatur und Psychoanalyse im Wien der Jahrhundertwende.* Frankfurt am Main, 1983.

Wotke, K. "Kant in Österreich vor hundert Jahren." *Zeitschrift für die österreichischen Gymnasien* 54 (1903): 289–305.

Zohn, Harry. " . . . ich bin ein Sohn der deutschen Sprache nur . . .": Jüdisches Erbe in der österreichischen Literatur.* Vienna, 1986.

Otto Weininger

Primary Sources

Eros und Psyche: Studien und Briefe, 1899–1902. Ed. Hannelore Rodlauer. Vienna, 1990.

Gedanken über Geschlechtsprobleme von Otto Weininger. Ed. Robert Saudek. Berlin, 1907.

Geschlecht und Charakter: Eine prinzipielle Untersuchung. 1903. Reprint, Munich, 1980.

Sex and Character. Authorized translation from the sixth German edition. London and New York, 1906.

Taschenbuch und Briefe an einen Freund. Ed. Artur Gerber. Leipzig, 1919.

Über die Letzten Dinge. Preface by Moriz Rappaport. Vienna, 1907.

Secondary Sources

Abrahamsen, David. *The Mind and Death of a Genius.* New York, 1946.

Baron, Lawrence. "Theodor Lessing: Between Jewish Self-Hatred and Zionism." *Leo Baeck Institute Yearbook* 26 (1981): 323–340.

Biro, Paul. *Die Sittlichkeitsmetaphysik Otto Weiningers: Eine geistegeschichtliche Studie.* Vienna, 1927.

Cavaglion, Alberto, and Michel David. "Weininger und die italienische Kultur." In *Otto Weininger: Werk und Wirkung.* Ed. Jacques Le Rider and Norbert Leser, 37–49. Vienna, 1984.

Centgraf, Alexander. *Ein Jude treibt Philosophie.* Berlin, 1943.

Dallago, Carl. *Otto Weininger und sein Werk.* Innsbruck, 1912.

Gilman, Charlotte Perkins. "Review of Dr. Weininger's Sex and Character." *Critic* 12 (1906): 414–417.

Gilman, Sander L. *The Case of Sigmund Freud: Medicine and Identity at the Fin de Siècle.* Baltimore, 1993.

Harrowitz, Nancy A., and Barbara Hyams. *Jews and Gender: Responses to Otto Weininger.* Philadelphia, 1995.

Janik, Allan. "Viennese Culture and the Jewish Self-Hatred Hypothesis: A Critique." In *Jews, Antisemitism and Culture in Vienna.* Ed. Ivar Oxaal, Michael Pollak, and Gerhard Botz, 75–88. New York, 1987.

Klaren, Georg. *Otto Weininger: Der Mensch sein Werk und sein Leben.* Vienna, 1924.

Kohn, Hans. *Karl Kraus, Arthur Schnitzler, Otto Weininger: Aus dem jüdischen Wien der Jarhundertwende.* Tübingen, 1962.

Köhnke, Klaus Christian. *The Rise of Neo-Kantianism: German Academic Philosophy between Idealism and Positivism.* Cambridge, 1991.

Kraus, Karl, and August Strindberg. *Die Faeckel,* 1903 and 1907. Munich: Kösel Verlag Munich, 1968–1976 and Frankfurt: Zweitausendeins, 1977.

Le Rider, Jacques. *Le Cas Otto Weininger: Racines de l'antiféminisme et de l'antisémitisme.* Paris, 1982.

———. *Der Fall Otto Weininger: Wurzeln des Antifeminismus und Antisemitismus.* Trans. Dieter Hornig. Vienna, 1985.

Le Rider, Jacques, and Norbert Leser. *Otto Weininger: Werk und Wirkung.* Vienna, 1984.

Lewin, Kurt. "Self-Hatred among Jews." In *Resolving Social Conflicts; Selected Papers on Group Dynamics (1935–1946).* Ed. Gertrud Weiss Lewin, 186–200. New York, 1948.

Lucka, Emil. *Otto Weininger: Sein Werk und seine Persönlichkeit.* Vienna, 1905.

Luft, David S. "Being and German History: Historiographical Notes on the Heidegger Controversy." *Central European History* 27, no. 4 (1994): 479–501.

———. "Otto Weininger als Figur des Fin de siècle." In *Otto Weininger: Werk und Wirkung.* Ed. Jacques Le Rider and Norbert Leser, 71–79. Vienna, 1984.

Monk, Ray. *Ludwig Wittgenstein: The Duty of a Genius.* New York, 1990.

Petrément, Simone. *Simone Weil: A Life.* Trans. Raymond Rosenthal. New York, 1976.

Scheichl, Sigurd Paul. "Contexts and Nuances of anti-Jewish Language." In *Jews, Antisemitism and Culture in Vienna.* Ed. Ivar Oxaal, Michael Pollak, and Gerhard Botz, 89–110. London, 1987.

Sengoopta, Chandak. *Otto Weininger: Sex, Science, and Self in Imperial Vienna.* Chicago, 2000.

Sobol, Joshua. *The Soul of a Jew: The Death of Otto Weininger: Weininger's Last Night.* Trans. Betsy Rosenberg and Miriam Schlesinger. Tel Aviv, n.d.

Spire, André. *Quelques Juifs.* Paris, 1913.

Sturm, Bruno. *Gegen Weininger: Ein Versuch zur Lösung des Moralproblems.* Vienna, 1912.

Swoboda, Hermann. *Die gemeinnützige Forschung und der eigenützige Forscher: Antwort auf die von Wilhelm Fliess gegen Otto Weininger und mich erhobenen Beschuldigungen.* Vienna, 1906.

———. *Otto Weiningers Tod.* 2d ed. Vienna, 1923.

Thaler, Leopold. *Weiningers Weltanschauung im Lichte der kantischen Lehre.* Vienna, 1935.

Toews, John. "Refashioning the Masculine Subject in Early Modernism: Narrations of Self-Dissolution and Self-Construction in Psychoanalysis and Literature, 1990–1914." *MODERNISM/modernity* 4, no. 1 (1997): 31–67.

Weininger, Richard. *Exciting Years.* Hicksville, N.Y., 1978.

Willey, Thomas E. *Back to Kant: The Revival of Kantianism in German Social and Historical Thought, 1860–1914.* Detroit, 1978.

Wistrich, Robert S. "Social Democracy, Antisemitism, and the Jews." In *Jews, Antisemitism and Culture in Vienna.* Ed. Ivar Oxaal, Michael Pollak, and Gerhard Botz, 111–120. London, 1987.

Robert Musil

Primary Sources

Briefe, 1901–1942. Ed. Adolf Frisé. Hamburg, 1981.

The Enthusiasts. Trans. Andrea Simon. New York, 1983.

Five Women. Trans. Eithne Wilkins and Ernst Kaiser. New York, 1966.

Gesammelte Werke. 9 vols. Ed. Adolf Frisé. Hamburg, 1978.

The Man without Qualities. 2 vols. Trans. Sophie Wilkins and Burton Pike. Ed. Burton Pike. New York, 1995.

On Mach's Theories. Trans. Kevin Mulligan. Washington, D.C., 1982.

Precision and Soul: Essays and Addresses. Ed. and trans. Burton Pike and David S. Luft. Chicago, 1990.

Selected Writings. Ed. Burton Pike. New York, 1986.

Tagebücher. 2 vols. Ed. Adolf Frisé. Hamburg, 1976.

Young Törless. Trans. Eithne Wilkins and Ernst Kaiser. New York, 1955.

Secondary Sources

Allen, Roy F. *Literary Life in German Expressionism and the Berlin Circles*. Ann Arbor, 1983.

Appignanesi, Lisa. *Femininity and the Creative Imagination: A Study of Henry James, Robert Musil, and Marcel Proust*. New York, 1973.

Ash, Mitchell G. *Gestalt Psychology in German Culture, 1890–1967: Holism and the Quest for Objectivity*. New York, 1995.

Beard, Philip Harper. "Der 'andere Zustand' im *Mann ohne Eigenschaften* und in der Musil-Kritik." Ph.D. diss., Stanford University, 1971.

Bonacchi, Silvia. *Die Gestalt der Dichtung*. Bern, 1998.

Coetzee, J. M. "The Man with Many Qualities." *New York Review of Books*, March 18, 1999, 52–55.

Cohn, Dorrit. *Transparent Minds: Narrative Modes for Presenting Consciousness in Fiction*. Princeton, 1978.

Corino, Karl. *Robert Musil: Leben und Werk in Bildern und Texten*. Hamburg, 1988.

———. *Robert Musils "Vereinigungen" : Studien zu einer historisch-kritischen Ausgabe*. Munich, 1974.

Dahan-Gaida, Laurence. *Musil: Savoir et fiction*. Saint-Denis, 1994.

Ego, Werner. *Abschied von der Moral*. Freiburg, Switzerland, 1992.

Hehner, Cay. *Erkenntnis und Freiheit: Der Mann ohne Eigenschaften als "Übergangswegsen."* Munich, 1994.

Henninger, Peter. *Der Buchstabe und der Geist: Unbewusste Determinierung im Schreiben Robert Musils*. Frankfurt am Main, 1980.

Jonsson, Stefan. *Subject without Nation: Robert Musil and the History of Modern Identity*. Durham, N.C., 2000.

Luft, David S. *Robert Musil and the Crisis of European Culture, 1880–1942*. Berkeley, 1980.

Mulot, Sibylle. *Der junge Musil: Seine Beziehung zu Literatur und Kunst der Jahrhundertwende*. Stuttgart, 1977.

Payne, Philip. *Robert Musil's "The Man without Qualities": A Critical Study*. Cambridge, 1988.

Pike, Burton. *Robert Musil: An Introduction to His Work*. Ithaca, 1961.

Rogowski, Christian. *Distinguished Outsider: Robert Musil and His Critics*. Columbia, S.C., 1994.

Webber, Andrew. *Sexuality and the Sense of Self in the Works of Georg Trakl and Robert Musil*. London, 1990.

HEIMITO VON DODERER

Primary Sources

Commentarii 1951 bis 1956: Tagebücher aus dem Nachlass. Ed. Wendelin Schmidt-Dengler. Munich, 1976.

The Demons. Trans. Richard and Clara Winston. New York, 1961.

Der Fall Gütersloh: Ein Schicksal und seine Deutung. Vienna, 1930.

Der Grenzwald, Roman No. 7, Zweiter Teil. Munich, 1967.

Die Daemonen, Roman Studien I, II, III; Ser. n. 14.238–14.240. In the Doderer Nachlass in the Handschriftensammlung der Österreichischen Nationalbibliothek, Vienna.

Die Dämonen: Nach der Chronik des Sektionsrates Geyrenhoff. Munich, 1956.

Die erleuchteten Fenster oder die Menschwerdung des Amtrates Julius Zihal. Ein Umweg. Zwei Romane. Munich, 1970.

Die Erzählungen. Ed. Wendelin Schmidt-Dengler. Munich, 1972.

Die Merowinger oder Die totale Familie. Munich, 1962.

Die sibirische Klarheit. Ed. Wendelin Schmidt-Dengler and Martin Loew-Cadonna. Munich, 1991.

Die Strudlhofstiege oder Melzer und die Tiefe der Jahre. 1951. Reprint, Munich, 1980.

Die Wasserfälle von Slunj. Munich, 1963.

Die Wiederkehr der Drachen: Aufsätze/Traktate/Reden. Ed. Wendelin Schmidt-Dengler. Munich, 1970.

Ein Mord den jeder begeht. 1938. Reprint, Munich, 1964.

Every Man a Murderer. Trans. Richard and Clara Winston. New York, 1964.

Frühe Prosa. Die sibirische Klarheit/Die Bresche/Jutta Bamberger/Das Geheimnis des Reichs: Roman aus dem russischen Bürgerkrieg. Ed. Hans Flesch-Brunningen, Wendelin Schmidt-Dengler, and Martin Loew-Cadonna. Munich, 1996.

Gassen und Landschaft. Vienna, 1923.

Gedanken über eine zu schreibende Geschichte der Stadt Wien. Ed. Erich Fitzbauer. Vienna, 1996.

Heimito von Doderer, 1896–1966: Selbstzeugnisse. Intro. by Wendelin Schmidt-Dengler. Ed. Martin Loew-Cadonna. Munich, 1995.

The Lighted Windows or The Humanization of the Bureaucrat Julius Zihal. Trans. John S. Barrett. Riverside, 2000.

Meine neunzehn Lebensläufe. Munich, 1966.

The Merowingians, or The Total Family. Trans. Vinal Overing Binner. Los Angeles, 1996.

Tagebücher: 1920–1939. 2 vols. Ed. Wendelin Schmidt-Dengler, Martin Loew-Cadonna, and Gerald Sommer. Munich, 1996.

Tangenten: Tagebuch eines Schriftstellers, 1940–1950. Munich, 1964.

The Secret of the Empire: A Novel of the Russian Civil War. Trans. and with a forward and afterword by John S. Barrett. Riverside, 1998.

"The Strudlhof Steps, or Melzer and the Depth of the Years." Trans. Vincent Kling. *Chicago Review 26* no. 2 (1974)

Treml, Reinhold, ed. *Briefwechsel, 1928–1962.* Munich, 1986.

The Waterfalls of Slunj. Trans. Eithne Wilkins and Ernst Kaiser. New York, 1966/1987.

Unter schwarzen Sternen: Erzählungen. Munich, 1966.

Von Figur zu Figur: Briefe an Ivar Ivask über Literatur und Kritik. Ed. Wolfgang Fleischer und Wendelin Schmidt-Dengler. Munich, 1996.

"Zur bürgerlichen Geschichtsschreibung in Wien während des 15. Jahrhunderts." Ph.D. diss., University of Vienna, 1925.

Secondary Sources

Bachem, Michael. *Heimito von Doderer.* Boston, 1981.

Eisenreich, Herbert. *Reaktionen: Essays zur Literatur.* N.p., 1964.

Erinnerungen an Heimito von Doderer. Ed. Xaver Schaffgotsch. Munich, 1972.

Excentrische Einsätze: Studien und Essays zum Werk Heimito von Doderers. Ed. Kai Luehrs. Berlin, 1998.

Falk, Thomas H. "Heimito von Doderer's Concept of the Novel. Theory and Practice." Ph.D. diss, University of Southern California, 1970.

Fleischer, Wolfgang. *Das verleugnete Leben: Die Biographie des Heimito von Doderer.* Vienna, 1996.

———. *Heimito von Doderer: Das Leben. Das Umfeld des Werkes in Fotos und Dokumenten.* Vienna, 1995.

Fischer, Roswitha. *Studien zur Entstehungsgeschichte der "Strudlhofstiege" Heimito von Doderers.* Vienna, 1975.

Hatfield, Henry. "Vitality and Tradition. Two Novels by Heimito von Doderer." In *Crisis and Continuity in Modern German Fiction.* Ed. Henry Hatfield, 90–108. Ithaca, 1969.

Heimito von Doderer, 1896–1966. Symposium anlässlich des 80. Geburtstages. Wien 1976. Ed. Wendelin Schmidt-Dengler and Wolfgang Kraus. Salzburg, 1978.

Helmstetter, Rudolf. *Das Ornament der Grammatik in der Eskalation der Zitate: "Die Strudlhofstiege," Doderers moderne Poetik des Romans, und die Rezeptionsgeschichte.* Munich, 1995.

Hesson, Elizabeth C. *Twentieth Century Odyssey: A Study of Heimito von Doderer's Die Dämonen.* Columbia, S.C., 1982.

Kastner, Siegmund. "Thomismus und Roman. Studien zu Heimito von Doderers Roman 'Die Dämonen' in Zusammenhang mit den 'Commentarii 1951 bis 1956.'" Ph.D. diss., University of Vienna, 1977.

Kerscher, Hubert. *Zweite Wirklichkeit: Formen der grotesken Bewusstseinsverengung im Werk Heimito von Doderer.* Frankfurt am Main, 1998.

Leinkauf, Simone. *Diarium in principio: Das Tagebuch als Ort der Sinngebung.* Frankfurt am Main, 1992.

Loew-Cadonna, Martin. *Zug um Zug: Studien zu Heimito von Doderers Roman "Ein Mord den jeder begeht."* Vienna, 1991.

Luger, Helmut. "Eine ideologiekritische Analyse der theoretische Schriften Heimito von Doderers." Ph.D. diss., University of Innsbruck, 1990.

Luft, David S. "Austrian Intellectuals and the Palace of Justice Fire." In *The Austrian Socialist Experiment: Social Democracy and Austromarxism, 1918–1934.* Ed. Anson Rabinbach, 151–156. Boulder, Colo., 1985.

———. "Eros and Apperception in Heimito von Doderer's *Tangenten.*" In *Philosophie, Psychoanalyse, Emigration: Festschrift fur Kurt Rudolf Fischer zum 70. Geburtstag.* Ed. Peter Muhr, Paul Feyerabend, and Cornelia Wegeler, 194–209. Vienna, 1992.

Pfeiffer, Engelbert. *Heimito Doderers Alsergrund-Erlebnis: Biographischer Abriss, Topographie, Interpretation.* Vienna, 1983. [*The Writer's Place: Heimito von Doderer and the Alsergrund District of Vienna.* Trans. Vincent Kling. Riverside, Ca., 2001.]

———. "Heimito von Doderer in Döbling," *Literatur und Kritik* 123 (April 1978): 158–170.

Politzer, Heinz. "Heimito von Doderer and the Modern Kakanian Novel." In *The Contemporary Novel in German.* Ed. Robert R. Heitner, 37–62. Austin, 1967.

Reininger, Anton. "'Die Dämonen': Totaler Roman und antirevolutionärer Traktat." In *Literatur und Kritik* 80 (1973): 599–608.

———. *Die Erlösung des Bürgers: Eine ideologiekritische Studie zum Werk Heimito von Doderers.* Bonn, 1975.

Rütger, Herbert. "Antisemitismus in allen Lagern." Ph.D. diss., University of Graz, 1989.

Schmid, Georg. *Doderer Lesen. Zu einer historischen Theorie der literarischen Praxis: Essai.* Salzburg, 1978.

Schmidt-Dengler, Wendelin. "'Analogia entis' oder das 'Schweigen unendlicher Räume': Theologische Themen bei Heimito von Doderer und Thomas Bernhard." In *Gott in der Literatur.* Ed. Gottfried Bachl and Helmut Schink. Linz, 1976.

Schneider, Karl Heinrich. *Die technisch-moderne Welt im Werk Heimito von Doderers.* Frankfurt am Main, 1985.

Schupp, Ulrike. *Ordnung und Bruch: Antinomien in Heimito von Doderers Roman Die Dämonen.* Frankfurt am Main, 1994.

Schröder, Hans Joachim. *Apperzeption und Vorurteil: Untersuchungen zur Reflexion Heimito von Doderers.* Heidelberg, 1976.

Spiel, Hilde. *Kleine schritte: Berichte und Geschichten.* Munich, 1976.

———. *Welt im Widerschein: Essays.* Munich, 1960.

Stieg, Gerald. *Frucht des Feuers: Canetti, Doderer, Kraus und der Justizpalastbrand.* Vienna, 1990.

Weber, Dietrich. *Heimito von Doderer*. Munich, 1987.

———. *Heimito von Doderer: Studien zu seinem Romanwerk*. Munich, 1963.

Wolff, Lutz-W. *Heimito von Doderer*. Hamburg, 1996.

———. *Wiedereroberte Aussenwelt. Studien zur Erzählweise Heimito von Doderers am Beispiel des "Romans No 7."* Göppingen, 1969.

Zeemann, Dorothea. *Jungfrau und Reptil: Leben zwischen 1945 und 1972*. Frankfurt am Main, 1982.

INDEX

Abrahamsen, David, 47–49
absolutism: in Austria, 14
Adler, Victor, 26, 30
aestheticism: in Vienna, 20–21
aesthetics: Musil on, 98–99, 107–8, 115
Allers, Rudolf, 230n. 68
androgyny: Musil on, 132–33; Weininger on, 55, 57–59, 63–64, 184. *See also* bisexuality
Anschluss, 96, 116, 126; Doderer on, 138, 149, 151; map of, 157
anti-Semitism: of Doderer, 138–39, 148–50, 156, 170–71; in Europe, 3, 30, 185; in Vienna, 46, 149–52; of Weininger, 46, 48, 81, 86–87, 150. *See also* Judaism
apperception: Doderer on, 158–59, 161, 163, 166
Aristotle, 73, 162
Arnstein, Fanny von, 16
art: in Vienna, 20–21
Augustine, Saint, 51, 64
Austria: absolutism in, 14; anti-Semitism in, 46, 149–52; Catholicism, 23; civil war in (1934), 138, 149; and Enlightenment, 15, 23; and German nationalism, 30, 185; Jews in, 17–18; National Socialism in, 137–39, 149–52; revolution in (1918–19),

115–16; science in, 23; women's suffrage in, 39–40. *See also* Anschluss; Vienna
avant-garde, 105
Avenarius, Richard, 50–51, 72

Bahr, Hermann, 196–97n. 30
Balázs, Béla, 110
Bauernfeld, Eduard von, 39
Beauvoir, Simone de, 152
Berlin, 97, 105–6. *See also* Germany
Bildung, 13, 15, 158
biology: and human nature, 29, 35; and scientific materialism, 25–26
bisexuality: and gender difference, 3; Weininger on, 50–51, 54–55, 57–59. *See also* androgyny; homosexuality
Blei, Franz, 106, 160
Böhme, Jakob, 84
Bolzano, Bernard, 23
bourgeois society, 17, 99, 186
Brentano, Franz, 24, 27, 94
Breuer, Josef, 42, 50
Broch, Hermann, 20–21, 33, 46, 192n. 10
Brücke, Ernst von, 26
Buber, Martin, 33
Büchner, Ludwig, 7, 22, 25–26
bureaucracy: and modernity, 17, 24